D1293295

DANGEROUS TALK
AND STRANGE BEHAVIOR

DANGEROUS TALK
AND STRANGE BEHAVIOR:

WOMEN AND POPULAR RESISTANCE
TO THE REFORMS OF HENRY VIII

Sharon L. Jansen

St. Martin's Press
New York, New York

ISBN 0-312-16090-9

Library of Congress Cataloging-in-Publication Data

Jansen, Sharon L., 1951-
    Dangerous talk and strange behavior : women and popular resistance
to the reforms of Henry VIII / Sharon L. Jansen.
        p.   cm.
    Includes bibliographical references and index.
    ISBN 0-312-16090-9
    1. Women in politics—Great Britain—History—16th century.
    2. Great Britain—Politics and government—1509-1547. I. Title.

HQ1236.5.G7J36 1996
320'.082—dc20   96-918
                                                                 CIP

Book design by Acme Art, Inc.

CONTENTS

For Professor George E. Arbaugh,
Friend and Colleague

Glory and honour, Virgil Mantoan,
Be to thy name! and I shal, as I can,
Folwe thy lanterne, as thow gost byforn. . . .
—Geoffrey Chaucer,
The Legend of Good Women, F. 924-26

ACKNOWLEDGMENTS

Without two influential books that served to guide me, *Dangerous Talk and Strange Behavior* would not have been possible. Geoffrey Elton's *Policy and Police* and Keith Thomas's *Religion and the Decline of Magic* changed the direction of my interests and research, and to these eminent historians I am profoundly grateful.

I would like to express my gratitude to the Public Record Office, London, for permission to cite PRO documents and to the British Library for permission to cite British Library manuscripts. I am also appreciative for the help I received from staff members at both of these institutions; their patient assistance was generously extended to me while I was at work on this project.

For his enthusiastic interest in *Dangerous Talk and Strange Behavior* and for their efforts in bringing this book to print, I would like to thank, respectively, Michael J. Flamini, Senior Editor, Suzanne Oshinsky, Editorial Assistant, and Ruth Mannes, Assistant Production Editor, of the Scholarly and Reference Division at St. Martin's Press. Professor Arthur F. Kinney, Department of English, University of Massachusetts, offered me very helpful suggestions about the shape and development of this book.

I would like to acknowledge the consistent support for my research from Pacific Lutheran University. I am especially appreciative of a Regency Advancement Award, granted by PLU's Board of Regents, which helped to fund a research period in England. For his encouragement and support, I owe a debt of gratitude to Paul Menzel, formerly the Dean of Humanities and now Provost. And for her sincere dedication, consistent enthusiasm, and tireless effort to find even the most obscure sources, I would like to thank Laura Lewis of the Interlibrary Loan Department at PLU's Mortvedt Library.

On a more personal level I am indebted to a number of very special women who have contributed in various ways to this book, including my mother Jean Jansen (a woman to be noted for her own "dangerous talk and strange behavior"), my neighbor Georgina Burlingame (who listened to progress reports on the book as we took our regular walks through the streets of Steilacoom), and my dear friends Suzanne Rahn and Barbara Temple-Thurston, both members of the English Department at PLU. Also on a personal level a special thank you to Phil Nordquist (History, PLU), for his interest in my work, to Tom Campbell (English, PLU), who believed in my ability to write this book and who checked in almost daily to see how it was going, and to George Arbaugh, to whom this book is dedicated, for his strength and courage, always an inspiration, and for his patience in listening to endless details about Margaret Cheyne!

And for help, encouragement, enthusiasm, and loving support of the most enduring kind, a special thank you to my son, Kristian Jansen Jaech.

A NOTE ON THE TRANSCRIPTIONS

I have used many kinds of sixteenth-century documents in this study: personal letters, trial records, public pronouncements, official memos and notes, and printed books, among them. I have made an effort to preserve the flavor and texture of the original sources yet to make them readable and accessible for modern readers. In this effort I have modernized and standardized the spelling and punctuation of quotations that appear in the text, even when these quotations have been made from modern editions of sixteenth-century documents and letters. Quotations appearing in the notes have been preserved in their original form. In using the state papers of Henry VIII, I have almost always consulted the original documents themselves, instead of relying on the abstracts that appear in the *Letters and Papers of Henry VIII (LP)*. In general I have quoted from the original documents, though on occasion—where the originals have been badly damaged, for instance—I have also used the summaries in *LP*. When the information I have cited is supportive or supplementary, however, I have at times relied on the *LP* abstracts alone.

Dangerous Talk and Strange Behavior: Women and Popular Resistance to the Reforms of Henry VIII

Late in the spring of 1992, I began work on a conference paper that told the story of a woman named Margaret Cheyne and her arrest for treason in 1537. Evidence about her crime had been gathered from neighbors and family members, whose opinions of her character and her activities varied considerably—even the statements her husband made about her were confused and confusing. I read carefully through the surviving records of her case, trying to discover just who Margaret Cheyne was and what it was she had said and done that had resulted in the charge of treason.

Although the words and deeds of a woman as obscure as Margaret Cheyne wouldn't seem to pose much of a threat to royal power and authority, the accusations against her were taken quite seriously by Henry VIII's Council of the North, investigating the series of rebellions that had broken out late in 1536 and early in 1537, first in Lincolnshire, then in Yorkshire, and finally throughout the northern counties. The action against her was swift and decisive. She was first taken into custody in early April by the duke of Norfolk in Newcastle; by 8 April she had been sent to London; by 21 April her husband had joined her in the Tower, and surviving documents record the charges and evidence against the two of them; on 14 May she was arraigned; on 16 May she pleaded guilty to the charge of high treason; on 25 May she was burned at the stake.

What had begun as a brief and unusual conference paper materialized into something quite unexpected. I found that I quickly filled many pages with the story of the official investigation into Margaret's activities, a narrative that now makes up the first chapter of this book. As I worked my way through the documents detailing her case, I slowly came to see that many of my assumptions about her were wrong; the more I learned about her, for example, the more I realized that she was not the obscure and insignificant woman I had at first assumed her to be. And the further I followed the threads of the government's investigation, the more I came to see why she might have been executed for treason. Yet, as I searched the records for answers to my questions about Margaret and her treason, I found only more, and more intriguing, questions. At last I came to see a much larger project, one examining the role of women like Margaret Cheyne in political resistance during the early modern period of English history.

As my title suggests, this book explores the roles of women in a period remarkable for religious, political, institutional, and social change. In many obvious ways women are intimately involved with the disruptions taking place within Henry VIII's kingdom. The king's struggle for a divorce from his first wife, Katherine of Aragon, and his subsequent matrimonial career have become so much a part of popular culture that they have provided the plots of plays and novels, movies and television shows, from Shakespeare to the British Broadcasting Corporation and Hollywood. While Henry's wives clearly played their part in the events of the early sixteenth century, real political power was exercised in their own names by the Tudor queens, Mary and Elizabeth, and by Mary Stuart, Queen of Scots, in the succeeding generation.

In *Dangerous Talk and Strange Behavior* I focus on the political activities of women very different from Henry's wives and daughters, however. I am interested in those whom we might call the "other women" in Henry's England—women who were far removed from the power and influence of the royal court. This book explores politically motivated activity undertaken by women from across a broad spectrum of Tudor society. Margaret Cheyne herself may, or may not, have been the wife of a well-connected knight, while other women investigated for what they said and did were the mothers, wives, widows, and daughters of gentlemen, husbandmen, tradesmen, poor servants, landless laborers, and homeless wanderers.

As a way of focusing this discussion of women's political activities, I have concentrated on the cases of several women charged with the crime of treason.

Despite their differences, all involve "crimes" that might best be called "dangerous talk and strange behavior": Margaret Cheyne, executed for the part she had played in a failed rebellion; Elizabeth Barton, executed for her prophecies against the king's divorce; Elizabeth Wood, executed for spreading "treasonous rumors" about the king; and Mabel Brigge, executed for a "black fast" she somehow "directed against" the king. These women posed no direct, physical threat to Henry; unlike some of their male contemporaries, their husbands and sons, for example, they did not take part in armed rebellion. Nevertheless, to Henry's government they also represented a danger to the stability of the realm. Their stories are used here as detailed case studies around which to organize a wider discussion of the types of political activities undertaken by women, for many of whom the extant records are not so complete. My aim has been to explore as fully as possible particular women's acts of protest and resistance and to analyze how, why, and when these sorts of actions were judged to threaten the peace and order of the realm.

The presence of so many women in the popular resistance to Henry's reforms has been largely overlooked, even in revisionist analyses of the Tudor revolution and Reformation. In the last decade G. R. Elton's foundational work in Tudor politics and reform has been challenged by a number of historians, among them John Guy and David Starkey. A reevaluation of women's roles in sixteenth-century political and religious changes has further transformed traditional political and administrative history. Two recent biographers, for example, argue that Anne Boleyn was a more informed participant in the Tudor Reformation than has been traditionally accepted.[1] Barbara J. Harris has extended that argument by suggesting both a range of political activity by women of the nobility and a failure of modern historians to assess their activity: "The very definition of politics underlying the dominant historiography has . . . made it seem both natural and inevitable to write history as if the world of high politics, the world that really counted, were exclusively male. . . . [O]nly historians who include women in their accounts can fully elucidate the inner workings of early Tudor politics and society."[2]

Dangerous Talk and Strange Behavior is part of this new effort to consider the part played by women in sixteenth-century political history. My intention here has been to explore women's dangerous talk and strange behavior and the predicaments in which women found themselves as a result of what they said and did. In the records that remain these women often speak directly to a secretary. Although their stories are thus filtered through the pens of the men who transcribed them, these first-person narratives, however mediated, offer us an opportunity to hear what survives of the long-silent voices of women and to glimpse, if only briefly, their reactions to the momentous changes taking place all around them. Their individual stories are fascinating, and my aim here is to place them once more within the larger narrative of political and social turmoil during the period.

ONE

A Woman's Treason: The Case of Margaret Cheyne

On 25 May 1537 Margaret Cheyne was taken from the Tower of London, where she had been imprisoned since early April, and dragged on a sledge to Smithfield, in the old City of London, a site known for its meat market and its public executions. There she was burned alive at the stake.

Only ten days earlier she had been indicted of high treason by Henry VIII's government, the charge arising from the role she was accused of having played in a series of rebellions that had erupted in the northern counties. Although she did not admit to acting or speaking against the king or his government while she was being investigated and examined, she still pleaded guilty to the charge. Her sentence—burning at the stake—was the prescribed method of execution for any woman convicted of high treason. Even so, it was not the usual sentence carried out on those who were found guilty. Just a few months earlier, in an act of relative mercy, Anne Boleyn had been beheaded after her conviction for the same crime.[1]

Margaret Cheyne's execution followed several others on that Friday. Earlier in the day six prisoners also judged guilty of high treason had suffered public execution at Tyburn. Sir Stephen Hamerton and Sir John Bulmer, enjoying the privilege of knighthood, had been hanged and beheaded. The others—Nicholas Tempest, esquire; James Cockerell, the former prior of the Augustinian priory of Guisborough; William Thirsk, the former abbot of Fountains Abbey; and John Pickering, a Dominican of Bridlington—had suffered the full penalty of the law. They had been hanged, disemboweled, and quartered, their heads, according to a contemporary chronicle, "set on London Bridge and diverse gates in London."[2]

Like Margaret, these men had been convicted for their participation in the northern rebellions of the preceding fall and winter.[3] The series of risings, known collectively as the Pilgrimage of Grace, had begun in Louth, in Lincolnshire, on 1 October 1536; within days similar riots had broken out in surrounding market towns. Although the rebellion in Lincolnshire collapsed by the middle of the month, sparks had spread in the meantime. On 4 October the East Riding of Yorkshire erupted, rebellion there led by Robert Aske, a lawyer and gentleman. By 16 October Aske occupied York, and Lord Thomas Darcy had surrendered Pontefract Castle to the rebels. By 24 October between 20,000 and 40,000 rebels had assembled in a camp at Doncaster. By the end of the month the rising had engulfed virtually all the northern counties, roughly one-third of the country.

To counter the self-styled "Pilgrims," Henry sent troops north under the duke of Norfolk, Thomas Howard, and the duke of Suffolk, Charles Brandon. Vastly outnumbered (one estimate placed his force at no more than 8,000), Norfolk was to temporize with the rebels: he agreed to carry their demands himself to Henry, and he waited while they drew up their articles at Pontefract. Finally, on 6 December Norfolk met at Doncaster with the rebel leaders, whose petition included, along with a long list of grievances, their request for pardon and for a meeting of Parliament in the north. Empowered by Henry to negotiate with them, Norfolk assured the rebels of the king's pardon. Robert Aske took off his Pilgrim badge, dispersed the Pilgrim force, and was persuaded to travel south to meet with the king in London. Norfolk, too, headed for London, where he was to report on the situation in the north.

Although the Pilgrims disbanded, the northern counties remained tense. When Norfolk failed to return promptly with the promised pardon, and when a number of northern gentlemen who had been involved in the risings were summoned to London, the sparks of rebellion reignited; on 15 January Sir Francis Bigod dispatched a series of letters calling for a new rising and began to muster the rebels again, this time under his leadership. But the effort to renew the rebellion quickly collapsed. By 19 January Bigod had abandoned the cause, and those who had gathered to support him had surrendered. Although rebellion had also flared up in places like Durham and Richmond, by 25 January the king's commissioners had regained control in most places. Norfolk headed north once more, arriving in Lincoln on 30 January and continuing on to York, which he reached on 5 February. Indictments against the rebels began on 10 February; by 20 February Norfolk had achieved a decisive victory over the remaining rebels at Carlisle. Acting under martial law, Norfolk had immediately condemned seventy-four to death for their rebellion. But those who were the alleged leaders of the rebellions were sent for trial to London, among them Lord Thomas Darcy, Lord John Hussey, Sir Thomas Percy, and Sir Francis Bigod. Also dispatched to London for their role in the rebellions were the seven prisoners executed for treason on 25 May.

What part had Margaret Cheyne played in all this?

Margaret Cheyne's relationship with Sir John Bulmer is what connected her to the northern rebels. The Bulmers were "an ancient and honourable family" whose holdings in Wilton dated to the reign of Edward II. Sir John Bulmer, the son of Sir William Bulmer, was closely connected with many of those involved in the northern risings, those who remained loyal to the king as well as those who participated in the rebellion. Ultimately taken into custody by the duke of Norfolk as he restored order in the north, Bulmer himself had, some years earlier in his career, served under Norfolk, then earl of Surrey, in Ireland. Bulmer had married Sir Ralph Bigod's daughter Anne, while Sir Francis Bigod, the leader of the January rising, was not only Bulmer's nephew but was also related to Bulmer by his marriage to Catherine, the daughter of Lord William Conyers of Hornby (Sir John Bulmer's mother was Margery, daughter of Sir John Conyers of Hornby). Bulmer's eldest son, named Ralph, had married into the Tempest family. His wife was Ann Tempest, the daughter of Sir Thomas Tempest of Brough. Nicholas Tempest, a member of the same family, and Sir John Bulmer were both executed at Tyburn on the same day. Bulmer's brother, also named Ralph, had married Anne Aske, the daughter and coheir of Sir Roger Aske of Aske. Robert Aske of Aughton, the Pilgrim leader, was convicted of treason, along with Bulmer, on 17 May 1537.[4]

While Bulmer was thus intimately connected in various ways to a number of prominent and influential northern families, not much has been written about Margaret Cheyne's origins. While her parentage is uncertain, what has been suggested about her family ties is notable: she has been most consistently identified as the daughter of Edward Stafford, duke of Buckingham, who is known to have had at least one illegitimate daughter.[5] Since Sir John Bulmer's father, William, had been one of Buckingham's loyal supporters, Sir John might well have become acquainted with Margaret during the time his father served the duke.[6]

Just as the circumstances of Margaret Cheyne's birth remain somewhat obscure, so does the status of her marriage to Sir John Bulmer. At the time of her arrest what connected her to him was their claim to be husband and wife, a claim Henry's government consistently refused to acknowledge. Sir John Bulmer had first been married, probably in 1509, to Anne Bigod, while Margaret, whatever her origins, had at one time been married to a William

Cheyne of London.[7] However and whenever they first became acquainted, Margaret Cheyne and Sir John Bulmer had at least two daughters born to them before their marriage.[8]

Despite what Henry's government would later claim, there can be little doubt that Margaret Cheyne and Sir John Bulmer did marry. Genealogical research indicates that this marriage took place around 1534. At the time Bulmer's neighbors and family clearly recognized this second marriage. Early in January 1537, for example, while Norfolk was pursuing his investigations of the northern rebellions, Sir Ralph Evers had written to Sir John, assuring him that "the king is gracious and pities his offending subjects" and acknowledging Bulmer's recent "diligent service," for which, according to Evers, Henry had "determined you a letter of thanks." Sir Ralph closed his letter with a greeting for Margaret: "I pray you have me recommended to my lady your wife."[9] Later in the month, on 25 January, Sir William Bulmer, one of Sir John's younger brothers, sent a letter full of rumors and fears to his brother; before turning his attention to his worries, though, William congratulated Sir John and his wife on the birth of their son, John.[10]

So much can be said for Margaret's personal connection to Sir John Bulmer. But how was she connected to the northern rebellions? About Sir John's involvement with the rebels there is ample evidence. Bulmer had taken the side of the Pilgrims in the October risings; he was numbered among the prominent rebels who had met with Norfolk on Doncaster bridge in October to discuss the Pilgrims' grievances.[11] He had, moreover, become involved with affairs at the monastery of Guisborough, maintaining the prior in his office at the direction of the Pilgrims' council in York.[12] During his investigations of the northern rebels, Norfolk had also seized some of Sir John's personal papers as evidence. In forwarding these "lewd" and "malicious" letters, now lost, to London, Norfolk concluded that they proved "no man had a more cankered heart."[13]

All of this evidence related to what had taken place in October, however, before the Pilgrims had disbanded, by then assured of their pardon. In the following months, while proclaiming his loyalty to the government, Bulmer had nevertheless been drawn into a series of increasingly desperate plots. On 31 December, after receiving a letter from his son Ralph in London, Sir John had written to his brother William, warning him that the king and Norfolk were moving north once more and that several former rebel leaders had betrayed them: "the king has rigged thirty ships to come upon us . . . my lord of Norfolk is coming down . . . Aske has accused diverse persons, and . . . Sir George Darcy has accused his father and Sir Robert Constable." The young Ralph had advised his father and uncle not to leave the county "for no fair letters nor words."[14] Sir

John was frightened. He asked his brother to lay a watch along the coast and to prepare beacons, "for I fear it is high time."

While Bulmer apparently tried to keep the commons quiet during Bigod's rising in January, his own servants had attended rebel musters. Sir John himself, meanwhile, had been busy amassing a collection of the treasonable "bills" then being circulated. In a statement he made after his arrest, Bulmer implied that his search had been deliberately undertaken on behalf of the king; he indicated that he had dutifully copied the texts and sent them on to Norfolk. Although the details are confusing, one of the bills Bulmer collected seems to have outlined a plot for "seizing" Sir John himself, by which act the rebels somehow planned to "take my lord of Norfolk, and either make him keep his promises at Doncaster or take their part."[15]

In his desperation Sir John at last seems to have considered taking up arms once more against the king. Apparently terrified at his summons to London, received about the middle of March, he decided not to go. (One witness against him later testified that Sir John had said he would rather die in battle than in London, as many others had.) Instead, Sir John proposed joining forces with Lord John Lumley in a new insurrection planned for Easter Sunday.[16]

All of this indicates something of why Sir John Bulmer was ultimately taken into custody by Norfolk, but it says nothing about Margaret Cheyne. In fact, no evidence for Margaret Cheyne's activities during the fall of 1536 or January 1537 has survived. But clearly she had also come to Norfolk's attention at some point during his investigations.[17] In a letter of 8 April addressed to the king from Newcastle, Norfolk noted that he had Sir John in custody and that he was sending Margaret, "his pretended wife," to London. Norfolk wrote that he was enclosing evidence he had already collected about Margaret and Bulmer in his letter. The "bearer" of this evidence, Gregory Conyers, was to accompany Margaret; Conyers, related by blood to Bulmer (whose mother was a Conyers) and by marriage to Margaret, must have known more about the couple than was included in the written document, since Norfolk indicated that Conyers could tell the king "how the matter first came to light." The duke planned to dispatch Sir John to London as well, waiting only for instructions about what "other persons," presumably witnesses against Bulmer and Margaret, were to be sent along with him.[18]

Three days later, on 11 April, Norfolk wrote again, this time from Durham, addressing himself to Cromwell. He related the details of a meeting with Sir William Bulmer, Sir John's younger brother; on hearing that Sir John was in custody, William had presented himself to Norfolk "to see if anything could be laid to his charge." Norfolk and the Council of the North had examined the younger Bulmer, concluding that he was "a true man." William was being sent to London, bearing Norfolk's letter, the duke advising Cromwell "to be his good lord . . . if you cannot detect ill matter against him."[19]

On the following day, still in Durham, Norfolk wrote again directly to the king, reporting on the executions of rebels he had sentenced. In his letter he calculated that Bulmer, already dispatched on his way to London, would "be with you before Sunday come sevennight."[20] By late in April, then, Sir John and Margaret must have both been in the Tower; after their executions a list of prisoners and charges for their maintenance indicated that they had been lodged there for a total of six weeks before their deaths on 25 May.[21] Ralph Bulmer, Sir John's son by his first wife, had been in the capital throughout the early spring; around the time Sir John Bulmer and Margaret Cheyne arrived in London from the north, he had also been taken into custody.[22] Thus, in relatively short order Sir John Bulmer, his wife, Margaret, his oldest son, Ralph, and his younger brother, William, were all being detained in London.

Among the depositions, charges, reports, and confessions related to the January rising and collected in the state papers in late April is a statement in Sir John Bulmer's hand recording the events that had transpired in those difficult days of the preceding January.[23] Bulmer recalled fragments of conversations he had had with his neighbors and with his brother William about the rebellions. He also dutifully reported his interest in the various incendiary writings that were being circulated in the neighborhood, indicating that he had copied some of the texts and sent them to Norfolk. He spent considerable time, in fact, detailing his efforts to track down the treasonable texts he had heard or read. Above all he emphasized his loyalty to the king, noting that he had publicly declared at the time that one particular text would "make the gentlemen and the commons fall forth." As he saw it, once the rebels were thus divided, the king would "take up the matter," emerging triumphant from the division: "when two dogs fight for a bone, the third will take it up."[24] The analogy may not have been particularly flattering to the king, but Bulmer clearly intended to distance himself from the rebels and their troublesome bills.

Bulmer's statement is followed in the state papers by the "confession" of one John Watts, the parson of Essington, Yorkshire, who was likely one of the "other persons" sent to London by Norfolk to act as a witness against Sir John Bulmer and Margaret Cheyne. This document also sheds some light on the uneasy spring that had followed the failed rebellion and suggests how and why Margaret Cheyne had come to Norfolk's attention. Worried about what he knew, Watts had come forward to offer his evidence to Norfolk's investigators: "I, knowing all this, some men would think I had no cause to be very merry at my heart. . . . I could not compass in my mind how I should disclose this hideous and perilous cause which passeth my rude understanding." So Watts copied out, in his own hand, a confession detailing a long conversation he had had with Bulmer's chaplain, Sir William Stainous, at the end of March.[25]

On 29 March, having decided not to obey the royal summons to London, Bulmer had sent William Stainous to visit neighboring priests to see whether the commons would rise again. When Watts asked Stainous why Bulmer would consult priests, "many of them foolish," rather than "any other temporal man," Stainous had replied that Bulmer thought "they might know the mind of the commons more secretly than any other." Watts was one of the priests Stainous consulted. The chaplain had told Watts that the Bulmers had been summoned to London but that Sir John was afraid to travel south. Watts's statement suggested why Bulmer had failed to answer his summons: "he believed he should never come again, for the which he was as good be slain and die in the field as be martyred as many was above at London." Bulmer was reportedly waiting for his son Ralph, then in the capital, to send him word; according to what Stainous had told Watts, if Ralph's "tidings were good then [Sir John] said he trusted . . . all should be well." Otherwise, according to Watts, Bulmer planned to take up arms again, gathering his own men and the men of Guisborough. With this combined force he would join Lord John Lumley at Wilton Castle: "He said my Lord Lumley had promised him if he came to him he would succor to his power." When Watts had challenged William Stainous about this new insurrection—"Surely, Sir William, there is not one man in all England [who] will take your master's part"—the Bulmers' chaplain had replied, "Thus it is, if my master mistrusted that the commons would not be up at a wipe, surely he will fly in to Ireland, and he trusts to get his lands again within a year."

In his version of events Watts placed the blame for Bulmer's planned rebellion squarely on Margaret Cheyne:

> Then I said "Fie, Sir William, that ever your master should be tempted against his prince . . . for I dare say in my conscience he would never have been tempted with such matters but that she is afraid that she should be departed with him forever." I said she peradventure will say, "Mr. Bulmer, for my sake break a spear," and then he like a dow will say, "Pretty Peg, I will never forsake thee." Thus I said she . . . makes him believe that he may do that things that is impossible. . . . Some of Sir John Bulmer's folks say that they heard their master say that he had rather be racked than to part from his wife.

Except for Margaret, Watts claimed, "I dare say in my conscience he [Sir John] would never have been tempted with such matters."

When the Bulmers' chaplain had ventured a word of support for Margaret, Watts reported having turned on him: "I said, 'Sir William, take heed for yourself and . . . beware you fall not in love with her, for if you do, you will be made as wise as your master and both will be hanged then.'" From Watts's point of view, then, Margaret was a dangerous woman—the source of Sir John's original treason, the reason for his refusing to answer the king's summons, and the motivating force for him to commit further treason by joining the rebellion once more. And, beyond all that, Watts believed that she represented a danger to other men as well—men like Bulmer's chaplain, who had simply offered a word in her defense.

Watts's long tale is followed in the state papers archive by a statement taken directly from Bulmer's chaplain, Sir William Stainous. Like Watts, Stainous seems to have been sent to London to act as a witness against Bulmer and his wife. Despite John Watts's testimony—all his information about the Bulmers had come from his conversation with Stainous—Stainous's initial statement makes no mention of Bulmer or his wife at all but, rather, accuses the parson of Loftus, one Sir Thomas Franck, of being "a captain" at the rebellion.[26]

The three statements made by Bulmer, Watts, and Stainous represent the initial stage of the legal proceedings against Sir John Bulmer and Margaret Cheyne. The three men were questioned again in the Tower, while Margaret Cheyne seems to have made her first statement at that time. These formal examinations were recorded by John ap Rhys, acting as notary. In their original statements the three men had recorded their own individual recollections of events, but, once the formal deposition process began, the accused and the witnesses against them could only respond to the interrogatories of their examiners.[27]

In his formal deposition Sir John admitted that he had had a letter from his son Ralph in London indicating that "as far as he could perceive all was falsehood that they [the rebels] were dealt withal" and that he had received other seditious correspondence as well, which he had not disclosed to the king or to his council.[28] In addition, he confessed that he had plotted with Lord Lumley, inviting Lumley to join him "until they might provide some way for themselves" and sending Lumley a copy of "the said seditious letter," evidently referring to one of the letters he had admitted keeping from the king and the council. Sir John's deposition also contains the admission that he had "concealed the treason" of his chaplain William Stainous, who had once said "if one would stir, all would up," and that he had sent Stainous out to canvas priests "to inquire if the commons would rise again, which they [the priests] should know by men's confessions."

In this examination Sir John himself seems unwittingly to have supplied an important piece of evidence against his wife. The recorded deposition, however, never identifies Margaret as Bulmer's wife or as Lady Bulmer; instead, the notary John ap Rhys has referred to her throughout as "Margaret Cheyne," noting parenthetically, "whom [Sir John] calls his wife." According to the surviving abstract of his statement, Sir John admitted that he had "concealed the treason of Margaret Cheyne"; she had "counselled him to flee the realm" if the commons would not rise again, fearing "that he and she should be parted." Bulmer also reported Margaret as having urged him to join Bigod in January and of saying that, if Lord Lumley "and all the gentlemen arose, he must do the like."

Margaret Cheyne's formal statement is the only testimony from her that has survived.[29] In her very brief deposition she indicated that she had told her husband that the "commons wanted but a head" and that she had encouraged him "to flee" if the commons did not rise; she attributed her advice to her fear that she would be separated from him. In her statement she added a few scant details of the plan she had counseled; she wanted Bulmer to "get a ship to carry her and him into Scotland." She also admitted knowing her husband's son had sent word to his father in March that all the king's promises of pardon were false.

John Watts was formally deposed in the Tower as well, and his testimony is considerably more subdued than the long and detailed statement he had first offered in his confession. Watts responded only to questions about the Bulmers' decision not to answer the king's summons to London and about Sir John's plan to fly to Wilton Castle, where he and the commons would then "go and take the Duke's grace [Norfolk]."[30]

The Bulmer chaplain, Sir William Stainous, was also examined again, and his statement shows that the examiners must have pressed him on the same questions. He added a bit more to the account given by Sir John and Margaret; he deposed that Margaret had asked him whether the commons would rise and that she had told him that "she would rather be torn into pieces than to go to London," almost the exact words the parson John Watts had earlier attributed to Bulmer. Another damaging bit of evidence against her was the chaplain's statement that Margaret Cheyne had "enticed" Sir John to raise the commons and that she had, several times, said that she hoped Norfolk's head "were off."[31]

Evidence against them having been gathered, Margaret Cheyne and Sir John Bulmer were arraigned along with the other northern rebels on 14 May. They were indicted in the court of the King's Bench the next day, the record once again emphasizing the official view of their marital status: "Sir John Bulmer of Wilton, Margaret Cheyne, wife of William Cheyne, late of London, esquire . . . Ralph Bulmer of London, son and heir apparent of the said Sir John." The indictment claimed that all of the rebels charged, including the three Bulmers,

> did, 10 October 28 Henry VIII, as false traitors, with other traitors, at Sherburn, Yorkshire, conspire to deprive the king of his title of Supreme Head of the English Church, and to compel him to hold a certain Parliament and Convocation of the clergy of the realm, and did commit diverse insurrections . . . at Pontefract, diverse days and times before the said 10th of October. And at Doncaster, 20 October 28 Henry VIII, traitorously assembled to levy war, and so continued a long time. And although the king in his great mercy pardoned the said Darcy, and others (named) their offences committed before 10 December 28 Henry VIII, nevertheless they, persevering in their treasons, on 17 January 28 Henry VIII, at Sedrington, Temple Hirst, Flamborough, Beverly, and elsewhere, after the same pardon, again falsely conspired for the above said purpose and to annul diverse wholesome laws made for the common weal, and to depose the king, and to that end sent diverse letters and messengers to each other, 18 January 28 Henry VIII, and at other days and times after the said pardon. And that Sir Francis Bigod and George Lumley, 21 January 28 Henry VIII, and diverse days and times after the said pardon . . . with a great multitude in arms, did make diverse traitorous proclamations to call men to them to make war against the king, and . . . did, 22 January 28 Henry VIII, levy war against the king.
>
> And thus the said jury say that Bigod and Lumley conspired to levy cruel war against the king. And moreover the said jury say that the others above named, 22 January 28 Henry VIII . . . falsely and traitorously abetted the said Bigod and Lumley in their said treasons.[32]

On Wednesday, 16 May, at Westminster, immediately following the trials of Lord Thomas Darcy and Lord John Hussey, the rebels Sir Robert Constable, Sir Francis Bigod, Sir Thomas Percy, George Lumley, and Robert Aske were brought into the court, where they pleaded not guilty to the charge of treason. While the jury retired to consider verdicts in their cases, Sir John and Margaret pleaded guilty to the same charge. The jury returned with a guilty verdict for Bigod and the others. Judgments against all of those who had been charged in the indictment were immediate: Cheyne to be burned, the rest to be executed at Tyburn. In a curious move the jury was relieved of delivering a judgment regarding Ralph Bulmer, Sir John's son: "As to Ralph Bulmer they are with the assent of the court and of the king's serjeants-at-law and attorney exonerated from giving any verdict."[33] He was returned to the Tower.

The executions, as we have seen, took place promptly and publicly.[34] Historians have analyzed, and argued about, the extent to which each of the men convicted and executed for treason was actually guilty. And they have also addressed the question of whether those executed were any more or less guilty than many others who had participated in the rebellions but who had avoided prosecution.[35] But they have been noticeably silent on the subject of Margaret Cheyne's crime and guilt.

If Margaret were judged strictly by the terms of the indictment, the case against her seems at first a tenuous one. The indictment charged those named with having taken part in the October rising of 1536—for their insurrection and for their intention to "levy war" as well as for having opposed the king's authority as "Supreme Head" and for having acted to "compel" the king to hold a parliament in the north. And, while the indictment acknowledged the king's pardon of the rebels for all of the "offences committed before 10 December" 1536, it carefully recorded the treasonous acts that followed in January 1537: the conspiracy to annul the king's laws and to depose Henry; the sending of "letters and messengers" to one another; the publication of "traitorous proclamations" to raise the people against the king once more; and the final claim that on 22 January 1537 Bigod and Lumley did "levy war against the king," while the others "above named . . . falsely and traitorously abetted [them] in their said treasons."

These charges do not seem to apply to Margaret Cheyne at all, nor do they seem to correspond in any way to the testimony of witnesses about what she had said or what she had done during the risings. The only case that could be made against her under this indictment would relate to the vaguely worded final charge encompassing those who had "falsely and traitorously" incited the "said treasons."

Sir John Bulmer's formal deposition in the Tower did, in fact, implicate his wife in just such an act. Sir John had stated that Margaret had encouraged him to join in a new insurrection or, failing that, to leave the country. In effect, then, she had "abetted" him in his treason.

When she was examined in the Tower, Margaret Cheyne admitted that she had hoped that the commons would rise again and, more significantly, that when they had failed to rise, she had "advised" her husband to leave England for Scotland. She also admitted having known that Bulmer's son had told his father not to obey the king's summons to London. Since refusing to answer the king's summons was itself an act of treason, her knowledge of Bulmer's refusal to answer the summons might also be construed as complicity, if not incitement. But during this formal examination Margaret could only respond to the questions she was asked by the official examiners; we have no statement from her which corresponds to the statement made by Sir John before his formal examination. We have no idea of what else she might have wanted to say and no explanation of why she had done what she admitted to doing.

Aside from the Bulmers' admissions, the evidence against Margaret came, first, from their chaplain, William Stainous, whose testimony more or less confirmed what the Bulmers had themselves already admitted. Stainous repeated that he had heard Margaret advise Sir John to try raising the commons again. He had also heard her say she would rather "be torn into pieces" than obey the summons to London. The only additional evidence he offered against Margaret Cheyne was his report that she had, on numerous occasions, wished that Norfolk's head was "off."

The remaining evidence about Margaret's treason, thirdhand at best, came from the parson John Watts, who hadn't actually heard or seen anything himself. His first statement to the examiners was a rambling report in which he merely repeated what he had heard Stainous say about what Stainous had heard from Bulmer about Bulmer's activities during the January risings. Most of what Watts repeated, in fact, had more to do with Bulmer than with Margaret: Bulmer had failed to answer his summons to London because he was afraid he'd never return to the north, he was waiting for his son's advice from London, and he would try to raise the commons or leave the country if the word he finally received was bad.

What emerges most strongly from Watts's testimony, in fact, isn't so much what Margaret Cheyne might have said or done; what emerges is the hostility and fear she had somehow inspired in the parson. Watts made Margaret responsible for Bulmer's role in the Pilgrimage of Grace. According to the parson's statement, Margaret had made Sir John "believe that he may do things that is impossible," she had asked him to "break a spear" for her "sake," and she had begged him to ignore the king's summons because of her fear of separation.

But, whatever he had claimed in this first confession, the parson John Watts's formal deposition, recorded in the Tower by the government's examiners, didn't contribute to the case against Margaret Cheyne. Although his original statement hadn't offered any evidence "of his own knowledge" about Margaret, the hearsay testimony that he had initially offered might have been introduced as evidence.[36] Watts's formal deposition, however, did not address the question of Margaret Cheyne's treason. Thus, Sir John Bulmer himself and the Bulmer parson, William Stainous, must be viewed as the principal witnesses against Margaret Cheyne.[37]

Yet, even without the testimony of any witnesses, Margaret herself admitted she did "incite" at least one of the rebels, her husband. Was that, then, the reason for including her in the indictment?

If so, it could be argued that her actions fell within the limits of the indictment, under the final clause charging "the others . . . named" with having "falsely and traitorously" abetted the rebels "in their said treasons." But, technically, at any rate, she could not have been guilty even under this charge, since the indictment specifies only those who "abetted the said Bigod and Lumley," not any of the other rebels. No one accused Margaret Cheyne of inciting either Bigod or Lumley.

Leaving aside this technicality, which has to do with the wording of the indictment rather than with Margaret's incitement, the question of whether Margaret Cheyne was actually guilty of any treason, as treason was defined by law, is still not clearly answered. The law of treason had been newly expanded by the 1534 Succession Act, the 1534 Treason Act, and the 1536 Succession Act.[38] Beyond the "overt" acts of levying war against the king or plotting his death, treasons first defined in the treason law of 1352, this more recent series of statutes expanded the list of treasons specifically to include "constructive" treason; that is, it was possible to "construct" treason by words only.[39] While Margaret herself did not join the northern rebels in the field, she did admit to encouraging her husband to commit at least two acts of treason, joining armed rebellion against the king and refusing to answer the king's summons. But the 1534 Treason Act carefully specified that, in order to construct treason, words had to be spoken "maliciously."[40]

In reading Margaret's testimony and the statements of those who testified about her, we obviously cannot decide whether her words were uttered with malice. Rather than malice, her words, at least those that have survived, suggest instead a woman who wanted desperately to get out of the way of danger, not to plunge her husband or herself into it any further. As they have been preserved, her words suggest that her interest in any renewal of rebellion was motivated less by political interest than by personal fear: she didn't want to be separated from Bulmer. When he was summoned to London, she encouraged him to ignore the summons, and she supported him in his plans for a new insurrection. Failing a new rising, she advised her husband to leave the country; she wanted him to "get a ship to carry her and him" to Scotland. But her interest in Sir John's remaining in the north, in his planning a new insurrection, or in his leaving the country may simply have come from her fear of being separated from him, not from any political motivation. There is nothing in any of the surviving testimony that indicates with certainty that her words were spoken with "malice"—and malicious intent, as specified by the 1534 Treason Act, was necessary for words to construct treason.

Her incitement, if that was the principal reason for including her in the indictment along with the other rebels, was distinctive in another way as well. Margaret Cheyne was not accused of having been a prominent participant in the northern rebellions, actively and openly involved. She didn't incite or encourage rebels publicly or inclusively—certainly not Bigod or Lumley, as the indictment charged. The only person she spoke to was her husband. The Bulmers' chaplain said she had "enticed" Sir John, but there is no indication in the statement Stainous made that her words had been spoken to anyone but her husband. Her "treason" was thus very different from the active and public treasons of her husband and other men such as Aske and Bigod.[41]

Margaret's words and behavior were foolish, perhaps even wild. But were they treasonable? At least given our analysis thus far, they don't seem very dangerous, nor do they seem to offer any real threat to Henry VIII. In fact, strictly on the basis of the evidence against her that has survived, it is hard to see how or why she came to be accused of the crime of treason in the first place. And it is even harder to see why she pleaded guilty to the charge when the case against her seems so weak.

We might be tempted to conclude that the accusations against Margaret Cheyne were unjustified or that the charge against her was a terrible mistake, the result of the overcharged atmosphere following the northern rebellions. We might also decide that her guilty plea was a mistake, a miscarriage of justice; a strong and informed advisor might have counseled her that, whatever she had done, it didn't fall within the limits of the charge. If Margaret herself had been as sharp or as articulate as some Tudor prisoners appearing before the bar, she might have challenged, and perhaps defended herself against, the charges of treason made against her.[42]

But a careful review of her life and her "crime" makes it almost certain that she was not caught up by accident in the prosecutions that followed the rebellions. The charge against her wasn't a mistake. Her inclusion with prominent traitors such as Aske and Bigod was both deliberate and calculated, and, instead of arguing her case, she probably had good reason for pleading guilty to the crime.

TWO

A Woman's Treason: Why Margaret Cheyne?

O n 22 May 1537, just five days after Margaret Cheyne was convicted of treason and three days before she was executed, Thomas Cromwell wrote to the duke of Norfolk with a series of instructions about matters that needed to be cleaned up in the north, chief among them money matters:

> The King's Highness also desireth your lordship that ye will make due search of such lands, offices, fees, farms, and all other things as were in the hands and possession of the Lord Darcy, Sir Robert Constable, Sir Francis Bigod, Sir John Bulmer, Sir Stephen Hamerton, Sir Thomas Percy, Nicholas Tempest, and all the persons of those parts lately attainted here and to certify the same to His Grace, to the intent the same may confer them to the persons worthy accordingly, and likewise to cause a perfect inventory of their goods, lands, and possessions to be made and sent up with convenient speed as shall appertain.[1]

On 6 June, only days after the rebels were executed, Cromwell wrote to Sir Thomas Wyatt, then serving as Henry's ambassador to the imperial court of Charles V. He sent Wyatt news of the executions:

> For although the Lords Darcy and Hussey, Sirs Robert Constable, Francis Bigod, John Bulmer, Stephen Hamerton, knights, the Lord Lumley's son [George Lumley], Robert Aske, Nicholas Tempest, the abbot of [Jervaux],

the prior of Bridlington, and some others, also Sir Thomas Percy, had
their pardon, yet because they have been openly . . . attainted of certain
conspiracies and high treasons most ingrately, spitefully, and heinously
committed against his benign and so gracious merciful Majesty . . . [and]
have been condemned of high treason, and some of them already executed,
whereof if there is any communication moved unto you, you may as-
suredly affirm that if they had not highly offended since the king's pardon,
his Majesty had never remembered their precedent offences, nor imputed
the same to their charge, being a . . . most honorable observator of his
word. But seeing their cankered . . . hearts he could no less do than to
suffer them to have his laws to the example of such ingrate and irremedi-
able obstinate hearts.[2]

Only a month later he mentioned the traitors again in a letter to Wyatt, this
time reporting on their executions:

Nothing is succeeded since my last writing but from good quiet and peace
daily to better and better. The traitors have been executed, the Lord Darcy
at Tower Hill, the Lord Hussey at Lincoln, Aske hanged upon the
dungeon of the castle of York, and Sir Robert Constable hanged at Hull.
The residue were executed at Tyburn.[3]

Despite Cromwell's silence about Margaret Cheyne, the news of her
treason had spread. One surviving account of the reaction to her fate
demonstrates the extent to which her story had become known throughout the
country.

Late in July 1537 Sir John Daunce was in Thame (Oxfordshire) investigating a small group of "seditious persons" and a conversation that had taken
place the previous May in the chantry of Thame.[4] There, on Whitsunday (20
May), only four days after the northern rebels had been convicted of treason, a
group of men had met for a breakfast gathering. As they spent their time
"making merry and spending their money," their conversation turned to "the
state of the North" and the news that "ten should suffer as proditors [traitors]."
According to John Strebilhill, who had taken part in the conversation, "it was
said, 'Lady Bulmer of the north country is attainted and shall die.'" Robert
Johns, also present in the group, had expressed a degree of sympathy for the
unfortunate woman: "It is a pity that she should suffer." Strebilhill had replied,
"It is no pity, if she be a traitor to her prince." Johns had then ended the
conversation with a carefully worded warning: "Let us speak no more of this
matter, for men may be blamed for speaking of the truth."

Although the conversation had been brief, and although it had been some weeks since it had reportedly taken place, Sir John Daunce was sent to investigate, and in Thame he took a series of depositions from the men who had been present about just what had been said and by whom. It doesn't seem as if any of the deponents got into further trouble for their "seditious conversation," and there is no indication about how it had come to the attention of the government in the first place, but the incident provides telling evidence of the impression Margaret Cheyne's death had made on the average man (and, presumably, woman) outside the capital.

What is remarkable about this incident in Oxfordshire, apart from the survival of its record in the archives, is that the conversation of ordinary men about extraordinary events focused not on prominent traitors such as Aske and Bigod but, rather, on the single woman accused of treason. Once the rebels had been convicted, Thomas Cromwell, the king's chief minister, could turn his attention to the serious business of gaining control of the possessions forfeited by the attainted prisoners. But the men who gathered in Oxfordshire to enjoy a breakfast together did not speak about the rebel leaders or captains; they spoke about Margaret Cheyne. In the midst of their "making merry" the mention of her fate reminded them of the need for silence and obedience.

Her fate was also noted by contemporary "historians," those careful chroniclers who recorded the day, place, and manner of her death. Surviving accounts vary widely in their attitudes toward her and in the degree of sympathy they expressed for her fate.

The compiler of the *Chronicle of the Grey Friars of London* observed the arrival in the capital of those accused of treason during the northern risings, and he briefly described what he knew of their trials as well. The chronicler took note, for example, that there was some confusion about the place where Margaret Cheyne was to stand trial: "Also . . . was brought from the Tower unto the Guildhall Sir Robert Constable and Lady Bulmer, but they were carried from the Guildhall unto Westminster with all the rest, and there had their judgment."[5] Interestingly, this chronicle is the only contemporary account that recognized Margaret's claim to be Lady Bulmer. "And at that time was drawn from the Tower . . . the Lady Margaret Bulmer, wife unto Sir John Bulmer," the chronicler noted on her execution day. But he could not mention her title without including what he had heard about the circumstances of her relationship with Sir John: "and he made her his wife, but she was the wife of one Cheyne, for he sold her unto Sir Bulmer; and she was drawn when she came to Newgate into Smithfield, and there burned the same forenoon." If this story is typical of the gossip current about Margaret Cheyne, it suggests how completely she and Sir John were being discredited.

Edward Hall, a lawyer at Gray's Inn and a staunch supporter of both Henry VIII and his policies, also recorded the trial of the northern rebels, among them "Sir John Bulmer and his wife, which some reported was not his wife but his paramour."[6] Following her trial he also reported on Margaret Cheyne's death, but his note is remarkable for the summary way he refers to both the woman and her execution: "and Sir John Bulmer's paramour was burned in Smithfield in London."

Charles Wriothesley, Windsor herald, evidently witnessed Margaret Cheyne's death. On 16 May he noted the arraignment at Westminster of the northern rebels, including, among them, Margaret Cheyne. Like the Grey Friars chronicler, he hinted that there was something wrong about her marriage, referring to her as "Margaret Cheyne, afterwards Lady Bulmer, by untrue matrimony." His account of her execution is brief: "Margaret Cheyne, other wife to Bulmer called, was drawn . . . from the Tower of London into Smithfield and there burned." He observed that she had died "according to her judgment, God pardon her soul." Wriothesley nevertheless concluded his note of her execution with a sympathetic observation: "she was a very fair creature and a beautiful."[7]

Modern historians, like Thomas Cromwell, have been more interested in the drama of high politics than in the brief story of Margaret Cheyne. The great nineteenth-century Tudor historian James Froude did at least note the "dreadful death awarded by the English law" to "Lady Bulmer." But without any explanation, he concluded, "Lady Bulmer seems from the depositions to have deserved as serious punishment as any woman for the crime of high treason can be said to have deserved."[8]

More recent historians have concerned themselves even less with Margaret Cheyne, failing to note the singularity of her position among the rebels. In his classic biography of Henry VIII, A. F. Pollard didn't mention her at all. In the standard Oxford history of England, J. D. Mackie's only reference to her comes at the end of his discussion of the northern rebellions. Her name then appears out of nowhere: "Lady Bulmer was burnt." The preeminent Tudor historian G. R. Elton has been no more inclusive in his volume of the *New History of England;* finishing his narrative of the Pilgrimage of Grace, he refers to her for the first and last time when he writes, "On the same day [that the leaders were executed at Tyburn], Lady Bulmer was burned for treason at Smithfield." Finally, Tudor revisionist John Guy has revised her out of history altogether: "Leaders executed included Lords Darcy and Hussey, Sir Robert Constable, Sir Thomas Percy, Sir Francis Bigod, Sir John Bulmer, and Aske. Clerical victims were James Cockerell of Guisborough Priory, William Wood, prior of Bridlington, Friar John of Pickering, Adam Sedbar, abbot of Jervaux, and William Thirsk of Fountains Abbey."[9]

In fact, the only historians who have paid any attention to the remarkable story of Margaret Cheyne were Madeleine Hope Dodds and Ruth Dodds. In their 1915 history of the Pilgrimage of Grace they took note of the singular presence of this woman among the traitors, concluding that she had "committed no overt act of treason." They argued that the "reason for her execution" was not "the heinous nature of her offence" but, rather, her death's usefulness: "her punishment . . . was intended as an example to others." Margaret Cheyne's execution was, in their view, "politic," an "object-lesson to husbands," the purpose of which was to "teach them to distrust their wives." It was also to be a lesson to women, "to teach them to dread their husbands' confidence."[10]

It is certainly possible to argue that Margaret Cheyne's execution was a cautionary example about the proper relationship of husbands and wives. Margaret's personal attractions seem to be of particular significance in this regard. There seems to be little doubt of her beauty. After noting her execution in his chronicle, for example, Charles Wriothesley added that she was "a very fair creature and a beautiful." But her beauty was dangerous. In John Watts's eyes "Pretty Peg" had seduced her husband into foolishness. According to the parson's evidence, Bulmer had agreed to his wife's suggestions as mindlessly as if he were a talking bird. Watts had even accused William Stainous, the Bulmers' chaplain, of falling prey to Margaret's charms. Margaret Cheyne's sexual power was thus suspect; women like her could lure their husbands into danger. Men needed to submit to their princes, and they also needed to control their wives, their mothers, their daughters, their female servants. Margaret Cheyne had violated the contemporary notion that wives should be chaste, silent, and obedient, and her death could certainly have been intended as a warning about the proper behavior of women.[11]

Thus, Henry's decision to proceed against Margaret Cheyne might have been a politic one, as Dodds and Dodds suggested—just as the decisions about all of the rebels who were to be tried for treason were, to a greater or lesser extent, political.[12] Regardless of her guilt or innocence, her conviction and public execution for the crime of treason would have been a powerful reminder that treason was not limited to acts of armed rebellion. Her sentence to the ghastly death of burning at the stake would also have been important in this regard. The public and horrifying spectacle of her execution reinforced the double horror of her betrayal—her violation of her duty to both king and husband, her challenge to the social order as well as to the political order.[13]

Yet Margaret Cheyne was not the only woman—or wife—involved with the rebels during the Pilgrimage of Grace. Women of the lower classes were most certainly present at rebel assemblies and with rebel forces, though reports sent to the king and Cromwell about "certain lewd persons," "an unlawful assembly," and "certain traitors," for example, make it impossible to tell just how many of those involved in the gatherings were women. Even reports that calculate numbers do not distinguish between men and women; in his accounting of the Lincolnshire rebels, for example, Christopher Askew reported on 6 October 1536 that "the insurgents . . . number 10,000 or 12,000 spears, well harnessed, and 30,000 others, some harnessed and some not."[14] Such calculations, as well as references in other reports to "all the commonalty," "the commons," "the great assembly in Lincolnshire," and "the people," suggest that women might have been present among those "others" and commons gathered for rebellion.

Two further examples, both dated 6 October, can be cited. On that day the earl of Huntington wrote to Henry VIII reporting that "diverse of your disobedient servants have assembled contrary to their allegiance, but where I do not know." Meanwhile, on the same day the king wrote to the earl of Shrewsbury, encouraging him to "raise . . . tenants, servants, and friends" against "the evil-disposed persons lately assembled in those parts."[15] Such inclusive references suggest that women might have been among those intended to receive the call. In his recent analysis of the social status of those who had participated in the Pilgrimage of Grace in the Lake Counties, Scott Harrison addressed just such a question in calculating the size of the northern gatherings. He concluded that women were numbered among the rebels: "Including women and children the greatest assembly was that of fifteen thousand at the Broadfield. Twenty thousand men, women and children may have actively supported the rebellion at some stages, and many more may have taken the rebel oath before returning to their homes."[16]

The presence of women among the rebels is made certain in several accounts of the northern rebellions. Among the records in the state papers, for instance, is a statement made by Thomas Kendall, vicar of Louth, whose Sunday sermon on 1 October seemed to have incited the Lincolnshire risings, which began the next day.[17] Along with many of the principal insurgents in the October risings, Kendall was deposed early in November. Although the surviving document is mutilated just where Kendall's testimony becomes important, from our point of view, enough remains to suggest that women had indeed been among those first rebels. Kendall's deposition consists of his answers to the questions of his examiners; in response to the sixteenth article, Kendall explained why he had left Louth, and although his answer is fragmentary, it involves a woman and child who had been killed during the riots, "in token whereof some of the parishioners sent their children and part of their goods" away. When he had heard about these deaths, Kendall claimed to have left the county.

Another state papers document, a letter from the king to the duke of Norfolk, also indicates that women were to be numbered among the rebels.

Despite his promised pardon to them, Henry urged Norfolk to advance on Aske and his followers, "for the utter extinguishment of these traitors, their wives and children, with fire and sword accordingly.[18]

As a final example, in April 1537, just as the Bulmers were being taken into custody and transferred to London, some sort of disturbance broke out in Taunton (Somersetshire). In his chronicle Wriothesley asserted that the rising was in response to a visit of the king's commissioners: "certain commissions were sent into the west country in Somerset for to take up corn, whereupon the people of the country began to rise and make an insurrection." While this short-lived rebellion was not part of the northern risings, it did erupt during the tense weeks when the northern rebels were being examined in London. Significantly, women had also participated in the Taunton rising. Wriothesley noted, "the chief beginners thereof were taken, and sixty of them condemned, whereof fourteen persons were hanged and quartered, one being a woman, and the rest had their pardon."[19]

Despite their involvement in the unrest late in 1536 and early 1537, these women remain unknown, both numberless and nameless. We cannot determine what part they played in the rebellions, much less who they were. But the names of a number of much more prominent women had also come to the attention of investigators during the aftermath of the Pilgrimage of Grace, and about their activities we can discover a great deal.

At the end of November 1536 Harry Osborne of Gloucester reported on a kind of spy mission he had undertaken among the rebels.[20] He had been serving with the king's army when he had decided "to go among the northern host to know the fashion of them." According to his report, he spent three or four days with the rebels; they had "meat and drink enough" as well as "many of them harness of deer skins." But Osborne's most interesting tidbit concerned the arrival of "Lady Rysse," that is, Katherine Howard, the widow of Sir Rhys ap Griffith, among the rebels. Osborne claimed that Lady Rhys had brought 3,000 men to the rebel company, as well as "half a cartload of plate, which they are coining among themselves." Osborne thought the coins the rebels were making looked as good as any of "King Harry's groats."

Osborne's is the only evidence that seems to have survived about Katherine Howard, Lady Rhys. Since her husband had been executed by Henry VIII for trying to incite a treasonous rebellion in 1531, her efforts on behalf of the rebel cause (if Osborne's report is true) would be both understandable and dangerous.

Much more is known about Lady Anne Hussey, the wife of Sir John Hussey. However reluctant a rebel her husband might have been, Lady Hussey was not at all hesitant about making her own convictions known.[21] Sir John

Hussey had been Princess Mary's chamberlain, his wife one of Mary's closest friends. By 1535, after Mary's household had been disbanded, Hussey was living in Sleaford (Lincolnshire), where he was gradually drawn into the plots that would eventually erupt in 1536 in the Pilgrimage of Grace. But earlier in 1536 John Hussey had traveled south to attend Parliament. His wife, Anne, had accompanied him and had taken advantage of the trip south to visit her former mistress.

During this visit, which had taken place on 5 June, Anne Hussey was overheard calling Mary "the Princess" on more than one occasion, a title that Mary had been deprived of by the 1534 Act of Succession. Lady Hussey was arrested, and she was detained in the Tower for several weeks. At the beginning of July Sir Thomas Audley wrote to Cromwell about her, indicating that a servant from Lady Hussey "has been twice with me this day, desiring that she [Lady Hussey] might go abroad to the chapel and take the air, as she is very sick. I wish your opinion on this matter." Audley continued, "Her offence was nought [wicked], but ye perceive how she abhorreth it, with that she never spake it but by event [accident], and not of will deliberate nor malice."[22]

Lady Hussey was still in the Tower on 3 August, when she was examined by Sir Edmund Walsingham.[23] She admitted to having given "the Lady Mary" the wrong title; she said she had once called "for drink for 'the Princess,'" and she had said, "'the Princess' was gone walking." Lady Hussey indicated that on both occasions she had been referring to Mary. But she emphasized that she had called Mary by her royal title only "by inadvertence," that she had heard no one else using the title, and that she had heard no one affirm the validity of the king's first marriage or of Mary's status as the king's lawful daughter. Although she also admitted having sent and received "tokens," she claimed never to have received written messages from Mary.

Lady Hussey was eventually released from the Tower; by October 1536, the time of the first risings in the north, she was back in Lincolnshire. According to Lord Hussey's statement to the Council of the North, his wife had been more than a little involved in the northern rebellions. Hussey testified that, when the rebel forces had heard early in the rising that Hussey had fled, they had threatened to burn his house at Sleaford; his wife, "like a fool," had promised the rebels she would bring him back.[24] She was also said to have supplied the rebels with "a cart of food."[25] Later, while her husband was in the Tower awaiting trial, she had been allowed to visit him; Hussey had been present at Lord Darcy's first examination and told his wife what Darcy had replied in answer to the investigators' questions. Lady Hussey then repeated what her husband had told her to her servant Catharine Cresswell; she, in turn, told her husband, Percival Cresswell, who, in his turn, repeated Darcy's responses to others. Before long the whole story had spread further abroad until it, too, was being investigated.[26] Although her husband was executed for treasons committed during the northern rebellions, Lady Anne Hussey was investigated no further.

In the midst of the northern rebellions Christopher Stapleton's wife, Elizabeth, also made her sympathies clear. The Stapleton family was from Wighill, not far from York. Suffering from a chronic illness, Christopher Stapleton often spent time in the summer and fall at the house of the Grey Friars in Beverly. In 1536 he was there with Elizabeth; Sir Brian Stapleton, his son by his first wife (Alice, the daughter of William Aske); and his brother, William Stapleton, who was a lawyer of Gray's Inn and a friend of Robert Aske. In October, just as William Stapleton was about to return to London, the northern risings began in Beverly, and he was chosen as captain of the commons.[27]

Later deposed about his activities, William Stapleton gave a day-by-day account of events in Beverly.[28] He vividly described the beginning of the rising on Sunday, 8 October. Although she had been instructed to stay inside, Elizabeth Stapleton had gone outside so she could watch the commons on their way to the musters at West Wood Green. As they passed, she called out, "God's blessing have ye, and speed you well in your good purpose." When she was asked why her husband and his son were not joining them, she replied: "They be in the [Grey] Friars [house]. Go pull them out by the heads." When her husband heard what she had said, he asked, in some despair, "What do ye mean, except ye would have me, my son and heir, and my brother cast away?" To which she answered that the commons' cause "was God's quarrel."

The next day, Monday, 9 October, she continued her involvement with the rebels. By then, according to William Stapleton's statement, the commons had become "wild people," threatening to burn the Grey Friars with Stapleton, his son, and his brother in it. One of the friars, who "rejoiced in their rising," was "very busy going betwixt the wife of the said Christopher and the said wild people." William swore that he had been coerced into taking the rebels' oath and becoming their captain, but he said that "the wife of the said Christopher" had been "very joyous" at his selection. Although his deposition continues in detail through the end of the month, William Stapleton had no more to say about his sister-in-law Elizabeth, who must have remained with her husband while Sir William had gone on with the Pilgrims to Doncaster.

In Doncaster William Stapleton had joined with rebel leaders, among them Sir Thomas Percy, who was ultimately convicted of treason. In his testimony Percy, too, indicated the involvement of a woman in the rebellions. When he was examined in the Tower, he testified that he had been staying with his mother in Yorkshire when rumors had reached them about the October risings in Lincolnshire. He claimed that he, too, had been coerced into joining the rebel muster at Malton. He had refused to join Bigod's rising the following January, though, and his explanation for his refusal is intriguing.[29]

During his 10 February examination in the Tower, Percy deposed that he had first heard of Bigod's insurrection through a letter the rebel leader had sent to his mother; Percy's mother had forwarded Bigod's letter to him, accompanied by the message that he "should take a substantial way in that matter upon her blessing." The rebels promised to put him into possession of the title and lands of his brother, Henry Percy, earl of Northumberland. This must have been a tempting offer. Sir Thomas Percy, next in line for the earldom, had been disinherited by his childless brother; in 1535 the earl had made the king his heir—an act of Parliament had granted Henry Percy the right to grant his possessions to the king when he (the elder Percy) died. Although it sounds as if Thomas Percy's mother was encouraging her son to join with Bigod in a new insurrection, Percy went out of his way to exonerate her in his statement, saying that he had interpreted her message to mean he "should not meddle" in the new rising.

Most surprising in some ways are the stories that survive about Sir Ralph Evers's wife. Sir Ralph Evers the younger had been a loyal supporter of the king throughout the northern rebellions. As keeper of the king's castle at Scarborough (Yorkshire), he had held out against the Pilgrims throughout the weeks of the rising in late 1536, and he continued to serve the king during Bigod's insurrection in January 1537. But he ran into some trouble as Norfolk attempted to settle the north. In July he fell under suspicion for having written a letter to Sir John Bulmer the preceding March, when Bulmer was worrying about whether to answer the king's summons or to try to renew rebellion. The letter Evers was alleged to have sent included disparaging remarks about both Cromwell and Norfolk. Norfolk himself questioned Evers about the letter in early July and reported on the examination to Cromwell later that month: "As to Evers, no man has more cause to be angry with him if the letter was written by his consent."[30]

Evers, however, denied that he had written the letter, claiming that he couldn't have written it because "he can neither read nor write more than his own name." Evers was sent to Cromwell, who examined him and then returned him to Norfolk.[31] It was during this period—the period of weeks when Evers was under suspicion and in London—that his wife uttered words that very well could have involved her in a charge of treason.

In September Cromwell received one more letter accompanied by a set of "confessions," this time about Lady Evers. According to one Edmund Wright,

Lady Evers and two servants had broken into Wright's home, fearing that Wright's wife "would reveal words she [Lady Evers] had spoken concerning the king" late in August (about the time of St. Bartholomew's Day, 24 August). According to Wright's confessions, Lady Evers had said, "There is twenty of the best in Yorkshire hath sent me word that if my husband were in any danger, that they would rise and fetch him out, or else to die therefore."[32] She had also warned that "if her husband were in any danger . . . they would it would turn to a worse business than the death of any man that died within Yorkshire as yet." Wright, seeing that Lady Evers had "threatened and reviled his wife and her servants," got the justice of the peace, who removed Lady Evers from his home. At the time that Wright wrote to Cromwell, Lady Evers had been reunited with her husband, and the two were in Pickering.

Some days later Norfolk wrote to Cromwell about the couple. He had been unable to find out who was responsible for sending the letter in Evers's name, evidently satisfied that Sir Ralph's claim that the letter had been forged was true. Norfolk had also followed up the charges made against Lady Evers, but these, too, he dismissed, saying that he had "examined an accusation of light words against" her but that he could "find no proof."[33]

All of these women might well have been charged with treason, for they had all gotten themselves involved, in one way or another, with the rebel cause during the Pilgrimage of Grace. Their dangerous talk and strange behavior might seem relatively insignificant when viewed against the background of open and armed rebellion, but they seem no less guilty than Margaret. They had all surely incited rebellion, their words, it could well be argued, "constructing" treason against the king.

Katherine Howard, lady Rhys, was reported to have taken troops and supplies to the rebel army. In addition to supplying 3,000 men, she was said to have delivered "half a cartload" of plate so that the Pilgrims could coin their own money.

Lady Anne Hussey had also been in direct contact with the Pilgrims. Aside from her references to "Princess" Mary, she had told the rebels she would bring her husband to them, and she had also supplied them with food. Despite the time she had spent in the Tower under suspicion, she couldn't keep silent even when her husband was imprisoned; her stories about Darcy's testimony may not have been treasonous, but they were indiscreet, and they certainly hadn't helped Hussey's situation.

Elizabeth Stapleton, Christopher Stapleton's wife, cheered on the rebels during the rising of Beverly and insulted her husband for failing to join them. She was also involved in her brother-in-law's "decision" to become a captain in the rebel army.

The dowager countess of Northumberland was also, at the very least, indiscreet. In sending the rebel leader Bigod's letter to her son, she had probably already compromised herself. But, along with the letter, she had sent the ambiguous message enjoining him to "take a substantial way in that matter" and giving him her blessing.

Finally, in spite of her husband's continued loyalty to the king, Lady Evers had not only reacted strongly when Sir Ralph Evers was under suspicion—breaking into a house and threatening its occupants—but she had also "spoken against" the king. She had even threatened to incite rebellion if her husband was not released.

While the tone of Margaret Cheyne's words remains uncertain, all of these women seem to have spoken with some degree of "malice." If malicious intent were necessary for words to be considered treasonous, their words seem more clearly to have constructed treason than anything Margaret Cheyne was reported to have said.

Moreover, all of these women seem to have been much more open and active than Margaret Cheyne—delivering men and food to the rebels, encouraging the rebel forces or promising them support, spreading tales, or sending messages. Margaret Cheyne, on the other hand, was accused only of having spoken to her husband in the presence of the family chaplain. For Madeleine Hope Dodds and Ruth Dodds what separated women like these from Margaret Cheyne was not what they said or did but, rather, who they were. Each of these women had the personal support and protection offered by a powerful web of family connections.

Katherine Howard was the widow of an executed traitor, but she was also a member of the powerful Howard family, and was the duke of Norfolk's own half-sister. Anne Hussey was the daughter of George Grey, earl of Kent, a woman of notable reputation. Loyal to Queen Katherine and the Princess Mary, she was, according to Charles V's ambassador Eustace Chapuys, "a lady of a great house, and one of the most virtuous in England."[34] The Stapletons were a well-connected Yorkshire family, loyal followers of the earl of Northumberland. Katherine Percy, the dowager countess of Northumberland, was the daughter and heiress of Sir Robert Spencer; although she favored her younger son, Sir Thomas Percy, she was also mother of Henry Percy, the current earl of Northumberland.

Margaret Cheyne, on the other hand, was a woman of "no family and irregular life, dependent on the head of a falling house," according to Dodds and Dodds. In her very "insignificance" was her "danger": she had no family to protect her, no "avenger" to come to her defense.[35]

At least in part, Dodds and Dodds were correct in their view of Margaret Cheyne: the Bulmer family certainly offered Margaret no support, either out of fear or from dislike. William Bulmer seems particularly to have failed his older brother and his wife. In his letter of January 1537 William sounded on cordial terms with Sir John, and he certainly indicated no suspicions about the validity of the marriage; although he was worried about the risings and his own involvement with them, he sent his congratulations to his brother and Margaret on the birth of their son.

Surviving evidence demonstrates that William Bulmer had been a active participant in the risings—and had shared his brother John's fears after the failure of Bigod's rebellion—but he lost no time after Sir John's arrest in making his way to Norfolk in order to clear himself of any suspicions. Norfolk wrote to Cromwell on 8 April that he had detained Sir John Bulmer and his wife; by 11 April William Bulmer had met with Norfolk, and the duke had sent him to Cromwell in London.

In fact, Norfolk sent his own letter to Cromwell along with William Bulmer and requested that Cromwell act as William's "good lord." It is tempting to think that William Bulmer had been spared and then sent to London to provide some kind of evidence against Sir John and Margaret Cheyne. Such a suspicion seems less unfounded in light of events that took place early in February 1538, long after the northern rebels had been executed. On 27 February Cuthbert Tunstall, bishop of Durham, and John Uvedale, who served on Norfolk's Council of the North, reported to Henry VIII that William Bulmer's wife, Elizabeth, had just put into their hands "a letter sent unto the said Sir William Bulmer from Your Grace's late rebel Sir John Bulmer, written all with his own hand."[36]

The story Tunstall and Uvedale told was an ugly one; William Bulmer had recently joined his wife in Durham, where she was then living (she was the daughter and heir of William Elmedon of Elmedon, Durham), and "at his there being he made much search amongst the evidence of his said wife's inheritance." Having finished his search, Bulmer then "departed unkindly from her." Fearing that her husband had "conveyed" something valuable from her, Elizabeth and a friar, together with her servant, made "a new search to see whether any of her said evidences [legal documents] were embezzled." During their search the three found a letter implicating not only Sir John in a treasonous plot but William Bulmer as well. In "discharge of her fidelity" William Bulmer's wife had sent the letter to Tunstall and Uvedale, who advised the king that: "whatsoever shall stand with your most gracious pleasure to be further done in the same, we shall with all good effect and diligence cause it to be accomplished to the best of our power."

In spite of everything, Sir John Bulmer and Margaret Cheyne had held fast to each other—during rebellion, during the unbearable stress of rebellion's aftermath, and during their imprisonment in the Tower. They had been tried for treason together, and together they pleaded guilty. They were executed on the same day, separated at the end only by the time and place of their execution. On the other hand, William Bulmer and his wife, Elizabeth, survived the aftermath of rebellion and escaped being implicated in treason, only to have turned on each other. Elizabeth Bulmer was more than willing to accuse her own husband of treason.

Norfolk may have concluded that William Bulmer was, in fact, a "true man" with "no fault in him," or he may well have known that William had evidence he was willing to offer against his brother if he could save himself. In either case William Bulmer does not seem to have been the kind of man on whom Margaret Cheyne could have relied if she had to. Nor was he the kind of man likely to use his family's remaining connections to save her. Throughout the Pilgrimage and its aftermath both Sir John and Margaret were so remarkably aware of the dangers of separation that they must have known that the Bulmer family could not be relied on to come to their aid.

Following the collapse of the Pilgrimage of Grace, Margaret and Sir John were to find the legality of their marriage under attack. The government made the most of their irregular past, every official reference emphasizing the ambiguity of their relationship. Margaret was never acknowledged in official documents as Lady Bulmer. She remained Margaret Cheyne—wife of the late William Cheyne, Sir John Bulmer's "paramour," a woman whom he simply "call[ed] his wife," the woman to whom Sir John was linked only "by untrue matrimony." A contemporary chronicler even recorded that her first husband had sold her to Bulmer.[37]

Yet Margaret Cheyne was not without some obvious family connections. She and her husband had three daughters, and in 1537 she had just given birth to another child, a boy, born in January. Yet not once in any of the surviving accusations, reports, or examinations is Margaret's physical condition mentioned. Her baby must have been born shortly before William Bulmer sent his congratulations on 25 January. She would thus have been pregnant during the Pilgrimage of Grace, her fears for her husband and of being separated from him all the more understandable. And when the Bulmers had been summoned to London in early March, Margaret's hesitations and fears are equally understandable; having just recovered from childbirth, she must have found the prospect of being separated from Bulmer disturbing.

There is no clue about what arrangements were made for the care of this child, named John after his father, while Margaret spent six weeks imprisoned in the Tower or where and how he was cared for after her death. Until now historians have been as uninterested in this child as Henry's investigators and the Tudor chroniclers were. Although I have been unable to discover any details about his early life, he did live, marrying Agnes Crathorne, the daughter of James Crathorne, of Crathorne. During the Yorkshire Visitations of 1584, Margaret Cheyne's son told examiners that, although his mother had first lived with Bulmer *pro concubina,* he had been born *post matrimonium et intra matrimonia;* the many attacks against his parents' marriage made at the time of their arrest and trial must have been behind his assertion. John Bulmer, the son of Sir John Bulmer and Margaret Cheyne, had survived the treason that had destroyed his parents. He died on 6 February 1608.[38]

In addition to the children he had with Margaret, Sir John also had children from his first marriage, and the fate of his oldest son, Ralph, has also intrigued me. Ralph Bulmer's part in his father's activities was relatively minor, but it was enough to have him charged with treason. Ralph's exact age is unknown; he was probably born about 1510, and he married Anne Tempest, daughter of Sir Thomas Tempest, about 1530. In 1537 Ralph was sent to London and while there had reported to his father rumors flying in the capital. In March he wrote to Sir John, warning him not to answer the king's summons.

At the time of their trial, while the jury retired to consider verdicts against the accused, who had pleaded not guilty to the charge of treason, the three Bulmers, along with Sir Thomas Percy and Sir Stephen Hamerton, remained behind. Once the jury had gone, Percy, Hamerton, Sir John Bulmer, and Margaret Cheyne pleaded guilty to the charge of treason. But there was no decision made about Ralph Bulmer: "As to Ralph Bulmer they [the jury] are exonerated from giving any verdict." He was returned to the Tower.[39]

We next hear of him in the fall of 1537; he had spent the intervening months still in the Tower. On 7 October Norfolk wrote to Cromwell, and in a postscript to his letter Norfolk mentioned the younger Bulmer, indicating that he had come to suspect that it was Ralph Bulmer who had counterfeited the letter Sir Ralph Evers was earlier alleged to have written: "I lately wrote to you to keep Ralph Bulmer . . . in ward, whom I suspected of counterfeiting Sir Ralph Evers's letter and hand; I have made inquiry and think at my coming up I shall lay so evident matter against the said Sir Ralph that it shall not be for his honesty to have so obstinately denied his hand as he has done."[40] Ralph Bulmer was still being held at the end of March 1538, when his name was included on a list of prisoners being held in the Tower.[41]

Charles Wriothesley provides the next clue about what happened to Ralph Bulmer; in summarizing the decisions about the northern rebels, he noted: "but Ralph Bulmer, the son of John Bulmer, was reprieved and had no sentence."[42] Although Ralph Bulmer had remained in the Tower for some time, at least through early 1538, he must have been, as Wriothesley reported, reprieved and eventually released. He lived to be restored to his father's estate in the first year of Edward VI's reign, dying in 1558.[43] It is very tempting to suspect that Sir John Bulmer and Margaret Cheyne's guilty plea may have had something to do with Ralph Bulmer's survival.

Yet these were not the kinds of family connections Madeleine Hope Dodds and Ruth Dodds had in mind when they tried to account for Margaret Cheyne's execution. Lady Rhys, Lady Hussey, the dowager countess of Northumberland, Elizabeth Stapleton, and Lady Evers were, in Dodds and Dodds's words, "all ladies of blameless character and of respectable, sometimes powerful, families." Given the peculiar circumstances of Margaret's marriage to John Bulmer, the Bulmer family's lack of support, and her own illegitimate birth, they judged that she was, by contrast, a woman of "insignificance," isolated and thus vulnerable to being used as an example.

But such conclusions ignore the fact that Margaret *did* have family connections and that they were connections of great significance. I would argue that Margaret Cheyne was arrested for treason and execution not because she lacked family connections but, rather, because of those family connections.

Contemporary reports and historical evidence, as we have seen, indicate Margaret Cheyne was the daughter of Edward Stafford, third duke of Buckingham.[44] Through his father, Henry Stafford, second duke of Buckingham, Edward Stafford was directly descended from Thomas of Woodstock, Edward III's youngest son. Edward Stafford's mother was Catherine Woodville, the sister of Elizabeth Woodville, Edward IV's queen. Edward Stafford's grandfather, Humphrey Stafford, had been married to a Beaufort, and through this Beaufort grandmother the third duke of Buckingham was descended from John of Gaunt, fourth son of Edward III. Through his great grandfather (Henry Stafford, the first duke of Buckingham) Edward Stafford was related to the Neville family. His wife was Eleanor Percy, the sister of Henry Percy, fifth earl of Northumberland; through the marriages of his children Stafford had strengthened his ties with the powerful Neville, Howard, and Pole families. Margaret Cheyne may have been illegitimate, but, if she was Buckingham's daughter, as seems probable, she had royal blood in her veins and, through her father, connections with the most influential—and potentially dangerous—families of the north.

Through her father and grandfather Margaret also had a family history of treason. The second duke of Buckingham had been proclaimed a traitor by Richard III in 1483.[45] The third duke, Margaret's father, had been executed for treason in 1521, the indictment against him charging that he "did . . . imagine and compass the deposition and death of the king," thus "intending to exalt himself to the crown."[46] Did treason, like royalty, run in the blood?

Margaret Cheyne's relationship to Buckingham may have given Sir John Bulmer a strong reason to ally himself with her. Bulmer would have known Margaret's background, and he might have been even more interested in her blood and connections than he was in her personal attractions.

As we have seen, Sir John's father, Sir William Bulmer, had served the third duke of Buckingham, and the strength of this relationship had been the source of a serious breach between Buckingham and Henry VIII. In November 1519 Sir William had been summoned to the Court of Star Chamber.[47] Bulmer was a royal retainer "pledged to serve none but the king." But Bulmer was accused by an enraged Henry of having "refused the king's service" and of having become "servant to the duke of Buckingham," even appearing at court wearing Stafford's badge. Henry declared that he "would none of his servants should hang on another man's sleeve" and that he was "as well able to maintain him as the duke of Buckingham." Henry was suspicious of both Bulmer's and Buckingham's intentions: "what might be thought by his [Bulmer's] departing, and what might be supposed by the duke's retaining him, he would not then declare."[48]

Sir William had ultimately been pardoned for his offenses, but Buckingham had not taken this affair lightly. According to evidence presented at the duke's trial for treason:

> when the king reproved the said duke for retaining Sir William Bulmer in his service, he [Buckingham] thought he should have been committed to the Tower of London; and he said that, if he had perceived it was to be so, the principal actors therein should have little joy of it, for he would have done what his father intended to do to Richard III at Salisbury, when he made suit to come to the king's presence, having upon him secretly a knife, so that when kneeling before the king he would have risen suddenly and stabbed him. In saying this, the duke put his hand treasonably upon his dagger, and said that if he were so ill treated he would do his best to execute his purpose.[49]

At some point after Buckingham's trial and execution, Sir William Bulmer transferred his allegiance to the Neville family, a tie that maintained his connection to the Staffords: Ralph Neville, earl of Westmorland, was married to Catherine Stafford, Buckingham's daughter (and, thus, Margaret Cheyne's half-sister), while Mary Stafford, another of Buckingham's daughters, had married George Neville, lord Burgavenny.[50]

Historians have long assumed that Margaret Cheyne was a woman of insignificance, overlooking the importance of her personal connections. Both Margaret Cheyne and Sir John Bulmer had strong ties to Edward Stafford and the Stafford family and, through the Staffords, to many of the remaining Yorkist claimants to Henry's throne. Buckingham's execution for treason in 1521 might well have given Margaret Cheyne a reason to wish for vengeance against Henry. Certainly, her presence among the rebels would have been noted with alarm by the king.

The evidence against Margaret Cheyne takes on a new significance when we consider her relationship with Buckingham. As the daughter of a convicted traitor, she had urged her husband to join Bigod, saying that, if "all the gentlemen arose, he must do the like." She admitted having urged Sir John to join Bigod, telling her husband that "the commons wanted but a head." John Watts claimed that Margaret had urged Sir John to "break a spear" for her sake. In light of her father's execution, she may have been appealing to Sir John for an act of vengeance rather than manipulating him simply to prove her sexual power over him, as the testimony against her at first suggests. And the family chaplain's evidence that Margaret had, on several occasions, wished that Norfolk's head "were off" is also of special significance in light of Margaret's family ties.

Margaret would have had very particular reasons for her antagonism to Norfolk, for Thomas Howard, duke of Norfolk, was married to Elizabeth Stafford, yet another of Buckingham's daughters. Norfolk's wife was thus Margaret's half-sister. At the time that he was investigating the northern rebellions, Norfolk was deeply involved in his own marital problems, having abandoned Elizabeth Stafford for his mistress, Elizabeth Holland. Margaret might have resented Norfolk's treatment of Elizabeth Stafford, and Norfolk, derided and insulted by his discarded wife, who was demanding support for her cause from both the king and Cromwell, might for his part have taken some measure of satisfaction in arresting Margaret, with her Stafford blood.[51]

Moreover, Norfolk had never been a friend to his father-in-law, Buckingham. As earl of Surrey, he had been in Ireland at the time of the duke's arrest in 1521, but his own father had been selected to preside over Edward Stafford's trial. Much later Norfolk would admit how strained his relationship had been with Buckingham; during the trial, Norfolk said, Buckingham had "confessed openly at the bar, my father sitting as his judge, that of all men living he hated me most, thinking I was the man that had hurt him most to the King's Majesty.[52]

Given what he must have known about both Margaret and Sir John's connections to Buckingham, Norfolk would have had ample reason to be suspicious of their participation in the January risings. At the time he took the two into custody, Norfolk indicated in a letter to the king that he had collected evidence against them, which he was enclosing with his letter, but he also wrote that the "bearer" carrying this letter had additional information about the two, including "how the matter [their treasonous activity] first came to light."[53]

Although the surviving evidence against Margaret Cheyne appears at first to be rather insubstantial, I would argue that the king probably did have good reason for proceeding against her. Her very presence among the rebels would have represented a challenge to the king's authority and legitimacy. Although the documents relating to Margaret that have been preserved are few, we cannot tell how much about her activities was committed to paper and how much was, like Norfolk's, left unwritten. Given who Margaret Cheyne was, there was every reason for the government to discredit her relationship with Bulmer and no reason to record her background and connections or to detail her motivations and actions.

Even the most sympathetic contemporary witnesses seem to have believed that she was guilty of treason. Though he thought her "a very fair creature," Charles Wriothesley wrote that she had been executed "according to her judgment, God pardon her soul." And, though Robert Johns had thought it was "a pity" that "Lady Bulmer of the north country" was to be executed, the men who spoke about her in Oxfordshire seemed to believe that she was "a traitor to her prince." They agreed to "speak no more" of her execution for treason not because they thought her wrongly judged but because they could be in danger even "for speaking of the truth."

And, when we consider what women such as Lady Rhys, Lady Hussey, Elizabeth Stapleton, and the countess of Northumberland had said and done during the Pilgrimage of Grace and its aftermath, we have one more factor to consider in assessing the extent of Margaret Cheyne's guilt. Despite their own actions and the actions of their husbands and sons during the northern rebellion, these women were never punished for their activities. If the king had chosen to treat them with mercy, we might conclude that Margaret Cheyne's actions, by contrast, precluded such mercy.

Though their assumptions about her insignificance were wrong, the arguments of Madeleine Hope Dodds and Ruth Dodds about the importance of family connections might, nevertheless, still be relevant to our assessment of Margaret Cheyne's guilt. What is notable about the families of Lady Rhys (who was, after all, Norfolk's half-sister), Lady Hussey, Elizabeth Stapleton, the countess of Northumberland, and Lady Evers was not their relative significance but, instead, the degree of support they offered. Margaret Cheyne's family connections were not insignificant, but the Bulmers were not willing to come to her support, and, as the duke of Norfolk must have known, no Stafford voice could be raised on her behalf. In her disputes with her husband even Elizabeth Stafford was not supported by her family; her appeals to her brother were ignored, and, as Barbara Harris writes, her "isolation during these years was emphasized by her estrangement from her elder son and her daughter both of whom sided with their father."[54] About Elizabeth Stafford's predicament, Harris concludes:

> the most striking features of the duchess of Norfolk's situation were her complete powerlessness vis-à-vis her husband and her inability to count on her relatives for any meaningful support against him. . . . Her father's execution for high treason in 1521 and the forfeiture of his estates to the crown undoubtedly left her in a particularly exposed position. The duke of Norfolk might well have refrained from some of the callousness, even cruelty, that marked his behavior toward his wife had she a powerful father to turn to for protection and to speak for her to the king. Were Buckingham still alive and in control of his estates, Elizabeth's relatives would also have had a political and economic interest in supporting her in her quarrel with her husband. Instead, they were anxious not to underscore their connection with her, especially since her defiant and outspoken conduct was uncomfortably reminiscent of her father's.[55]

If Elizabeth Stafford could not count on the support of her family in her marital dispute, certainly Margaret Cheyne would not have looked for support from the Staffords after she had been charged with treason.

Despite all of the evidence about Margaret Cheyne gathered here, there is still—and must necessarily be—some room to question the extent of her guilt. Coming upon her story four and a half centuries later, and finding only the most intriguing hints of her actions, we can never be certain. Nevertheless, as I have suggested, her execution for treason may well have been justified. I would argue that Margaret Cheyne's presence among the rebels during the Pilgrimage of Grace was deliberate rather than accidental, her participation in the rebellion much more significant than historians have realized.

Of all the historians who have written about the Pilgrimage of Grace, only Madeleine Hope Dodds and Ruth Dodds saw any significance in Margaret Cheyne's presence among the rebels. While I disagree with their assessment of her execution as a politic example to husbands and wives, I would like to return to their conclusions. Whatever Henry's motives might have been, I have deliberately decided to use Margaret Cheyne as an example. Against the logic of chronology, I have chosen to begin my discussion of women's dangerous talk and strange behavior with her story because it illustrates the issue I would like to address in the pages that follow.

Margaret Cheyne has been written out of the accounts of the Pilgrimage of Grace, the largest and most serious rebellion faced by any Tudor monarch. Although considerable effort has been made to analyze the roles of even minor figures in the Pilgrimage, historians have either overlooked Margaret Cheyne's participation in the northern risings or included her name as an aside or an afterthought. Yet she was judged to have committed an act of political resistance: she was involved in the great events of public life. Women have long been recognized as having been active in the religious conflicts of the sixteenth century, but they have rarely been placed within the context of more clearly political activity.[56]

Like a surprising number of women during the decades of Henry's religious, political, economic, and social reforms, Margaret Cheyne either stepped or was thrust into the turmoil that *circa Regna tonat*.[57] She lived and died when a nation was emerging and the very texture of culture was being radically altered. There are gaps in our knowledge of these changes. Margaret Cheyne's story, and the others in this book, can help to fill in the gaps of the larger narrative of Tudor history.

THREE

Elizabeth Barton:
The "Holy Maid of Kent"

We catch only a few brief glimpses of Margaret Cheyne's life, all of them in the weeks before her arrest and trial—a letter congratulating her husband on Margaret's safe delivery of a son, separate reports from her family chaplain and a local priest about what Margaret had said and done during the turmoil of the Pilgrimage of Grace, the explanation of her actions offered by her husband to investigators, and a very brief deposition recorded as she was examined in the Tower. Margaret Cheyne's only statement is preserved in the very few lines of this document, which tells us almost nothing of her own view of the events in which she had come to be involved. The opinions and intentions of Elizabeth Barton, by contrast, were widely reported. Of all the women involved in political resistance during Henry's reign, Elizabeth Barton's story is uniquely well documented.[1]

Elizabeth Barton's final public statement was made as she stood on the scaffold at Tyburn. She was reported to have addressed these words to the crowd gathered there to witness her execution by hanging:

> Hither I am come to die, and I have not been the . . . cause [only] of my
> own death, which most justly I have deserved, but also I am the cause
> of the death of all these persons which at this time here suffer. And yet,
> to say the truth, I am not so much to be blamed considering it was well
> known unto these learned men that I was a poor wench without
> learning—and therefore they might have easily perceived that the things

that were done by me could not proceed in no such sort, but their capacities and learning could right well judge from whence they proceeded, and that they were altogether feigned. But because the things which I feigned was profitable unto them, therefore they much praised me and bear me in hand that it was the Holy Ghost and not I that did them. And then I, being puffed up with their praises, fell into a certain pride and foolish fantasy with myself and thought I might feign what I would, which thing hath brought me to this case, and for the which now I cry God and the King's Highness most heartily mercy, and desire all you good people to pray to God to have mercy on me and on all them that here suffer with me.[2]

The chronicler Edward Hall recorded Elizabeth Barton's words and described her execution, which took place on 20 April 1534. Five men, believed to be her "accomplices," were hanged and beheaded with her on that day: her spiritual director Dr. Edward Bocking, of the priory of Christ Church, Canterbury; John Dering, also monk of Christ Church; Henry Gold, the parson of St. Mary Aldermary, London, formerly the chaplain of Archbishop William Warham; and two Observant Franciscans, Hugh Rich, the warden of Richmond priory, and Henry Risby, the warden of the Grey Friars at Canterbury.[3]

At first glance Elizabeth Barton seems as unlikely a traitor as Margaret Cheyne. She was a Benedictine nun, but, in spite of her vocation, she was arrested for treason in September 1533. Her words and deeds were systematically and rigorously investigated, yet she was never to be tried and convicted for that crime. Instead, Parliament passed a special act of attainder against her, condemning her to death.[4]

How and why did she come to such an end?

According to a biography published in her own lifetime, Elizabeth Barton was born about 1506, although no details about her family or her early life seem to have been included in this brief pamphlet.[5] In all of the later proceedings against her, no mention was made of her family, nor in the exhaustive investigation of her activities and contacts were any family members questioned or even named. It seems likely, then, that she was a woman alone, a woman without close family connections of any sort.[6]

At some point, when isn't exactly clear, Elizabeth Barton was taken on as a servant by Thomas Cobb, the steward of Archbishop William Warham at Aldington, in Kent, about twelve miles from Canterbury. There, in 1525, she became violently and mysteriously ill:

About the time of Easter [16 April], in the seventeenth year of the reign of Henry VIII, it happened a certain maiden named Elizabeth Barton . . . to be touched with a great infirmity in her body, which did ascend at diverse times up into her throat, and swelled greatly, during the time whereof she seemed to be in grievous pain, in so much as a man would have thought that she had suffered the pangs of death itself, until the disease descended and fell down into the body again.

Thus she continued by fits the space of seven months and more, and at the last, in the month of November (at which time a young child of her master's lay desperately sick in a cradle by her) she, being vexed with the former disease, asked (with great pangs and groaning) whether the child were yet departed this life or no; and when the women that attended upon them both in their sickness answered no, she replied that it should anon. Which word was no sooner uttered, but the child fetched a great sigh and withal the soul departed out of the body of it.

This her divination and foretelling was the first matter that moved her hearers to admiration.[7]

With this first prediction about the imminent death of the young child who lay ill by her side, Elizabeth Barton's life was transformed. She was no longer to live in obscurity as a servant; instead, she was catapulted into a very public and increasingly influential life as a prophet.

News of her strange illness traveled throughout the parish. One of those most obviously aware of Elizabeth's condition was the parish priest of Aldington, Richard Master, who reported the story of Elizabeth Barton to his superior, then Archbishop William Warham: "upon this occasion" Master traveled to Canterbury, where he met with Warham and "informed him that the said Elizabeth Barton had spoken certain words of high and notable matters in her sickness to the great marvel of the hearers."[8] Warham instructed Master to listen for any "more such speeches," indicating that, if her prophecies continued, Master should "be at them as nigh as he could and mark them well."

Among the visions Elizabeth had during those months of illness was one that "she should at a certain day appointed go to the chapel of Our Lady of Court-of-Street" where she would be "restored to health by miracle, through the power of God and His Blessed Mother Mary."[9] She traveled to the chapel, a little over two miles from the Cobb farm in Aldington, expecting her cure, but it did not take place on that day.

On 25 August, the Feast of the Assumption, she returned to the chapel. She found a small commission sent by Warham waiting there for her; the archbishop had sent his controller, Thomas Wall, and two monks of Christ

Church, Canterbury, Edward Bocking and William Hadley. Their task was "to see this woman, and to see what trances she had." They seem to have approached their task with some skepticism; Thomas Goldwell, the prior of Christ Church, was later to write that "they went thither at the beginning, as I suppose, somewhat against their minds, and also against my mind, except the obedience that I do owe unto my lord of Canterbury; and he had not been [my master], I would not have sent them thither."[10]

On their arrival the examiners found that a crowd had gathered to wait for the young woman; Elizabeth's biographer claimed they numbered about 3,000 people, while the formal denunciation made by the king's government after her attainder numbered the crowd at 2,000. In either case there was a sizable gathering at the chapel, indicating something of how quickly and widely reports of her visions had spread.

The archbishop's examiners must have been impressed after witnessing the events that took place at the chapel of Court-at-Street: "There fell she eftsoons into a marvelous passion before the image of Our Lady, much like a body diseased of the falling evil, in the which she uttered sundry metrical and rhyming speeches."[11]

Later, in a long letter describing what had happened to the young woman in the chapel on that occasion, Thomas Cranmer gave an account of what he called the "great miracle" that had been wrought in "a maid by the power of God and our Lady."[12] He described in some detail the physical symptoms of her "grievous and continual sickness": "her face was wonderfully disfigured, her tongue hanging out"; her eyes were "in a manner plucked out and laid upon her cheeks"; a voice was heard "speaking within her belly, as it had been in a tun [cask]," with "her lips not greatly moving." These trances lasted "the space of three hours and more."

In this state the voice within Elizabeth's "belly" spoke about the "joys of heaven" in a voice "so sweetly and so heavenly that every man was ravished with the hearing thereof." When it spoke of hell, the voice "spake so horribly and terribly that it put the hearers in great fear." In this prophetic state Elizabeth spoke of "the confirmation of pilgrimages and trentals [a set of masses], hearing of masses, and confession, and many such other things." When her visions were complete, Cranmer reported, "she came to herself again, and was perfectly whole."

During her vision at the chapel Elizabeth Barton was instructed about "her own bestowing in some religious house." In reporting back to Warham, Bocking requested the archbishop to "declare the same for a miracle" and to arrange for Elizabeth's sequestration at St. Sepulchre's, a Benedictine foundation in Canterbury. Warham seems to have acted on these recommendations only after careful consideration. Even the hostile official sermon preached against the nun at her public humiliation just before her execution mentioned his caution: "the said archbishop answered, that he would not be hasty therein, but would counsel thereupon with the prelates and clergy of his diocese and with his learned counsel."[13]

Elizabeth became a postulant at St. Sepulchre's in 1526, and Edward Bocking became her spiritual advisor, following the instructions she had received in one of her trances "that it was the pleasure of God that he should be her ghostly father." By midsummer 1527 she had taken her final vows. Her visions continued, becoming especially intense at the time of the Feast of the Conception of the Blessed Virgin (8 December). In the same year the Kentish gentleman Edward Thwaites published his account of Elizabeth Barton's early life and of her visions in *A Marvellous Work of Late Done at Court-of-Street in Kent.*[14]

Cranmer confirmed the nun's continued visions; Elizabeth Barton experienced, he wrote, "almost every week or, at the furthest every fortnight,"

> new visions and revelations, and she hath had oftentimes trances and raptures, by reason whereof, and also of the great perfectness that was thought to be in her, diverse and many as well great men of the realm as mean men, and many learned men, but specially diverse and many religious men, had great confidence in her, and often resorted unto her and communed with her, to the intent they might by her know the will of God.[15]

Her reputation spread abroad as well, reaching the reformer William Tyndale in Antwerp. By 1528 Tyndale was criticizing her prophecies in *The Obedience of a Christian Man,* claiming her visions were either feigned or the work of the devil.[16] Tyndale's skeptical views may have been shared by many; nevertheless, on 1 October 1528 Archbishop Warham wrote to the king's chief minister, Cardinal Thomas Wolsey, on Elizabeth Barton's behalf, recommending her as "a very well-disposed and virtuous woman." The nun had asked to speak personally with the cardinal and had made "very importunate suit" to Warham for the introduction.[17]

Her visions, it seemed, had come to focus on new subjects: "she had revelations and special knowledge from God in certain things concerning my Lord of Canterbury [Warham], my Lord Cardinal [Wolsey], and also the King's Highness."[18] Her career as a prophet was about to take a new course. Her religious prophecies had become political prophecies.

What prompted this change in Elizabeth Barton's career? While Protestant reformers like Tyndale viewed her prophecies as the work of the devil, her supporters regarded them as divinely inspired. Putting aside any judgments about her inspiration and motives for the moment, we will follow the narrative of her prophetic career—the progress of her "dangerous talk and strange behavior."

Before 1528, with religious reform becoming more widespread and controversial on the Continent, Elizabeth Barton's prophecies had been primarily religious: her voices had spoken of heaven and hell, but they had also addressed more specifically theological issues, confirming pilgrimages and the practice of Mass and confession, as Cranmer had noted, for example, all practices then being attacked by reformers such as Luther and Tyndale. While some care had been taken to check into her professed visions, such prophecies had confirmed orthodox Catholic teaching and practice. But by 1527 the king's "Great Matter" had become a public matter, and by 1528 Elizabeth Barton's prophecies had begun to focus on the king's marriage and the question of divorce.

Henry's desire for a male heir, his doubts about the validity of his marriage to Katherine of Aragon, and his intention to marry Anne Boleyn are still so intriguing as to have become the subject of "Masterpiece Theatre" dramas and Hollywood movies. If any British matrimonial disaster is as widely known in the twentieth century as Charles and Diana's, it is the lurid tale of Henry VIII's protracted divorce from his first wife and his brief and, ultimately, bloody marriage to his second. In 1528 this story was just beginning to unfold.[19]

In May 1527 a secret tribunal, headed by Wolsey, had begun an investigation into the validity of the king's marriage. William Warham, as archbishop of Canterbury, had attended these proceedings. Although the tribunal turned out to be a "false start," by 22 June Henry had informed Katherine of his scruples and of his intention to separate from her. A month later Wolsey was on his way to France, planning to convene a meeting of cardinals to negotiate peace on the Continent and, as he thought, to settle the matter of Henry's divorce. But, impatient to have the matter decided as quickly as possible, Henry chose not to wait for Wolsey's diplomatic solution; he sent his own representative direct to Rome.[20]

But neither Wolsey nor Henry would get the king's Great Matter settled quickly. The affair dragged on until 1533, long after Wolsey's death, when, on 23 May, Thomas Cranmer, the new archbishop of Canterbury, declared Henry's marriage to Katherine null and void. On 1 June 1533, Anne Boleyn was crowned queen. During the years of struggle in between, the life of Elizabeth Barton became inextricably linked to the king's suit for divorce.

But in 1528 Warham's letter to Wolsey on behalf of Elizabeth Barton indicated nothing of the substance of her new prophecies. In fact, he claimed not to know the reason for her desire to see the cardinal: "What she hath to say, or whether it be good or ill, I do not know, but she hath desired me to write unto Your Grace and to desire . . . that she may come into Your Grace's presence."[21] Later sources are more specific about her reasons for wanting to see Wolsey. Her "revelations" and her "special knowledge from God" concerned the king's first marriage and his desire for a divorce: "she . . . said that God commanded her to say to the . . . cardinal and also to the said archbishop of Canterbury that, if they married or furthered the King's Grace to be married [to Anne Boleyn], they both should be utterly destroyed."[22]

Elizabeth Barton did get her meeting with Wolsey, though the exact date it took place is not certain. At this first occasion "she was charged [through a vision] to go unto the cardinal when he was most in his prosperity and show him of three swords that he had in his hand: one of the spirituality, another of the temporality, and the other of the king's marriage." A second meeting took place in yet "another season," when an "angel commanded her to go unto the said cardinal and show him of his fall, and that he had not done as she had commanded him by the will of God."[23] Later, in writing about his own contacts with Elizabeth Barton, Sir Thomas More indicated that at the time they had taken place he had been fully aware of the nun's meetings with the cardinal.[24]

But Wolsey was not the only prominent man who had interviews with Elizabeth Barton. John Fisher, bishop of Rochester, met with her, by his own admission, three times.[25] Friar John Lawrence, whose deposition was taken during the later investigation of the nun, testified that Rochester had "wept for joy" when he heard of her prophecies against the king's divorce.[26] When questioned about the meetings, Fisher was more specific about the substance of Elizabeth Barton's predictions: she had told the bishop that she had a "revelation . . . from Almighty God" that, if the king went forward with his plans to marry Anne Boleyn, he "should not be king of England seven months after." Fisher claimed, "I conceived not by these words, I take it upon my soul, that any malice or evil was intended or meant . . . by any mortal man, but only that they were the threats of God, as she then did affirm."[27] Fisher's strongest argument defending his own meetings with the nun was that he knew Elizabeth had spoken directly to Henry himself.

Sir Thomas More, too, knew of the nun's meetings with the king. In recalling the circumstances of his own involvement with Elizabeth Barton, More wrote, "It is, I suppose, about eight or nine years ago since I heard of that huswife [worthless woman] first, at which time the bishop of Canterbury that then was [Warham] . . . sent unto the King's Grace a roll of paper in which were written certain words of hers, that she had, as report was then made, at sundry times spoken in her trances."[28] The king had sent this "roll" on to More, asking his opinion. When he later met with the king, More told Henry, "in good faith, I found nothing in these words that I could anything regard or esteem."

Sir Thomas did indicate something of the form and quality of Elizabeth's prophecies, however, writing that "some part fell in rhyme, and that, God wot [knows], full rude [unpolished]." He found nothing unusual in her words, nothing, in his judgment, "a right simple woman" could not speak of by "her own wit well enough." But, he averred,

> because it was constantly reported for a truth that God wrought in her and that a miracle was showed upon her, I durst not nor would not be bold in judging the matter. And the King's Grace, as me thought, esteemed the matter as light as it after proved lewed.

More indicated that, in the following years,

> there was much talking of her, and of her holiness, yet never heard I any talk rehearsed, either of revelations of her or miracles, saving that I had heard sometimes in my Lord Cardinal's [Wolsey's] days that she had been both with his Lordship and with the King's Grace.

More himself would not meet face to face with Elizabeth Barton until 1533; the king, in the meantime, had met with the nun on three separate occasions.

About Elizabeth Barton's first meeting with Henry little is known, not even when, exactly, it took place. Most likely the two met at some point late in 1528, after her prophecies had begun to be concerned with political events. It was later claimed that an angel had appeared to Elizabeth

> and bade the nun go unto the king . . . and say that "I command him to amend his life," and that he leave three things which he loveth and purposeth upon: that is, that he take none of the pope's right nor patrimony from him; the second that he destroy all these new folks of opinion and the works of their new learning; the third, that if he married and took Anne to his wife the vengeance of God should plague him.[29]

No evidence survives that explains how the nun might have come to the king's attention, though Wolsey would have been the logical connection.

The second meeting between the king and the nun, however, was more public. Elizabeth Barton traveled with her prioress, Dame Philippa John, and an escort of servants from her convent to the royal manor of Hanworth. There, probably some "two or three months" after their first encounter, she met again with the king and once more delivered her prophecies to him: "the angel appeared and bade her go again unto the king, and say that since her last being with His Grace, that he hath more highlier studied to bring his purpose to pass."[30]

On that occasion she might also have confronted Anne Boleyn; a later deposition reported that at this meeting the king had offered to make Elizabeth Barton an abbess, that Anne had asked the nun to remain at court, and that Lady Wiltshire, Anne's mother, had asked Elizabeth Barton not only to remain at court but to wait upon her daughter.[31] Elizabeth refused the offers.

The nun met with Henry one more time, probably just before he traveled to Calais in October 1532. The act of attainder passed against her claimed that, when they met on this final occasion, she at last made an even more vehement and direct threat to the king:

> she had knowledge by revelation from God that God was highly displeased with our said Sovereign Lord . . . and in case he desisted not from his proceedings in the said divorce and separation but pursued the same and married again, that then within one month after such marriage he should no longer be king of this realm, and in the reputation of Almighty God should not be king one day nor one hour, and that he should die a villain's death, saying further that there was a root with three branches, and until they were plucked up it should never be merry in England, interpreting the root to be the late Lord Cardinal [Wolsey], and the first branch to be the king, our Sovereign Lord, the second the duke of Norfolk, [Thomas Howard] and the third to be the duke of Suffolk [Charles Brandon].[32]

Elizabeth Barton would later claim that Henry had intended to marry Anne Boleyn in Calais and that he would have done so if she, Elizabeth, had not prevented it by delivering this final prophecy directly to him.[33]

In June of that year, meanwhile, she had finally met with Thomas More. Their face-to-face conversation took place while they were both visiting at Syon Abbey.[34] According to More's version of events, the monks "showed me diverse things that some of them misliked in her"; they wanted to know what More would make of her. The meeting was a private one: "At which communication had, in a little chapel, there were none present but we two." More discussed with Elizabeth a young woman named Helen, whom Barton herself had advised to ignore the "trances and revelations" she had begun to experience; Elizabeth had called Helen's visions "plain illusions of the devil." More regarded his conversation with Elizabeth as part of a "rude warning" to her. In response to More the nun told him that the devil, "in likeness of a bird, was fleeing and flickering about her in a chamber."

Aside from these topics, both of which seemed to indicate some caution about the source and inspiration of Barton's visions, they did not talk further about Elizabeth's prophecies. More wrote, "For conclusion, we talked no word of the King's Grace, or any great personage else, nor in effect of any man or woman but of herself and myself." Following this meeting More wrote to Elizabeth Barton, once again warning her of the danger of the kinds of political predictions she was making.[35] Although she tried to speak with him on at least two other occasions, More declined to meet with her again.[36]

By this time the nun's circle of acquaintances had widened. In April 1533 a papal diplomat, Silvestro Dario, had passed through Canterbury on his way to Dover. Elizabeth was later to claim that she had had a vision of the ambassador's arrival. Dario met with Elizabeth Barton, and the nun gave him a warning to deliver to the pope: "she sent by him the message of God unto the pope, how he should be scourged of God" if he did not condemn the king's divorce and remarriage.

At some point she also met with Antonio de Pulleo, apostolic nuncio to England, ordering him to write "the message of God unto the pope, to the which she did set her hand."[37] Again, she threatened the pope if he issued a decision against the validity of Henry's first marriage. About Elizabeth's communications to the pope, Cranmer would later write, "she wrote letters to the pope, calling upon him in God's behalf to stop and let the said marriage, and to use his high and heavenly power therein, as he would avoid the great stroke of God, which then hanged ready over his head, if he did the contrary."[38]

She also met with Gertrude Courtenay, marchioness of Exeter, the wife of Henry Courtney, marquis of Exeter. The Courtenays, along with the Nevilles and the Poles, were the last Yorkist claimants to the English throne; the contact between Gertrude Courtenay and Elizabeth Barton was thus dangerous to both of them. The marchioness had traveled from Kew to Canterbury, in disguise, to consult with Elizabeth.[39] There she had dined privately with the nun and Bocking, but the subject of their conversation is unknown.

Then, in June, the marchioness sent to Syon for the nun, wishing Elizabeth to return with the Courtenay servants to Horsley; the marchioness wished to consult the nun once more.[40] Receiving permission from her abbess to travel, Elizabeth Barton set out. Once at Horsley, Elizabeth reportedly went into a trance. According to her later confession, the "chief cause" for the interview was the concern of the marchioness that "she had had children before, who lived not after their birth [and] that, supposing herself to be with child again, the said Dame Elizabeth should pray for her to Our Lady, that she might have issue and fruit that might live." They also talked about the possibility of war and the future safety of Henry Courtenay.

Beyond her personal contacts Elizabeth's associates carried her prophecies and warnings to other gentlemen in the court and county as well as to merchants in London and to a number of religious houses. Hugh Rich, the warden of Richmond priory, admitted to showing Elizabeth's "revelations concerning the King's Grace's reign that he shall not be king a month after that he married the Queen's Grace [Anne Boleyn]" to Queen Katherine; to Princess Mary and to her chamberlain John Hussey and his wife, Anne; to Margaret Pole, countess of Salisbury; and, literally, to dozens of other members of the court and of religious houses. Henry Gold, who had been William Warham's chaplain, admitted showing "revelations concerning the King's Grace and his reign" to Queen Katherine twice as well as to members of several religious orders. Edward Bocking, John Dering, and Henry Risby, all attainted for treason along with Barton, Rich, and Gold, shared her prophecies widely with their own associates.[41] Elizabeth Barton was known and supported by the Observant Franciscans, the Carthusians of London and Sheen, and the Bridgettines of Syon, all hostile to the king's divorce.

Perhaps even more dangerous than the personal contacts of Elizabeth Barton and her supporters were the published accounts of her visions. The first of these, Edward Thwaites's *Marvelous Work of Late Done at Court-of-Street,* a booklet of twenty-four leaves, contained a brief life of Elizabeth Barton, an account of her disease, and something of her first visions. Whatever he had heard of Elizabeth Barton in 1528, when he first ridiculed her visions, by 1530 the reformer Tyndale had seen a booklet of her prophecies, perhaps even the one written by Thwaites. In *An Answer Unto Sir Thomas More's Dialogue,* he again attacked Elizabeth Barton's credibility as a prophet, ridiculing her "high learning which as a goodly poetess she uttered in rhyme." Her prophecies, he concluded, would be found "clean without rhyme or reason."[42]

There were other books as well, containing prophecies more dangerous than the religious visions Thwaites had preserved. By September 1533 Cromwell was pursuing a book he referred to as "the Nun's book," which had been printed by the London printer John Scott. Cromwell interrogated Scott, who said Edward Bocking had given him "all the Nun's book to print." Scott admitted to having 200 copies of this book still in his possession at the time that Cromwell questioned him; he had given the remainder, 500 copies, to Edward Bocking, who had probably written the text.[43] The act of attainder indicated that Bocking had written "a great book" of Elizabeth Barton's prophecies, while the sermon preached against her and those condemned with her attributed to him a book as well: "Dr. Bocking hath written this great book with his own hand."[44]

John Dering, also a monk of Christ Church in Canterbury, was responsible for yet another book detailing Elizabeth Barton's revelations. In a letter dated 5 January 1534 Cranmer wrote to Cromwell, "it was brought to my notice and knowledge that Monk Dering hath lately compiled and made . . . a certain treatise *de Duplice Spiritu.*"[45] Cranmer had "diligently examined" Dering, who "hath confessed that he hath made such a book, but he will in no wise be known where it is, saying that he hath burned the same." Cranmer set Dering the task of remembering and rewriting "the whole effect . . . of the same book." While Dering reconstructed the book he claimed to have destroyed, Cranmer urged that a search be made; he had heard that Henry Gold had been given Dering's book and "hath it still in his custody, wherefore I do think it very expedient that some good and politic mean be made for the trial and search . . . in the premises."

Both the sermon and the act of attainder, in fact, indicate that several books had been produced. The act claimed that the nun and her supporters "made write and caused to be written sundry books, both great and small, both written and printed." The sermon, meanwhile, lists a number of the specific predictions made in Bocking's "great book" but also refers to the contents of "the said books" and "these books," indicating that still other books were in existence.[46]

Besides printed books there were also manuscript copies of Elizabeth Barton's predictions. The attainder refers to books "written" as well as "printed." Clearly, when Henry VIII had initially received copies of the nun's prophecies, he had a manuscript collection compiled by Archbishop Warham; the king had sent More the roll that Warham had sent him.[47] In addition to the books by Thwaites and Bocking, the act of attainder named Thomas Lawrence, the registrar of the archdeacon of Canterbury, as having transcribed and circulated a copy of Bocking's manuscript. The act also referred to a heavenly letter Elizabeth had received from Mary Magdalene—a copy of which, complete with golden lettering, was made by a monk of St. Augustine's, Canterbury, named Hawkhurst. And later, when the public sermon was preached against the "nun and her adherents," both a printed book and a manuscript in Bocking's hand were exhibited.[48] Once printed books were in circulation, anyone who had access to a copy could, in fact, make a manuscript extract for still further circulation.

Matters began to move quickly after the king's secret marriage to Anne, which probably took place in January 1533. The new queen was crowned on 1 June—and the news reached England that Clement VII's long-threatened papal bull excommunicating Henry had finally been introduced in consistory. Shortly after the new queen's coronation Henry took his first steps to silence Elizabeth Barton. On 19 July Thomas Cranmer, who had become archbishop of Canterbury in March, wrote to Philippa John, the prioress of St. Sepulchre's, summoning the nun of Canterbury to his manor at Otford.[49]

The decision to move against Elizabeth seems to have come from the king himself; on 23 July, in a report to Henry, Cromwell indicated that he had directed Cranmer to act "according to your gracious commandment."[50] A report about Cranmer's questioning of Elizabeth was sent to Cromwell on 11 August: she had "confessed many mad follies," with Cranmer encouraging her, "as if he did believe her every word."[51]

After her examination Elizabeth was likely sent back to Canterbury. On 7 September Henry's new queen gave birth to a child, a girl, and sometime shortly thereafter Cromwell had Elizabeth Barton transferred to London. A series of letters to Cromwell indicates that her supporters, among them Edward Bocking, were also being rounded up "as secretly as possible."[52]

Between September and November Cromwell's personal "remembrances" are filled with reminders to himself about all the necessary details to be attended to as part of the investigation.[53] During these weeks Elizabeth Barton was held in the Tower and examined at Lambeth Palace by Cranmer, Cromwell, and Hugh Latimer, who would soon become bishop of Worcester. While in the Tower, Elizabeth Barton was reported to have had one final vision: "in which God willed her, by his heavenly messenger, that she should say that she never had revelation of God."[54] The nun seems to have followed the instruction of this final revelation; Cranmer reported, "she confessed all, and uttered the very truth, which is this: that she never had vision in all her life, but all that ever she said was feigned of her own imagination, only to satisfy the minds of them the which resorted unto her, and to obtain worldly praise."[55]

News of her confession spread. On 12 November Eustace Chapuys, the imperial ambassador, was writing to Charles V that Henry had "lately imprisoned a nun"; by 16 November one of Lady Honor Lisle's correspondents was reporting, "Our holy Nun of Kent has confessed her treason against God and the king," while Lady Eleanor Rutland wrote to her father, Sir William Paston, that she, too, had heard that "the Holy Woman of Kent" had confessed and that her "abominable matter" would "be published openly to all people within these three or four days at the furthest."[56]

By 20 November Elizabeth Barton had been examined by a larger group of officials. Writing again to Charles V, Eustace Chapuys reported on the public assembly that had taken place at Westminster:

> The king has assembled the principal judges and many prelates and nobles, who have been employed three days, from morning to night, to consult on the crimes and superstitions of the nun and her adherents; and at the end of this long consultation, which the world imagines is for a more important matter, the chancellor, at a public audience, where were people

from almost all the counties of this kingdom, made an oration how that all the people of this kingdom were greatly obliged to God, who by His divine goodness had brought to light the damnable abuses and great wickedness of the said nun and of her accomplices, whom for the most part he would not name, who had wickedly conspired against God and religion, and indirectly against the king. . . .

. . . On the chancellor proceeding to say that the nun and her accomplices in her detestable malice, desiring to incite the people to rebellion, had spread abroad and written that she had a divine revelation that the king would soon be shamefully driven from his kingdom by his own subjects, some of them began to murmur and cry that she merited the fire. The said nun, who was present, had so much resolution that she showed not the least fear or astonishment, clearly and openly alleging that what the chancellor said was true. . . . The chief business still remains, for the king insists . . . that the said accomplices of the nun be declared heretics for having given faith to her, and also be guilty of high treason for not having revealed what concerned the king. . . . To which the judges during the last three days will not agree . . . since the nun a year ago had told the king of it in person. It is to be feared, however, that they will do that which the king desires.[57]

The debates in the Star Chamber, at Westminster, had begun on 18 November. Henry intended that Elizabeth and her associates should be judged guilty of heresy for their faith in her prophecies and of high treason for having concealed these prophecies about the king, but, just as Chapuys reported, the assembled judges pointed out that the nun had revealed her prophecies to the king himself only the year before—clearly referring to the meeting between the two in 1532. Failing to win an indictment against Elizabeth, the king decided to proceed against her by means of a bill attainder in Parliament and not by an indictment in a court of common law.[58]

By Sunday morning, 23 November, a temporary platform and public seating had been erected at St. Paul's Cross, and a crowd of 2,000 had gathered to see the public penance of Elizabeth Barton and those attainted with her. The sermon preached on that occasion by John Salcot has been preserved; it runs to approximately 5,000 words.[59] Elizabeth Barton, Edward Bocking, John Dering, Henry Gold, Hugh Rich, Henry Risby, and Edward Thwaites stood on the platform throughout the preaching of the sermon. Following the sermon Elizabeth Barton stepped forward to deliver a public confession:

I, Dame Elizabeth Barton, do confess that I, most miserable and wretched person, have been the original of all this mischief, and by my falsehood have grievously deceived all these persons here and many more, whereby I have most grievously offended Almighty God and my most noble sovereign, the King's Grace.

Wherefore I humbly, and with heart most sorrowful, desire you to pray to Almighty God for my miserable sins and, ye that may do me good, to make supplication to my most noble sovereign for me for his gracious mercy and pardon.[60]

Following this confession the penitents were returned to the Tower. Reporting on the public penance, Chapuys wrote on 24 November:

It is said on the two next Sundays the nun and the above-mentioned persons will play the same part, and that afterwards they will be taken through all the towns in the kingdom to make a similar representation, in order to efface the general impression of the nun's sanctity, because this people is peculiarly credulous and is easily moved to insurrection by prophecies, and in its present disposition is glad to hear any to the king's disadvantage. The king has not yet prevailed on the judges to make the oration against those who have practised against him [with the] said nun in the form that I last wrote. He is going to have the affair discussed with them on Friday, and although some of the principal judges would sooner die than make the said declaration, yet, when the king comes to dispute, there is no one who will dare contradict him.[61]

Chapuys indicated that Henry planned to dispute the case against Elizabeth Barton "on Friday," which would be 28 November. Meanwhile, depositions were being taken from all of the accused.[62]

While the rumored tour "through all the towns in the kingdom" was never made, the public humiliation of Elizabeth Barton and her adherents was not yet over. Cranmer traveled to Canterbury, and there, on Sunday, 7 December, Elizabeth Barton and the others went through a second public penance, a repeat performance of the spectacle that had taken place on 23 November. Following this trip they were all returned to the Tower. There they waited.

It may be that Henry still wasn't quite sure what to do with Elizabeth Barton. As late as 14 January, Cromwell was reminding himself "to know what the king will have done with the nun and her accomplices."[63] Parliament opened on 15 January. A bill of attainder was introduced into the House of Lords on 21 February; on 26 February it passed its second reading, on 6 March its third. On 12 March it was given its fourth reading and passed by the Lords. On 17 March it was passed by the Commons. On Saturday, 21 March, the bill was completed in its final form and received royal approval, its substance being made known by proclamation to all "shires, cities, boroughs, and towns . . . to the intent that the . . . false and dissimulate offences of the offenders may be known and the people thereby to take an example." One further addition was made to the public proclamations:

> every such person and persons which hath in their custody and keeping any books, scrolls, or writings containing any [of] the false, feigned revelations and dissimulated miracles of the said Elizabeth . . . shall within forty days next . . . bring or cause to be brought the said books, scrolls, and writings unto the lord chancellor of England . . . and if any person or persons, after such proclamations had and made according as is above said, knowingly and willingly do retain and keep any such books, scrolls, or writings . . . then any person offending the same . . . shall suffer imprisonment and make fine to the king.[64]

On Monday, 20 April, Elizabeth Barton was executed. She was dragged on a hurdle from the Tower to Tyburn. There, after the speech she addressed to the crowd gathered to witness her execution, she was hanged. After she was dead, she was beheaded.

FOUR

Elizabeth Barton and Political Prophecy

Even before Elizabeth Barton's execution, her former supporters were scrambling to distance themselves from her. Their excuses and explanations came pouring in to the king. Typical of the apologies and pleas Henry received is one sent by Gertrude Courtenay, marchioness of Exeter. Late in November she wrote to the king, thanking him for his "most gracious, merciful, and benign letters" addressing the subject of her "abuse, lightness, and indiscreet offenses" with "that most unworthy, subtle, and deceivable woman, called the Holy Maid of Kent." The marchioness sought the king's "most gracious remission, pardon, and forgiveness":

> I shall now, most humbly prostrate at the feet of Your Royal Majesty, beseech [you] . . . not only first and chiefly to consider that I am a woman whose fragility and brittleness is . . . most facile, easily, and lightly . . . seduced and brought into abuse and light belief, yet being now the most sorrowful and heavy creature alive that ever my hap [fortune] . . . should be such to do that thing that in any manner of wise should offend or displease Your Majesty . . . or bring me into the danger or suspicion of Your Grace's indignation or displeasure.

The marchioness admitted having listened to the "seditious tales, blasphemies most execrable, and false prophecies" of the "false and unworthy" nun, but, she explained, "as God is my judge I ever thought the same to be so full of folly and untruth as me thought they were neither worthy to be revealed [or] in any part to be trusted and believed."[1]

In writing to the king and asking for his pardon, the marchioness had followed Cromwell's advice and instruction; she wrote to Cromwell as well, thanking him for his guidance and support. John Fisher, bishop of Rochester, on the other hand, did not follow Cromwell's instruction to seek the king's pardon. He chose, instead, to defend himself to Cromwell, giving seven reasons why he had not reported to the king on his involvement with the nun. In February Cromwell wrote him a scathing letter of rebuke:

> How you can declare yourself afore God and the world when need shall require I cannot tell, but I think verily that your declaration made by these letters is far insufficient to prove that you have deserved no heavy words in this behalf, and, to say plainly, I sent you no heavy words but words of great comfort, willing your brother to show you how benign and merciful the Prince was. And that I thought it expedient for you to write unto His Highness and to recognize your offense and desire his pardon, which His Grace would not deny you now in your age and sickness—which my counsel I would you had followed, rather than to have written these letters to me excusing yourself as though there were no manner of fault in you.[2]

Cromwell concluded his long letter to Fisher with a warning—"if the matter come to trial, your own confession in these letters, besides the witness which be against you, will be sufficient to condemn you"—and with further insistence that Fisher write to the king, admitting his "negligence, oversight, and offense."

Sir Thomas More, as we have seen, wrote at length to explain his own dealings with the nun. A letter to Cromwell detailed the whole of his acquaintance with her; at the same time he wrote to the king with his own "humble suit": "Wherefore, most gracious Sovereign, I neither will, nor well it can become me, with Your Highness to reason and argue the matter, but in my most humble manner, prostrate at your gracious feet, I only beseech Your Majesty with your own high prudence and your accustomed goodness consider and weigh the matter."[3]

While those who had known Elizabeth Barton personally were thus engaged, contemporary London chroniclers also wrote about the nun and her supporters. With few exceptions those who wrote expressed strong opinions, their widely divergent views reflecting their personal political and religious allegiances.

By far the longest version was offered by Edward Hall, whose extensive story of the "new-found saint and holy hypocrite" and her "juggling and crafty deceit" occupied many pages in his history. Hall's account followed closely the narrative of the act of attainder, but he also recorded Elizabeth Barton's speech "at the place of execution and the present time that she suffered."[4]

Charles Wriothesley, meanwhile, noted the public sermon preached at St. Paul's Cross and then the fact of the execution. His entry, by contrast with that of Hall, is brief and matter-of-fact: "the Holy Maid of Kent . . . [was] brought from the Tower of London to Paul's Cross, and there stood on a scaffold all the sermon time"; "the Holy Maid of Kent . . . [was] drawn from the Tower of London to Tyburn, and there hanged."[5]

Several other contemporary chroniclers mentioned Elizabeth Barton as well. Two anonymous London chroniclers are brief and neutral in their notations. Richard Hill also includes without comment the executions of the nun and her followers in his commonplace book. The chronicler of the Grey Friars is similarly brief in his note about the penance and the execution: "This year was the Maid of Kent . . . drawn to Tyburn and there hanged and headed."[6]

Given his political and religious biases, Hall's lengthy and spirited entry is understandable; given the danger to members of religious orders following the arrest and attainder of the nun and her adherents, the reticence of the Grey Friars chronicler is also understandable. The London chroniclers who noted the executions may well have decided that further comment about the nun was unwise. Curious, however, is the silence of a Spanish chronicler living in London whose strong Catholicism and ardent support for Queen Katherine would seem to have inspired some word about the nun's opposition to the divorce and to Anne Boleyn in his record of events.[7] Yet he mentioned neither Elizabeth Barton nor her prophecies in his narrative.

An inveterate plotter and gossip, Eustace Chapuys, Charles V's ambassador to England, was noticeably restrained in the accounts of Elizabeth Barton, which he forwarded to the emperor. His first reference to the nun's activities was made on 12 November 1533, when he reported to Charles that Henry had "lately imprisoned a nun." His several dispatches to the emperor detailing the interrogations of Elizabeth Barton and of the subsequent actions of Parliament to attaint her and her followers focused more on the legal maneuvering than on the nun's support of Queen Katherine.

The views of those who had had firsthand knowledge of the nun were equally mixed. The Kentish gentleman Edward Thwaites certainly thought her early visions had been made "devoutly and discreetly." The members of the commission of inquiry sent by Warham to Court-at-Street had been impressed enough to recommend her removal from Aldington to St. Sepulchre's. And, although his "mind was not to be familiarly acquainted with women," the prior of Christ Church, Canterbury, seemed to concur with these early reports that "she was a person much in the favor of God and had special knowledge of Him in many things."[8] As late as October of 1533, Christopher Warener, an anchorite of the Black Friars, Canterbury, had written to Cromwell that, because of Elizabeth's "perfect life and virtue," he had believed her prophetic career "a thing supernatural, and did judge it to the best that it should come of God."[9]

Certainly, she had impressed William Warham, archbishop of Canterbury, who had subsequently introduced her to Wolsey. By the time the investigation of her prophecies was coming to an end, nearly everyone agreed that her influence over Warham and Wolsey (both of whom were then dead) had been so great that they had backed off from their support for Henry's divorce proceedings.[10] And, in his response to John Fisher's explanations of his relationship with the nun, Cromwell not only referred repeatedly to the credence the bishop had given to her and her revelations (Fisher had referred to her "holiness") but also to the part Fisher's relationship with her had played in his opposition to the king's divorce and remarriage.[11]

In spite of his own danger at the time, even Sir Thomas More said that on the occasion of their interview Elizabeth Barton had given him a "very good and virtuous" answer when he asked her to pray for him. She seemed to him to have "much meekness in her soul" and was mindful of the "rude warnings" she had received about her prophecies. "I liked her in good faith better for this answer," More wrote, "than for many of those things that I heard reported of her."[12]

Although he generally wrote little about Elizabeth Barton herself, and nothing about the validity of her prophecies, Eustace Chapuys reported to Charles V that, until the time of her arrest, the nun "had always lived till this as a good, simple, and saintly woman." Even during the long attack on her made by Lord Chancellor Audley during the public address at Westminster, Chapuys reported that the "said nun, who was present, had so much resolution that she showed not the least fear or astonishment, clearly and openly alleging that what the chancellor said was true."[13]

But, certainly, not all the contemporary evaluations were so positive. In a letter written to her father, Sir William Paston, Eleanor Manners, lady Rutland, called Elizabeth Barton's activities "one of the most abominablest matters that ever I heard of in my life."[14] Perhaps understandably, given the close association of the nun with Canterbury, and the subsequent danger to all of her religious connections, the monk responsible for the Chronicle of St. Augustine's, Canterbury, wrote that Elizabeth Barton had "by marvelous hypocrisy mocked all Kent and almost all England." She had confessed "many horrible things against the king and the queen." At the time of the public sermon preached against her, she and her adherents, who had "authored" her "dissimulation," were "grievously rebuked" for their "horrible" deeds. The chronicler expressed no sympathy for the traitors.[15]

The government's official denunciations were, of course, even more strongly worded. The sermon preached at St. Paul's Cross is filled with references to her "false, forged, and feigned" prophecies, while the act of attainder is itself a vituperative piece of rhetoric aimed at thoroughly discrediting the nun, her "hypocrisy," and her "false revelations."[16]

Most of the more recent historians who have written about Elizabeth Barton have also, in their own ways, either defended her as a saint or condemned her as a charlatan. In the case of her most recent biographer, Alan Neame, the position is at least overt; his book *The Holy Maid of Kent* is intended, through careful and exhaustive narrative detail and, less fortunately, through sometimes wild speculation, to prove her a mystic and martyr. More often, however, the prejudices of historians are less explicit. References to Barton as a "deluded prophetess" or to Bocking as her "impresario" are as rhetorically charged as anything included in the sermon preached at St. Paul's Cross or the act of attainder approved by Parliament. Conclusions that she was a "poor woman," a "hysterical girl," a "bewildered young woman," "an innocent victimized by superstition and intrigue," or that she was "manipulated by opponents of the divorce" or "endoctrinée" are, in their condescension, equally devastating.[17]

One of the most balanced assessments of Elizabeth Barton is made by J. J. Scarisbrick in his biography of Henry VIII: "The sturdiest scepticism has, perhaps, not yet succeeded in dismissing the nun as a mere hysteric or fraud, nor the most favourable pleading lifted her above all suspicion." He concludes, "whatever else she may or may not have been, she was indisputably a powerful, courageous and dangerous woman whom the wracking anxiety of the late summer and autumn of 1533 required should be destroyed."[18]

In this assessment Scarisbrick suggests something of the approach to Elizabeth Barton I think most useful. Attempts to decide whether the nun was a true mystic or a deranged pawn are at once futile and misdirected. Amid all such arguments we lose sight of the woman herself, and either way she is assumed to have no independence of thought or action. I believe Elizabeth Barton is a woman whose dangerous talk and strange behavior deserves a much different kind of analysis than it has received. More specifically, we need to understand her words and actions in relationship to those of other women—and men—during the early sixteenth century.

Stories of English women and their strange predictions appear with some regularity though little detail in early-sixteenth-century historical records. In July 1502, for instance, a woman named Alianor Dulyne appeared before the

Court of the Commissary of London, charged with having practiced the art of divination. She was also under examination for having somehow used these arts in an effort to destroy her husband. It isn't clear from the surviving record whether her attempts to kill her husband had been successful—but Alianor produced two compurgators, Anna Mareys and Agnes Wenchecome, to swear on her behalf, and she was discharged, but not before bringing countercharges of defamation against Anne Miller, who had first circulated the stories of Alianor's divination.[19]

Similarly, in 1523 one Johanna Hebe was brought before the ecclesiastical court of Leicester, charged with assault. At the time of her court appearance it was also alleged against her that she had reported seeing visions of her dead father walking: *etiam asseritur officio quod asserit dicta Johanna quot pater suus naturalis iam post eius mortem dambulasset.* Nothing more seems to have come of these allegations nor of the charges against Mabel Priors made in the same court. She too was accused of divination, which she denied; the court determined that the case should be taken up again "in the neighbourhood where the accused lived."[20]

No details survive about the divination practiced by Alianor Dulyne or Mabel Priors, but records of similar cases do include such details. In 1525, for example, Joan Mores of East Langdon, Kent (some twelve miles from Elizabeth Barton's home in Aldington) was also cited before an ecclesiastical court for divining the future. In her case the record specified that she could foretell the future somehow by means of the croaking of frogs: *utendo sufflationibus ranarum.*[21]

Some sort of divination was also involved in a case described in Yorkshire in 1528, when Isabel Mure of Bishop Wilton was presented before an ecclesiastical court. The charge against her involved a ritual that allowed her to see the future:

> She took fire and two young women with her and went to a running water and lit a wisp of straw and set it on the water and said thus, "Benedicite, see ye what I see. I see the fire burn and water run and the grass grow and sea flow and night fevers and all unknown evils that evil flee and all other, God will," and after these words said fifteen paternosters, fifteen ave marias and three creeds.[22]

About the same time that Elizabeth Barton first became so mysteriously and terribly ill, a young woman in Suffolk was also stricken by an illness accompanied by strange visions. Anne Wentworth, the daughter of Sir Roger Wentworth, was "a very fair young gentlewoman of twelve years of age" when she was suddenly and unaccountably overcome "in marvelous manner." Her horrible attacks and the visions that accompanied them were believed to be the work of Satan; she was "vexed and tormented by our ghostly enemy, the devil," her mind "alienated and raving with despising and blasphemy of God."

But during one of her trances she received a vision from God that she was to go on a pilgrimage to the image of the Virgin at Our Lady at Ipswich, where she was "so grievously tormented, and in face, eyes, look, and countenance so grisly changed, with her mouth drawn aside and her eyes laid out upon her cheeks, that it was a terrible sight to behold." But her torments at Ipswich rid her of the devils that had possessed her. And by means of her new and "wonderful trances and visions,"

> she prophesied and told many things done and said at the same time in other places which were proved true, and many things said, lying in her trance, of such wisdom and learning that right cunning men highly marvelled to hear of so young [and] unlearned maiden, [who] herself wist [knew] not what she said, such things uttered and spoken as well learned men might have missed with a long study.[23]

Curiously, Sir Thomas More was interested in Anne Wentworth, just as he was interested in Elizabeth Barton. He believed that Anne's trances and visions were real, in part because her parents were "right honorable and . . . sore abashed," in part because "the maid herself [was] too young to feign, and the fashion itself too strange for any man to feign." When Sir Thomas published his description of Anne Wentworth in *A Dialogue Concerning Heresies* . . . in 1531, he indicated that, despite her father's efforts, Anne Wentworth had become a nun: she "forsook the world and professed religion in a very good and godly company at the Minories, where she hath lived well and graciously ever since."[24]

Sir Thomas More knew of yet another young woman who claimed to have similar visions. When he met with Elizabeth Barton at Syon Abbey in 1533, as we have seen, he reminded the nun of "one Helen, a maiden dwelling about Tottenham, of whose trances and revelations there hath been much talking." For reasons he does not explain he had recently met with Helen of Tottenham, who then told him that she, in her turn, had just recently met with Elizabeth Barton.

During her visit with the Canterbury nun Helen described the visions she had experienced. Elizabeth "showed her that they were no revelations but plain illusions of the devil and advised her to cast them out of her mind." Helen had given "good credence" to Elizabeth, More reported, and gave up "such visions."

Rather than taking credit for having helped Helen, Elizabeth replied that the change in Helen was due to the "much meekness in her soul" wrought by God.[25]

Stories detailing the religious ecstasies of young woman are not unusual in early modern Europe, but they are not the only kinds of connections I would like to explore here. Far more important for the case of Elizabeth Barton, I think, is some understanding of the long tradition of political prophecy in England. Elizabeth Barton would certainly have been familiar with such prophecies. When the events of her life became entangled in the king's complicated divorce proceedings, her predictions about his fate if he divorced Katherine and married Anne were in part expressed in the form and language of these popular expressions of political opinion.[26]

Political prophecies in verse and in prose flourished in England from early in the twelfth century until quite late in the seventeenth, and, although these "prophecies" pretended to be ancient predictions attributed to reputed prophets, they were really potent political propaganda circulated to influence popular opinion. The sibyl, Saint Jerome, Merlin, Bede, Thomas à Becket—all were used as authorities in these partisan texts. But the predictions that purportedly came from these prophets were anything but straightforward. They were deliberately obscure, filled with veiled topical allusions, disguised historical figures, and vague prognostications about future triumphs and calamities, intended to be both confused and confusing.

The most common devices used to complicate the prophecies were animal symbols, but alphabetic prophecies, astrological prophecies, prophecies by the dice, and even prophetic pictures were also popular. Filled with veiled topical allusions and disguised references to contemporary figures, these pieces were both lively and compelling—lively because they responded to the political fortunes and misfortunes of the moment, compelling because they predicted the fate of powerful men and women and foretold the future of England.

Political prophecies were always most popular during periods of crisis. Many surviving texts and manuscripts date from the Lancastrian-Yorkist civil wars, for example, while a number of prophecies circulated at the time of Henry VII's fight for the throne.[27] Henry VIII's reign had been untroubled by serious conflict—or by the powerful antigovernment propaganda that political prophecy threatened—until the 1530s.

Henry's struggle for a divorce began in the late 1520s and ended only in 1533, when Cranmer pronounced a sentence in the king's favor. But by the time Henry's Great Matter was resolved to his satisfaction, the question of the divorce had become only one issue in much greater theological, ecclesiastical, social, and political controversies.[28]

The failed engineer of Henry's divorce, Cardinal Wolsey, died in 1529, the so-called Reformation Parliament meeting for the first time the next month. During the next ten years, with the aid of Wolsey's successor, the indefatigable Thomas Cromwell, the king finally secured his divorce from Katherine, married Anne Boleyn, executed her, married Jane Seymour, who died after childbirth, and began negotiations for a fourth wife. He married Anne of Cleves as the decade closed in 1540. During the same period Henry declared his daughter Mary illegitimate, celebrated the birth of a second daughter, Elizabeth, then declared her illegitimate, and finally satisfied himself when a son, Edward, was born late in 1537.

These more personal upheavals were paralleled by political, institutional, and social changes. The Reformation Parliament met for the first time in November 1529. During the next seven years Parliament sat in seven sessions and enacted 137 statutes.[29] The first acts of the November 1529 session addressed various clerical abuses, among them pluralism and nonresidence. Parliament was adjourned in December 1529 and not called again for over a year, reassembling in January 1531. In the meantime, however, Henry had taken further action on his own behalf. After enlisting scholars from universities in England and throughout Europe to offer opinions about the validity of his marriage, and after failing to secure a papal decision, Henry moved.

When Parliament reconvened in January 1532, a bill to halt the payment of papal annates to Rome was introduced. In spite of strenuous opposition in both houses, the bill was passed. The king also engaged in a long battle with the Convocation of the Clergy over clerical abuses. Parliament was prorogued on 14 May 1532. On 15 May a surrender was forced from the Convocation, which finally passed the Act for the Submission of the Clergy. On 16 May Sir Thomas More resigned as lord chancellor.

Before Parliament met again in 1533 Cranmer had become archbishop of Canterbury, Henry had been married to Anne Boleyn, and Thomas Cromwell had secured his place as Henry's chief advisor. The February–April 1533 session of Parliament passed the Act in Restraint of Appeals, and there followed swiftly both a decision on Henry's first marriage in the king's favor in Convocation and a judgment on the validity of his second in Cranmer's court. In response, in July 1533, Clement VII prepared a sentence of excommunication against Henry.

The break of 1533 was completed by the acts of the next year. During its first session of 1534 (15 January–30 March) Parliament passed a series of critical statutes, among them the Act of Succession, which imposed an oath acknowledging the king's second marriage and its offspring. The second 1534 session (November-December) passed the Act of Supremacy and the new Treason Act, which, as we have seen, expanded the 1352 treason of "compassing the king's death" to include attempts to "imperil the king's person" and activities "to the prejudice, slander, disturbance and derogation" of his marriage to Anne. Treason by word was as serious as by deed; treason could be committed by "writing or imprinting."

By the end of the decade the king had dissolved the monasteries, been excommunicated by a pope he no longer recognized, faced political rebellion during the northern risings, and defended himself against threats of invasion from the Continent. He had executed those who opposed him, threatened him, or proved themselves inconvenient, including Anne Boleyn, Thomas More, John Fisher, and the remaining Yorkist claimants to the throne. Henry ultimately found he could even dispense with Cromwell's services; the king's assertion of royal supremacy extended to Cromwell's execution in July 1540.

Against this backdrop of turmoil and change the government announced its position through a campaign of proclamation, statute, and propaganda.[30] This official discourse was challenged by a bewildering array of strange political prophecies. Understanding these political prophecies is critical for understanding the predictions that Elizabeth Barton was to deliver publicly—to the king's political opponents but also to the king himself.[31]

As early as 1521, predictions about the king's death had been involved in the trial of Edward Stafford, duke of Buckingham, for treason. Among the charges against him was the claim that he had "imagine[d] and compass[ed] the deposition and death of the king." Involved in the case against him was a monk, Nicholas Hopkins from Henton, Somersetshire, whom the duke had consulted about more than religious matters. Over the course of several years Buckingham was said to have consulted Father Nicholas repeatedly, to be assured by the monk that the king "would have no issue male of his body" and that the duke himself "should have the rule of all England." The monk had received this information "by revelation."[32]

While these predictions were clearly regarded by Buckingham's contemporaries as dangerous "prophecies" of future events, they were not the kinds of riddling and ambiguous political prophecies that were later to flood the kingdom. More to the point is one of the charges made against Sir Rhys ap Griffith, executed for treason on Tower Hill on 4 December 1531. Among the accusations against him was that he had spread a seditious prophecy. According to the formal indictment preferred against him and his two servants, "*et inter se colloquentes sepius repetendo et dicebant quod hec antiqua subsequens prophecia existit in wallia videlicet* that king James with the red hand and the ravens should conquer all England."[33] In this prophecy the "red hand" referred to the Welsh hero Owen Lawgoch, the "ravens" to Griffith himself, whose arms bore the three ravens on a white field. In the words of the prophecy Griffith quoted, then, James of Scotland would lead a great army, the combined forces of Scotland and Wales, which would conquer England. Although no more of the text survives, it seems likely that Griffith was quoting a version of a political prophecy known as "The Sayings of the Prophets."[34]

Aside from the indication that political prophecies had been involved in these two very high-profile treason cases, concerns about political prophecies and prophets appear regularly in the state papers in the early 1530s. One supposed prophet, William Harlock, was brought from Somersetshire to the Tower in 1530, where he was examined before Sir Edmund Walsingham, lieutenant of the Tower. Harlock had been showing a "calendar of prophecy" around the county. He had interpreted its pictures to predict a battle of priests and the coming invasion of a "dreadful dragon." Harlock admitted showing his prophecies to a goldsmith named Richard Loweth, who had produced his own book of prophecies about a dragon, a blue boar, "bare-legged hens," and a "lion gentle," which represented the Scots king. No charges seem to have resulted from Harlock's examination.[35]

In 1532 William Neville, a younger brother of John Neville, lord Latimer, was also involved with political prophecies, specifically prophecies that he would not only succeed his older brother but that he would become, first, earl of Warwick and, ultimately, king of England. Among the animal symbols in his prophecies was one of "a bear which had been long tied to a stake" that would, he said, "arise and make peace and unity." A bear and a ragged staff were part of the Warwick arms. If Neville were to become the Warwick earl and then to bring England "peace and unity," he was perhaps fantasizing a role for himself along the line of the "kingmaking" earl of Warwick, Richard Neville.[36] Although he was held in the Tower for some time, William Neville was finally released.

Even Thomas Wolsey was plagued by the riddling predictions of political prophecy. As early as 1512, he had supposedly heard the prophecy that "one with a Red Cap" (Wolsey would become cardinal in 1515) would rise "from low degree to high estate" and would "rule all the land under the king." This "Red Cap" would "involve the land in misery" until "the land by another Red Cap [Reginald Pole]" would either "be reconciled or else brought to utter destruction." Cromwell was later reported to have taken careful note of this prediction.[37]

Wolsey's biographer and "gentleman-usher," George Cavendish, recorded a conversation he had with Wolsey in 1529 about another popular prophecy circulating throughout the kingdom: "When this cow rideth the bull, / Then, priest, beware thy skull." Cavendish then interpreted the prophecy, which neither he nor Wolsey understood when they first heard it:

> This prophecy was afterwards expounded in this wise: this dun cow, because it was the king's beast, betokened the king; and the bull betokened Mistress Anne Boleyn, who was afterwards queen and the king's wife, because her father, Sir Thomas Boleyn, had the same beast in his coat of arms. So that when the king had married her, which was unknown to my lord or to any other at that time, then was this prophecy thought by all men to be fulfilled. For what a number of priests, both religious and secular, lost their heads for offending against such laws as were then made to bring this prophecy to effect is not unknown to all the world. Therefore it was judged by all men that this prophecy was then fulfilled when the king and she were joined in marriage.[38]

That the king's interest in Anne Boleyn inspired many contemporary political prophecies is also made clear by Eustace Chapuys. In his dispatches to Charles V he referred several times to popular prophecies about Anne. His most extended account, however, was included in a letter to Charles's minister, Nicholas Granvelle, reporting on Anne Boleyn's imprisonment:

> Before her marriage to the king, and in order to enhance the love she bore him, the royal concubine used to say that there existed a prophecy that about this time a queen of England was to be burnt alive; but that, to please the king, she cared not if she was that queen. After the marriage she often said in jest that part of the prophecies had already been fulfilled, and yet she had not been condemned to death by fire.[39]

The diplomatic account of Anne Boleyn's execution, meanwhile, concludes: "It is said that she was condemned to be burned alive, but that the king commuted her sentence to decapitation. Thus, he who wrote this billet says that, according to old writings, he has seen the prophecy of M[e]rlin fulfilled."[40]

But from the point of view of our interest in Elizabeth Barton, the most striking investigation of political prophecy in the early 1530s involved the wife of John Amadas, a member of the king's household.[41] In July 1533 Amadas's wife was examined about "some part of such ungracious rehearsals as [she] at sundry times hath spoken before diverse persons."[42] During her examination Mistress Amadas described at some length, and with great gusto, the prophecies she had been examining for over twenty years. She had concluded, she said, that "this is the year that her matters shall come to pass."

Among the prophecies she helped to spread were claims that the king was cursed "with God's own mouth" and that he would soon be banished from his realm. According to her prophecies, the Scots would conquer Henry's kingdom, a "parliament of peace" would be called by a religious man known as "the dead man," and a battle of prelates would erupt, during which the king would be destroyed. After Henry's death the realm would be divided into four parts, "and there shall be never no kings in England" afterward. All this she had declared, seemingly, to anyone who would listen to her.

Like Elizabeth Barton, Mistress Amadas spoke against Anne Boleyn and Henry's second marriage, but her attacks seem to have been motivated at least in part by her own personal experience. She claimed that Anne was a harlot whose father, the earl of Wiltshire, had been "bawd both to his wife and his two daughters." This was certainly the stuff of common gossip, but Mistress Amadas went on to charge that Henry had also plied *her* "many times" with "tokens and large offering of gifts," intending to make her his "whore" as well. Mistress Amadas clearly identified with Henry's first wife, claiming that, "because the king hath forsaken his wife, he suffereth her husband to do the same": "she swore by the passion of Our Lord that she thought there was never a good wedded woman in England but Prince Arthur's dowager [Katherine], the duchess of Norfolk [Elizabeth Stafford, deserted by her husband for his mistress, Bess Holland], and herself." She predicted that the emperor would "deliver all good wives when he cometh, which shall be shortly" and that "my Lady Anne should be burned."

Mistress Amadas indicated to her examiners that she owned "a roll" on which was "painted and written all her prophecies." Many of the predictions she made were couched in the riddling language of political prophecy, referring, for example, to the cursed "moldwarp," to a dragon that would be "killed by midsummer," and to a mysterious dead man who would arrive from across the sea.[43] Mistress Amadas even knew of Elizabeth Barton and her prophecies; during her examination she referred specifically to Silvestro Dario, who, she knew, had met with both the king and "the holy maiden of Courthope Street."

No one who has thus far attempted to assess Elizabeth Barton's prophetic career has done so in light of the long tradition of political prophecy in England. Her predictions might, certainly, have been inspired by God. Or she might have been fed her "predictions" by the men who surrounded her. But I believe she could just as well have adopted and adapted popular political prophecies herself; like Mistress Amadas, Elizabeth Barton would have been quite familiar with such prophecies, and she could have drawn on the tradition of political prophecy to express her own political opinions.

Overlooked in all the accounts of Elizabeth Barton's prophecies is the fact that her predictions demonstrate that she was very much aware of the form and language of contemporary political prophecy. In addition to the visions that had come from "the angel" or in a "golden letter" sent by Mary Magdalene are, for example, prophecies "of 9, 9, 9, the reign of a king how long he shall reign" and prophecies "of three letters, A, F, G."[44] Although ignored by historians, such numerical and alphabetic predictions would certainly not have been ignored by Elizabeth Barton's contemporaries. Their significance would have been both familiar and recognizable in the 1530s.

For example, the calculation "of 9, 9, 9" as the length of the king's reign is not all that difficult to understand—and the twenty-seventh year of Henry's reign would have commenced in April 1535. Such a prediction, combined with Elizabeth Barton's earlier warnings that Henry would not long survive his marriage to Anne, is certainly a dangerous "imagining" of the king's death.

The alphabetic references "of three letters, A, F, G" are also typical of contemporary political prophecy. Prophecies referring to "A, B, C" (for Anne Boleyn and Cromwell) and to "K, L, M" (Katherine and Lady Mary) figured in the case of John Dobson, vicar of Muston, for example, who was executed for having spread such predictions. A contemporary version of "The Sayings of the Prophets" refers to "H, G, or I" as the deliverer of England, while an alphabetic prophecy of "L, M, N" is part of the case against the priest Henry Cowpar of Ockley, reported to Cromwell by Sir William Parr in 1537.[45] It's not clear now, at the distance of four centuries, who Elizabeth Barton might have been referring to by the initials *A, F,* and *G,* but the technique she used for her predictions is very clear indeed.

As the letters and reports that first came trickling, then flooding into Cromwell amply demonstrate that such political prophecies did not come only from divine voices or from insider politicians. They were made by common men—and women—throughout the kingdom. I would argue that Elizabeth Barton's career as a political prophet is not as singular as it has seemed to historians. During Henry's reign she was the first of many who would be executed for saying something that today seems merely strange: "he that bears the eagle . . . shall spread his wings over all this realm" or "the cock of the north . . . shall do great adventures" or "the scallop shells shall be broken" or that "more ill cometh of a small note as a crumb well set in a man's throat."[46]

Moreover, Elizabeth Barton's career as a political "prophet" needs also to be placed in the larger context of western Europe, where a number of otherwise quite ordinary women would become involved in secular politics in quite extraordinary ways. Like the "Holy Maid of Kent," they were less concerned with the spiritual life, theological debate, and religious reform than they were with social and political commentary.

In Italy, for example, the duke of Ferrara protected and promoted Lucia da Narni, whose visions, in turn, bolstered the duke's reputation.[47] He invited her to stay in his palace and later founded a convent for her (she was a Dominican tertiary), where he installed her as abbess.

Lucia da Narni earned her reputation as a visionary in Italy during the years between 1497 and 1505, just as the "Beata of Piedrahíta" rose to prominence in Spain.[48] María de Santo Domingo, the Beata, was "acclaimed by supporters as a great mystic and prophetess" but denounced by her opponents "as a vain, lascivious, and publicity-seeking fraud." Tried in 1509-10, she was exonerated because of the intercession of three powerful "protectors," the duke of Alba, King Ferdinand of Aragon, and Cardinal Cisneros, the head of the Spanish Church. In her analysis of their intervention on her behalf, Jodi Bilinkoff has argued that the relationship between the Beata and these powerful men was a "complex, reciprocal" one, "based upon mutual, if not equal, needs": María de Santo Domingo's words and actions "helped them consolidate their power, endorsed many of their policies, and bolstered their prestige and sense of identity."[49]

Beginning in 1575, Sor María de la Visitación would experience a series of visions that would involve her in secular affairs.[50] The prioress of the Convento de la Annunciada in Lisbon, the so-called Nun of Lisbon supported the exiled Portuguese heir to the throne after Portugal was annexed by Philip II of Spain in 1582. Among her public pronouncements was one that sounds remarkably as if it had come from the mouth of Elizabeth Barton: "If the king of Spain does not restore the throne that he has unjustly usurped, then God will punish him severely." Sor María was tried by the Inquisition, pronounced guilty of "trickery and deceit," and exiled to Brazil for life.

As a young woman, Lucrecia de León experienced a series of dreams that, in 1587, launched a prophetic career that led her to the court of Philip II and, eventually, to a trial by the Spanish Inquisition.[51] Lucrecia's reputation soared after her predictions about the defeat of the Spanish armada in 1588. She blamed Spain's multiple problems on the king, Philip II, becoming "a court celebrity" and gathering around her "a cult," known as the Holy Cross of the Restoration. In his extended study of Lucrecia and her dreams Richard L. Kagan writes: "the confraternity seems to have united various courtiers and other individuals, who, for various reasons, believed that the monarchy's policies required urgent reform. In this respect the confraternity may have constituted the nucleus of a court faction whose members faulted Philip."[52]

At first Philip seems to have dismissed Lucrecia as inconsequential, but he could not continue to ignore her. Her prophecies "continued to be publicized and openly discussed, and her supporters continued to represent her as a divinely inspired prophet."[53] In 1590 Lucrecia was arrested by the Inquisition. The investigation that followed, a "trial of faith," took over five years to complete. She was, at the last, judged guilty of blasphemy, falsehood, sacrilege, and sedition. Her punishment, considering these crimes, was relatively minor: one hundred lashes, banishment from Madrid, and two years' seclusion in a religious house.[54]

By widening the focus of our examination, I would argue that we can begin to assess Elizabeth Barton's career more accurately than it has been in the past. She may have been, as many of her contemporaries believed, a divinely inspired prophet, a religious mystic. When her prophecies turned political, she claimed that they too were visions that had come from God. Or, as many have argued, she may have been a woman who was manipulated by the men who surrounded her and used her to their advantage. But I believe there is another alternative to consider in coming to terms with the "career" of Elizabeth Barton. Her political predictions show that she was familiar with popular English political prophecy. Rather than being a visionary or a pawn, she might instead have deliberately chosen to address political issues about which she felt strongly, voicing at least some of her opinions in the language of these popular texts.

On the scaffold at Tyburn she would claim—or be forced to claim—that she was a "poor wretch without learning" who had been misled by "learned men" who should have protected her from "foolish fantasy." It was certainly to the government's advantage to have her confess that she had been deluded, that she was an ignorant woman who had been manipulated by powerful and calculating men. But it may well have been that she was, in truth, the powerful one.

The men who surrounded Elizabeth Barton—Bocking and the rest who died with her, the religious from whom she drew her support, and prominent men such as William Warham and John Fisher who opposed the king's divorce—had found in her a charismatic focus for their opposition. They certainly stood to gain from her influence. Like the powerful protectors of the "Beata of Piedrahíta," the men who supported the "Nun of Kent" found in her someone who could "consolidate their power," someone whose predictions "endorsed many of their policies," and someone whose visions "bolstered their prestige and sense of identity." But Elizabeth Barton had much to gain from this relationship as well.

When she had experienced her first paralyzing illness and had made her first successful prediction, Elizabeth Barton found the circumstances of her life radically altered. A servant, she found that, "as soon as she was able to sit up, her master cause her to sit at his own mess with her mistress and this parson of Aldington." The sermon preached at the time of her public penance may not have been wrong in concluding,

> thereupon she, perceiving herself to be much made of, to be magnified and much set by, by reason of the said trifling words spoken unadvisedly by the idleness of her brain, conceived in her mind how she (having so good success and furtherance of so small occasion, being nothing to be esteemed in deed) might further enterprise and essay what she could do, being in good advisement and remembrance, to illude [deceive] the people giving audience unto her, who were so ready to make so much of her idle and trifling words aforesaid.[55]

Stripped of its judgmental qualifiers, the sermon preached against Elizabeth Barton may have come close to the reality of her situation. There is no reason to condemn a young and obscure woman for having found herself the focus of attention. Nor is there any reason to condemn a servant for having been promoted to the dining table of her employer.

Although her continuing illnesses seem to have been frighteningly real, Elizabeth Barton must also have found it comforting not only to be cared for but, as a woman with no natural family, to have found herself with a "family" of real significance—a "father" in Edward Bocking, a "mother" in her superior at St. Sepulchre's, and all the "brothers" and "sisters" who came to surround her in the new life to which she was transported. Her biographer Edward Thwaites concluded, "Thus was Elizabeth Barton advanced, from the condition of a base servant to the estate of a glorious nun."[56]

A young woman like Helen of Tottenham could be dissuaded from her religious visions by the assurances that they came from the devil. The daughter of a gentleman "sore abashed" at her visions, Anne Wentworth, too, could be convinced to retire from a visionary career, though she could not be turned away from her wish for a religious life; over her father's objections she entered a convent. Elizabeth Barton's religious convictions seem to have been equally sincere, and she must also have found in the convent a very desirable life and position.

Her religious prophecies had attracted a great deal of attention. But her political prophecies brought her much more; they brought her into contact with important members of the church, with educated university men, with wealthy and prominent noblemen and noblewomen, and with the most powerful political figures in England—even, eventually, Anne Boleyn and Henry himself.

Why should we assume that a woman like Elizabeth Barton had no political views of her own that she was eager to express? That her views had to be fed to her, either by God or by the men around her? The scores of reports to Cromwell about political prophecies are evidence that ordinary people had very strong political opinions. And, as Eustace Chapuys wrote to Charles V, the English commons paid particular attention to such predictions; they were, he judged, "easily moved to insurrection by prophecies." By means of her singular reputation Elizabeth Barton had attained some measure of social and religious prominence for herself; when she turned her attention to the king's marriage and divorce, she gained a political voice, and she could use her reputation as a prophet to give authority to the opinions she expressed.[57]

Although Mistress Amadas was questioned about her involvement with prophecy at just about the same time as Elizabeth Barton, the investigation of John Amadas's wife and her activities ended very differently than the investigation into the nun of Canterbury's prophetic career. As her "ungracious rehearsals" make abundantly clear, Mistress Amadas spoke publicly and violently against the king's divorce and Anne Boleyn, but she did not have the contacts of the nun, nor had her political predictions been published, reaching an even wider audience. And, perhaps most significantly, the government would have had some reason, and means, to control her rather than to eliminate her. Her husband was a useful public servant and a member of the king's household; whatever the state of their marriage, John Amadas undoubtedly could be counted on to keep his wife out of further trouble.

Elizabeth Barton, on the other hand, was a woman with no family connections to shield her and her chosen family was deeply implicated in her disruption. There was no safe place to stow her, no husband or father to whom she could be entrusted, and even a convent had been insufficient to contain her. Her prophecies interested and inspired many, and, once in print, they could circulate even further. Given the extraordinarily tense political climate, she needed to be silenced. When the king moved against her, there was no one who could, or would, defend her.

Through her prophecies, religious and political, Elizabeth Barton had challenged the power of the church hierarchy and the authority of the king. Though a remarkable number of documents about her dangerous talk and strange behavior exist, we still cannot know precisely what she said; as we have seen, every effort was made to obliterate all remaining traces of her voice. The many accounts of her predictions that survive have all come to us, in Carlo Ginzburg's terms, as "hostile testimonies, originating from or filtered by" those who wished to disassociate themselves from her or those who wanted to control her.[58] Yet, though her voice may thus be "altered" or "distorted," we can assess something of its strength by taking note of the government's extraordinary efforts to control it.

Even before she was hanged, her powerful voice was weakened and choked. The spectacle of her public "confession" and penance were calculated to reestablish royal authority. Her scaffold speech reminded those who had come to hear her that she was only "a poor wench without learning," a woman from whom such words could not have come "in no such sort"; "puffed up" with the praises of the men who had misled her, she had, she claimed, fallen "into a certain pride and foolish fantasy." She ended by asking for God's and the king's mercy and by beseeching all the "good people" who had come to hear her final words to pray for her.[59]

Yet silencing her was not quite enough. She needed to be discredited as well. The public sermon preached at St. Paul's Cross while she stood nearby and the formal act attainting her of treason are filled not only with attacks upon the validity of Elizabeth Barton's prophecies but also with sexualized attacks on her reputation for virtue. The sermon and act both imply that the nun's chastity was as feigned as her visions. The public heard that she had originally been taken from Aldington to Canterbury by Bocking, the two arriving "in an evening"—but "Dr. Bocking brought her to the said Priory of St. Sepulchre's in the morning!"

Once she had become a nun, she was said to steal "forth of the dortour [dormitory] in the night (which was once or twice weekly)" not for "spiritual business" or to receive "revelations of God" but, rather, "for bodily communication and pleasure with her friends, which could not have so good leisure and opportunity with her by day." She would, according to her maid, "be absent for an hour and sometimes more, when she perceived her sisters in their deep sleep. And it is supposed that then she went not about the saying of her paternoster!"[60]

Having silenced Elizabeth Barton completely—executing her and effectively suppressing all texts circulated by her supporters—and having done its best to destroy her credibility, the government finished its job by taking control of all her "worldly" posessions. The meager contents of her cell at St. Sepulchre's were turned over to the government and inventoried faithfully.[61]

Elizabeth Barton's prophetic career showed how threatening a common woman with uncommon strength could be. After her death Henry's government would not ignore the threat a woman's dangerous talk and strange behavior could offer. Her life and influence were to have profound effects on women like Margaret Cheyne. Yet, as we shall see, the lesson Elizabeth Barton's humiliation and execution was intended to teach was not enough to dissuade women from having an interest in affairs of state—or in having strongly expressed political views.

FIVE

Elizabeth Wood and Her "Traitorous Words"

When Elizabeth Barton mixed her religious visions with her views on the king's marriage and divorce, she expressed herself, at least in part, in the language of political prophecies that had been popular throughout England for centuries—but she did not attribute her predictions to the sources that were traditional in such texts. The "truth" of political prophecies was generally credited to reputed "prophets" such as Merlin, Bede, or Thomas à Becket; Elizabeth Barton topped those more traditional sources, claiming that her political prophecies had come from God Himself. Such a volatile mixture of political commentary and religious authority was bound to be dangerous, and the government's efforts—first to silence her, then to destroy her credibility, and finally to seek out and destroy all of her words—were both systematic and extraordinary.

The career of the Nun of Kent was only the most spectacular of cases that led to the passage of a new Treason Act in 1534. Drafts of a new law had been written as early as 1530; the revised act was finally introduced in the November 1534 session of Parliament. After the passage of this bill there was danger in all kinds of words, even the kind we might typically ignore as harmless gossip, wild rumors, or foolish boasting.[1] Such "dangerous talk" was not overlooked, however, as the story of Elizabeth Wood makes clear. Elizabeth Wood's case is not nearly so complicated as Elizabeth Barton's. The evidence against her is, in many ways, very slight. Yet Elizabeth Wood was executed for what she said and what she did, no matter how inconsequential those words and deeds now seem.

On 26 April 1537, while Margaret Cheyne and the other northern rebels were still awaiting trial, Sir John Heydon of Baconsthorpe, Norfolk, and Sir Roger Townsend of East Raynham sent Cromwell "two ungracious persons," George and William Guisborough, along with confessions detailing their "heinous and malicious intentions." According to the information Heydon had received, the two, father and son, had been involved in a plan to raise the county in an insurrection; the Guisboroughs had reportedly "disclosed their minds of their mischievous purposes and intents" to a number of men in and around Walsingham, Norfolk.[2] Although they had threatened death to anyone who disclosed their "privy matters," Sir John Heydon's servant John Galant had gone to Heydon and revealed what he knew about the details of the plot.

According to Galant, the conspirators had met together "privily in the night to get a great number of people together"; their plan involved setting the coastal beacons alight, raising the commons in the county, cutting off the heads and taking the goods of all those who resisted them (whom they predicted would be the "gentlemen"), taking control of a bridge to disrupt travel to or from London, and then going to "the north country to aid and help the northern men."[3]

Although by April the northern risings had been put down and those accused of treason, Margaret Cheyne among them, were being held in the Tower, this new threat of insurrection was not to be ignored. Heydon acted with remarkable speed on Galant's information. Sir John involved Sir Roger Townsend immediately, and, on the same day that they had first heard of the plot, the two took into custody the five men whom Galant said were involved. Aside from the two Guisboroughs, Heydon and Townsend took depositions from Robert Hawker, John Semble, and Thomas Howse.

But Heydon discovered he hadn't yet rounded up all those involved in the conspiracy; he indicated in his report to Cromwell that a man named Ralph Rogerson had fled before he could be taken into custody, and it had been alleged that it was Rogerson who had first involved the Guisboroughs in the plot. Heydon sent all the depositions he had taken, along with the two Guisboroughs and their confessions, to Cromwell. Finally, he reported, he and Townsend were in pursuit of Rogerson. They believed that Rogerson was in truth the originator of the whole plan for the insurrection.[4]

At the same time, Heydon sent another letter, this one to his most "assured friend" Richard Gresham, a Norfolk merchant in London with numerous court contacts.[5] Heydon indicated to Gresham that he was sending his servant Galant to him in London: "I have sent him to you with his confession in writing to me . . . here enclosed, praying you to cause him to be examined by my Lord Privy Seal, whereupon he shall inform my lord more plainly in that behalf." Sir John indicated that he was taking still further action on that same day: "this night or early in the morning I intend to be at Walsingham to apprehend or take some of these rebellious, trusting to have knowledge from my lord how I shall order myself and do in this behalf, praying you to be so friendly that I may have short knowledge of my lord's pleasure."

The "great disturbance and insurrection" that had been planned in and around Walsingham never became more than a plan, but the conspiracy combined many elements of unrest—social, political, religious, and economic. And there had been a great deal of sympathy in Norfolk for the northern rebels at the time of the Pilgrimage of Grace. During the preceding November copies of the Pilgrims' demands had appeared in Walsingham, and in the weeks that followed several people had been under examination for expressing support for the northern rebels.[6] There was, then, a very real possibility of trouble erupting in Norfolk: in assessing the significance of the aborted Walsingham rising, G. R. Elton has concluded that it was "the most serious plot hatched anywhere south of the Trent in those years."[7]

When Cromwell learned of the conspiracy, he responded as quickly as Heydon and Townsend, immediately dispatching one of his agents, a Norfolk native named Richard Southwell, to undertake further investigations.

George and William Guisborough, meanwhile, were examined in the Tower by Thomas Wriothesley on 29 April.[8] George Guisborough, the father, deposed that he had met Ralph Rogerson, a yeoman farmer employed as a lay chorister by Walsingham priory, about two weeks earlier. They had talked together about five or six times and, over the course of their conversations, had discussed the suppression of the religious houses and the oppression of the commons by "the gentlemen." They had planned somehow to meet with the king about their grievances. George Guisborough had agreed with Rogerson that they should contact others to raise the county; he admitted having talked to Thomas Howse, a husbandman, John Symley, a mason, and "a glover whose name he remembreth not." William Guisborough's deposition confirmed his father's statement.[9]

While the investigation of the conspiracy was being thus pursued in London, on 30 April Richard Southwell, Cromwell's agent, was already reporting back to Cromwell from Baconsthorpe. He had traveled so hard to Norfolk, he wrote, that he had arrived at Heydon's house between four and five in the morning of the previous day. Heydon had informed Southwell that the "conspirators pass not in number as few as . . . twelve persons thereabout, and they

[are] all very beggers and men neither of honesty, wit, or conduct."[10] Southwell reported Heydon's conclusion that there was no likelihood of "any commotion" further in Walsingham: the county was in as "good and due obedience as ever it was." Southwell planned to round up the rest of those implicated in the conspiracy that day, leaving them in Norwich Castle and returning to London.

Southwell's investigation of the matter proceeded quickly. Within a few days he was reporting success to Cromwell.[11] In addition to those already being held, Southwell had taken into custody the elusive Ralph Rogerson as well as Nigel Mileham, subprior of Walsingham Priory, whose name had also emerged in the course of the investigations. As it turned out, Mileham had been one of the leaders of the intended rebels. Instructed by Cromwell to remain in Norfolk to examine all those involved "without sparing," Southwell reported again to Cromwell on 10 May. He was forwarding all the depositions and was waiting for further instructions.[12] Some twenty-five men were in custody in Norwich Castle.

On 25 May, the day Margaret Cheyne was executed for treason at Smithfield, the Walsingham conspirators were convicted of treason: Mileham, the subprior of Walsingham Priory; Rogerson, a farmer and lay chorister at the priory; the two Guisboroughs—the father, George, a yeoman peasant and a lay chorister at the priory, the son, William, a merchant; John Grigby, rector of Langham; Richard Henley, a plumber; Thomas Howse, a husbandman; Thomas Manne, a carpenter; Andrew Pax, a parish clerk; John Pecock, a Carmelite friar; Thomas Penne, a husbandman; John Punt, rector of Waterdon; John Sellers, a tailor; and John Semble, a mason.[13] Another three men were convicted of misprision of treason, while eight were "delivered by proclamation," the charges against them dropped.

Grigby and Punt were remanded to the prison without their sentences being carried out. The rest were sentenced to hanging, drawing, beheading, and quartering. The executions were carried out in several locations around the county: on Saturday, 26 May, in Norwich, Henley, Howse, Manne, Pax, and Rogerson; on Monday, 28 May, in Yarmouth, Sellers and Semble; on Wednesday, 30 May, in Walsingham, George Guisborough and Mileham; on Friday, 1 June, in Lynne, William Guisborough and Pecock.[14]

Southwell witnessed the executions in Norwich, writing to Cromwell that "by way from the castle [the condemned] confessed their crime. So lying on the hurdles, both by the way and at the place of execution, they exhorted the people, who, by reason of Trinity Fair that day, were very numerous, to take example by them."[15] But Rogerson remained rebellious to the last: "according to his cankered stomach [he] began to enter matter, wherein he was stayed, much after the infection of his heart."[16]

Although no further details emerge from the surviving records, two women—the wives of Richard Mariot, a mariner, and Andrew Pax, the parish clerk—were at least tangentially involved in the Walsingham conspiracy. The women, both named Agnes, were accused of misprision of treason for concealing what they knew about the plot. They were recorded as having been charged, but there is no record that either one was ever tried. It is impossible to know now what happened to them.[17]

While Southwell was thus wrapping up his investigation in Norfolk, writing to Cromwell while "riding towards Walsingham" on 29 May that he would return to court after the executions were completed, Sir John Heydon was writing another letter from Baconsthorpe on the same day, once again addressed to his "most especial friend" Richard Gresham in London.[18] He was enclosing a bill "declaring the detestable and traitorous words" spoken by a "lewd and ungracious woman" named Elizabeth Wood. Heydon had been informed of her words only the day before; he already had her in custody in Norwich jail and wanted Cromwell to tell him what to do with her.

In the most detailed examination of what he calls "the Walsingham conspiracy," C. E. Moreton refers consistently to "the Walsingham men," relegating to a footnote the name of Elizabeth Wood.[19] His brief reference includes nothing of her story—nor does he mention that she was executed for treason for her comments about the Walsingham plot. To be sure, Elizabeth Wood was not one of the conspirators involved in planning what was to be a rising in Norfolk, but she was caught up in the investigation nonetheless, and she lost her life as a result of what she said about the planned rising. I think she warrants more than a brief aside; I would like to move her name from the footnotes and return it to the narrative of the Walsingham story itself.

According to Heydon's report, two constables from the town of Aylesham, John Bettes (a "worsted weaver") and Thomas Oakes, had presented themselves before him and Sir James Boleyn on the previous day, 28 May.[20] The two were reporting "one Elizabeth Wood, the wife of Robert Wood of Aylesham" for publicly speaking "certain traitorous words as followeth."

According to Bettes and Oakes, John Dix and William Jeckes were responsible for the accusations against Elizabeth Wood. On 12 May, while the Walsingham conspirators were being held awaiting trial, Elizabeth Wood had spoken to Dix and Jeckes in Dix's shop. She was, they said, "resting upon the shop windows of the said John Dix" when she spoke. According to the two accusers, Elizabeth had commented that "it was pity that these Walsingham men were discovered, for we shall have never good world till we fall together by the ears, and 'with clubs and clouted shone / shall the deeds be done,' for we had never good world since this king reigned. It is pity that he filed any clouts more than one."

Elizabeth's reference to "clubs and clouted shone," clubs and "cloutshoes," seems to have been a quotation from a popular rhymed political prophecy. The second reference to "clouts" seems to be a pun on the slang expression "to file a cly or cloy," that is, to pick a pocket—perhaps to be understood as, "It's a pity the king has picked more than a single pocket."[21] Even though the exact meaning of her words has been obscured by time, it is still possible to see that they constituted an insult directed against the king and that they represented the same kinds of social unrest that the plans of the Walsingham conspirators had revealed.

After hearing these words, Dix became uneasy. The next day he had consulted with one Thomas Clampe, also of Aylesham, asking Clampe what, if anything, should be done. Clampe had advised Dix "to take his witness with him that heard the same words and so shortly as possible to show it unto the king's officers." And so Dix and Jeckes had presented themselves to Oakes and Bettes, who absolved themselves for any delay in reporting to Heydon and Boleyn by indicating that they had only been informed of the matter the day before, Monday, 28 May, the day following Trinity Sunday.

No record of Cromwell's response to all this survives, but we know Elizabeth Wood's words were taken seriously. She was already in Norwich jail when Heydon wrote on 29 May. On 26 July she was tried and convicted of treason.[22]

As in the case of Margaret Cheyne, almost nothing survives of Elizabeth Woods's own words. When Heydon sent his "information" to Cromwell, he recorded at some length what the two constables reported to him, but he sent no deposition from Elizabeth Wood herself. By contrast, when he had taken into custody those accused in the Walsingham conspiracy, he examined carefully all five of the men first mentioned, enclosing their depositions when he wrote to Cromwell—the one from George Guisborough fills half a folio, his son William's about the same length on a separate folio. Thomas Howse's statement fills a whole folio, while Robert Hawker's and John Semble's statements together are on a single folio, but each is about as long as the statements made by the Guisboroughs. George Guisborough's second statement, made in London, fills the front and part of the reverse of a folio, his son's second statement a full folio in length.

But, if one was taken, no statement from Elizabeth Wood has survived. Indeed, the indictment against her in the King's Bench document is word for word the same as the conversation Heydon had reported, thirdhand, on 29 May, so it may be that no statement from Elizabeth Wood was ever recorded. In this way the surviving documents in her case parallel the records of the case against Margaret Cheyne, in which lengthy statements are made detailing what men such as John Watts and William Stainous thought of her, but only a few brief lines (twelve, as preserved in the state papers) have survived from Margaret herself.

Also interesting in this case is the fact that Elizabeth Wood is consistently identified as the wife of Robert Wood, yet nothing further is said of him or by him. It might be that, since his wife spoke while leaning on the tailor's shopwindow, he had not been around to hear what she had said. Given the thoroughness of Heydon's investigations, however, it is curious that he didn't at least question Robert Wood about what he knew about his wife's sympathies (or about his own feelings, for that matter), particularly since Aylesham seems to have been a real focus for seditious talk; at the same time that Elizabeth Wood was reported for her traitorous words, James Boleyn was investigating the "sayings and opinions" of a whole group of Aylesham men, one of whom, John Tolwyn, claimed that he "knew a hundred traitors" in the town.[23]

Perhaps since Elizabeth Barton had said so much, and so much of what she had said had been written down and circulated, it was better not to preserve too much of Elizabeth Wood's dangerous talk. For whatever reasons, not much of what Margaret Cheyne and Elizabeth Wood were accused of having said has survived.

What has survived, however, are many reports of women's words—their gossip, rumors, and insults. Women expressed their opinions about the king's Great Matter, about Queen Katherine, and about Anne Boleyn, and their opinions about the king's marriage and his political and religious reforms were as much a source of concern to the government as men's views were. Nor were women assumed to be uninvolved in more active political resistance; there was a real possibility that women might be participants in conspiracy to rebel, and they were in due course investigated for their possible involvement. Strongly expressed political opinions and the potential for more active resistance were combined in the case of Elizabeth Wood. There are two threads to the investigation of her traitorous words that I would thus like to follow: one showing how women's words were a cause for concern, and a second showing the involvement of women in riots, risings, and plots like "the Walsingham conspiracy."

Reports about Henry's plans to divorce Katherine soon led to widespread rumors that "the king would for his own pleasure have another wife." In writing about these "foolish words" and "foolish communications," the chronicler Edward Hall attributed them generally to "the common people," who were "ignorant of the truth." But Hall also took occasion to make particular mention of women's opposition: "in especial women," he said, "favored the queen" and "spoke largely" against the king's plans.[24]

In a diplomatic report to Francis I similar comments about women's reactions to the king's Great Matter appear. In describing the divorce proceedings at Blackfriars in 1529, John DuBellay wrote, "If the matter were to be decided by women, he [Henry] would lose the battle, for they did not fail to encourage the queen [Katherine] at her entrance and departure by their cries, telling her to care for nothing, and other such words."[25]

While expressing strong support for Katherine, the common people spoke out strongly against Anne Boleyn. Contemporary chroniclers, whether they favored Katherine or Anne, agreed that Anne was not generally liked. Edward Hall reported, "surely the most part of the lay people of England, which knew not the law of God, sore murmured at the matter, and much the more, because there was a gentlewoman in the court called Anne Boleyn."[26] Cavendish, in his biography of Cardinal Wolsey, mentioned the rumors circulating about Anne as well: "And thus the world began to be full of wonderful rumors not heard of before in this realm." The reports were not in the lady's favor: "Then began other matters to brew and take place that occupied all men's heads with diverse imaginations, whose stomachs were therewith full filled without any perfect digestion. The long hid and secret love between the king and Mistress Anne Boleyn began to break out into every man's ears."[27] The Spanish chronicler, too, wrote about attitudes toward Anne: "It is a thing to note that the common people always disliked her."[28]

While such gossip is far from historical "fact," of course, it nevertheless tells us as much about the king's Great Matter as the opinions on Henry's first marriage solicited from scholars throughout Europe or all the details of the diplomatic maneuverings between England and Rome. The possibility of the king's divorce disturbed his subjects deeply, and his choice of a new queen appalled many of them. Displays of royal power and authority could not stop people from saying what they thought. Nor, it seems, could the threat of legal action.[29]

One thing in particular seemed to attract attention and comment, and that was Henry's riding with Anne in public. After the legatine proceedings at Blackfriars were dismissed, the king left the court with Anne Boleyn. "The king commanded the queen to be removed out of the court and sent unto another place," Cavendish wrote, "And His Highness rode in his progress, with Mistress Anne Boleyn in his company all the grease season."[30]

Such public display sparked not only attention but also negative response. The following spring, Chapuys was reporting on the king's reaction to one such incident:

> The king shows greater favor to the lady every day. Very recently coming
> from Windsor he made her ride behind him on a pillion, a most unusual

proceeding, and one that has greatly called forth people's attention here, so much so that two men have been, as I am informed, taken up and sent to prison merely for having mentioned the fact.[31]

Chapuys wrote to the emperor again, in July 1532, about a similar incident, this time remarking on the way that Anne had been treated by women along the king's route:

> The king was on his way to the northern counties where he intended to hunt . . . when he suddenly changed his purpose and came back to town. The causes of his return are variously explained. Some say that for the last three or four days after he started on his journey, wherever he went accompanied by the lady, the people on the road so earnestly requested him to recall the queen, his wife, and the women especially so insulted the royal mistress, hooting and hissing on her passage, that he was actually obliged to retrace his steps.

Chapuys himself wasn't certain of the exact reasons for Henry's return from the north, but he concluded, "I have, nevertheless, deemed it necessary to acquaint Your Majesty with all these rumors.[32]

Such reaction and comment were not confined to the north. During a sermon preached in support of the divorce at St. Paul's in May 1532, for example, a woman interrupted the proceedings. In reporting this incident to the Seigniory in Venice, ambassador Carlo Capello wrote that the woman "stood up and told him [the preacher] that he lied, and that this example in a king would be the destruction of the laws of matrimony." Capello reported that the disruptive and outspoken woman had been arrested.[33]

In the month following Anne Boleyn's coronation two women in London were punished publicly for words they had uttered: "The 23rd day of August were two women beaten . . . naked from the waist upwards with rods and their ears nailed to the standard for because they said Queen Katherine was the true queen of England and not Queen Anne. And one of the women was big with child. And when these two women had thus been punished, they fortified their saying still, to die in the quarrel for Queen Katherine's sake."[34]

Such reports about public reactions to political events became much more frequent after 1534, following Elizabeth Barton's execution and the passage of the new Treason Act. Defamation was, strictly, a church court offense, the terms most commonly complained of being "whore" and "heretic." But when such names were applied to Anne Boleyn, they became something more than the common ecclesiastical offense they had customarily been. Among the letters that came pouring in to Cromwell were dozens that relayed to the king's minister what people had been saying. Many of those reports focused on women's words.[35]

Such a letter was one sent by Sir Walter Stonor to Cromwell in June 1534.[36] John Dawson, a constable from Watlington, Oxfordshire, had presented himself before Stonor to relay to him the words of one Joan Hammulden, the wife of Walter Hammulden. Joan was a midwife who had been sent for "about Whitsuntide twelvemonth" by "one Burgyn's wife of Watlington, when she was with child." According to the midwife Joan, Mistress Burgyn had been so impressed by her services that she had praised her by saying that "for her honesty and her cunning she [Joan] might be midwife unto the queen of England, if it were Queen Katherine. And [if] it were Queen Anne, she [Joan] was too good to be her midwife, for she [Anne] was a whore and a harlot of her living."[37]

Joan Hammulden, the midwife, had reported Mistress Burgyn's words, after waiting a year, to Dawson and "several others," who then proceeded to question "the said Burgyn's wife." When Burgyn's wife was examined, she denied having said any such thing, but, in turn, she lodged a complaint against the midwife. According to Mistress Burgyn, "one Collins's wife" had said "about midsummer last . . . that it was never merry in England since there was three queens in it, and then the said Joan said there would be fewer shortly." The "three queens" were Katherine, Anne, and Henry's sister Mary, who had been married to Louix XII of France and was called "the French Queen" even after she had been widowed and returned to England as the wife of Charles Brandon, duke of Suffolk.

Back the justices went to Joan Hammulden, who denied having predicted that there would be "fewer" queens shortly. At this point, however, the midwife admitted that she would not have accused Burgyn's wife if Burgyn's wife had not first threatened her by claiming "she would burn the said Joan Hammulden's tail and do her other displeasure."[38] Stonor reported that he was holding them all "in ward" until he knew Cromwell's "pleasure."

It's impossible to know what Cromwell must have thought of all of this, for with Stonor's report the record ends. But in September Cromwell received yet another report from Oxfordshire, this one from Henley-on-Thames, full of the story of Alice Brown, the wife of John Brown.[39] In this case, though, it wasn't Alice herself who ultimately became the focus of the query, although initially she seems to have been the one under investigation.

According to the justices who wrote to Cromwell, Alice Brown traveled to Reading to receive payment for a kirtle she had sold to the wife of a laborer named Thomas Fen. When she arrived in Reading, according to her statement, she had a drink "there in the afternoon that day." After refreshing herself, she sought out Fen and his wife to ask for payment.

But Fen's wife had no intention of paying. She called in her neighbor's wife to help her get rid of Alice Brown. For having "made affray in the forest," Alice was "brought to the cage" in Reading, where she found the mayor, Thomas Evered, waiting for her. Alice first "made special request to the mayor to desire him that she might depart out of the cage in the honor of Our Lady," and, when that request was denied, she said she "would kneel before Queen Anne." To which the mayor replied, in Alice's words, "that if Queen Anne and I both were in the cage a-fire, he would make Anne a new cage."

Although Alice Brown's husband John had "commanded his wife to speak no such words in no wise," and although she told the justices in Henley-upon-Thames that she told her story to "no man but to her husband," the details of what had gone on in Reading somehow became known in Henley. Alice Brown was the one initially under investigation, but what was finally at issue wasn't what Alice Brown said about Queen Anne but, rather, what the mayor of Reading had said. Again, however, there is no record of what resulted. Presumably, the investigation of both Alice Brown and the mayor of Reading ended.

A similarly muddled case of who said what emerged later that same year. In early December Sir John Markham wrote to Cromwell about accusations that had been made during a domestic dispute.[40] Markham reported that "of late there fell certain variance between one Allen Hey and his wife." Hey's wife had left him, "as she hath done diverse times before," taking shelter with relatives. Hey, angered at the "sudden departing" of his wife, proceeded to speak out violently against her, "in diverse places saying she was a traitrix and that she had railed against the Queen's Grace." Markham reported that Hey's "wild words" included claims that his wife had predicted that Anne would die.

Not content, Allen Hey wrote a letter to those sheltering his wife, threatening that, if they did not "send her home to him, he would lay to her charge" the seditious words he claimed she had uttered. Sir John Markham evidently had Hey's letter in hand at the time he wrote to Cromwell; Markham reported that Hey had written such "lewd and evil words" that he couldn't even bring himself to copy them out to send to Cromwell. Along with two justices of the peace Markham had "taken diverse depositions whereby we thought to have come to the true knowledge whether they were his wife's words or that he feigned them of malice." Even though the matter still appeared "doubtful," Markham concluded, "we be of that opinion that he [Hey] feigned such matters thereby to put . . . the said wife's kinsmen in fear to cause them . . . rather to send her home again."

The outcome of all this obviously was not what Allen Hey had intended. Markham wasn't sure exactly what Hey's wife might have said, but it was clear that Hey, at least, had "uttered such lewd words at diverse and sundry times with his tongue" and that he had "written the same with his hand." Markham had Hey in custody, and he wanted to know what Cromwell wanted done with the angry and deserted husband.

Nothing further about Hey and his wife has been recorded. But what is most interesting about this domestic dispute is the fact that, in his anger, Allen Hey could think of no more dangerous accusation to make against the wife who had deserted him than to claim she had insulted and threatened Queen Anne. His accusations had, at least in part, accomplished his goal; ecclesiastical courts were usually the bodies that pursued investigations of marital disharmony, including cases of married couples who were living apart. Hey knew how to get his wife into more serious trouble, but he had miscalculated the conclusions Markham would draw after his investigation.

In January 1535 another woman was being investigated for her traitorous words.[41] In Sevenoaks, Kent, Margaret West had been taken into custody by Thomas Boleyn, earl of Wiltshire. Margaret "hath been, and was now at the time of her taking, a common keeper of them that hath been visited with the pestilence." Her accusers "also hath been very late visited with the visitation of the pestilence." They were recorded as John Potted, a weaver, and James Fuller. According to Boleyn's report, Margaret was being held "for certain traitorous words that she hath spoken against Our Sovereign Lord, the king, His Grace's person." As in all the cases so far noted, the motivations for the accusations are tantalizing. Why would two men who had just been ill "of the pestilence" have accused a woman whose job was taking care of those stricken? Nothing more is known about Margaret West; the last we hear of her is that she was held pending further instruction.

Motivations, or excuses, are a little more clear in the case of Margaret Chanseler of Bradfield St. Clare in Suffolk. Sir Robert Drury examined her on 11 February, indicating that she was a spinster and that she was also sometimes called Margaret Ellis.[42] According to Drury, Margaret admitted to "opprobrious words which she did speak in contempt of our said Sovereign Lord the king and the Queen's Grace." First, "she said that the Queen's Grace had one child by our Sovereign Lord the king which she [Margaret] said was dead born, and she prayed God that [the queen] might never have [an]other."

According to Drury's dutiful report, "Also, she said that the Queen's Grace was a naughty [evil] whore and that the King's Grace ought not to marry within his realm." But Margaret Chanseler, or Ellis, went further, and, for pure inventiveness, she is quite amazing. Those who accused her added: "the said

Margaret said that the queen was a goggle-eyed whore and said God save Queen Katherine . . . righteous queen' and that she trusted to see her queen again."[43]

These were certainly strong words, and Margaret Chanseler might not have escaped punishment for such dangerous talk. But, while admitting that she had uttered the words ("these words she denied not," Drury wrote; she agreed that "she did speak them"), Margaret pleaded that "she was drunk when she did speak them, and that the evil spirit did cause her to speak them—and she was very penitent for her offences."

A plea of drunkenness was made by Margery Cowpland as well. In early June Sir Walter Stonor wrote to Cromwell once more, from his "poor house at Stonor," not far from Henley-on-Thames.[44] On 8 June he had examined a number of witnesses, all of whom were accusing Margery of having spoken "against the King's Highness and the Queen's Grace." According to the evidence Stonor had gathered, Margery had said "the King's Grace was an extortioner and knave and . . . the Queen's Grace was a strong harlot." Another witness claimed he had heard Margery say that the king was a traitor, the queen a "strong whore." Some sort of fracas had also broken out between Margery and a man named Richard Heath, who had warned her that he was the king's servant, to which she had replied, "The king's servant, the devil's turd."

Stonor went to a great deal of trouble in reporting to Cromwell. He investigated Margery's principal accuser, John Wynbok, who, it turned out, had been brought up by Margery and who seemed to have some financial reasons for accusing the woman who had raised him. Stonor reported that, "for love that she bear unto him she hath granted and delivered to him a lease that her husband and she hath of . . . a mill, upon a certain covenant that she and her husband shall be found meat and drink and to have yearly a mark of money paid to them by Wynbok." Stonor suspected that Wynbok had broken these "covenants" and that the "variance" that had broken out between Wynbok and Margery "causeth Wynbok to utter the saying and the words," trusting that by accusing Margery he would rid himself of her.

Stonor recorded the accusations of Wynbok and two men who supported him, but he had also examined Margery. He reported that "she utterly denieth" having spoken the words, but he added his own view that "it is like that she spake them." He concluded, "she is a marvelous drunken woman, and as I perceive her she is somewhat straight out of her wits and her husband is out of his mind and hath been this twelve months and more."

Stonor apologized for his "tedious letter," indicating that he had sent Margery to the jail at Wallingford, where he intended to keep her until he knew what should be done. Despite the length of his letter, he added a postscript below his signature, repeating his request for advice: "Also I beseech you that I may know your pleasure for the said Margery Cowpland, for she is very aged and lacking wit, and also there is nobody to tend to her husband, which is mad as all her answers hath testified with her."

While Stonor had gone to great lengths to track down what Margery Cowpland had said—and to ascertain why her accusers had come forward—not all the letters to Cromwell were so detailed. At the same time that Stonor was writing to Cromwell about Margery, Thomas Cranmer was writing to the king's minister from Lambeth about yet another woman who was in trouble for what she had said.[45] Instead of writing the kind of "tedious letter" Stonor apologized for, he had simply sent Cromwell the two people accused of speaking against the king—the one a priest who had reportedly reacted to a new tax by saying, "a vengeance on the king," the second a "woman which said that since this new queen was made, there was never so much pilling and polling in this realm, asking a vengeance also upon her." As can be seen from the words of this anonymous women, the king was not only criticized for his personal life but for "pillaging" and "plundering" as well (literally "making bare both hair and skin"), his economic excesses being linked to his marital choices. Margery Cowpland, too, had linked money and sex when she had called the king an "extortioner" while accusing Anne of being a "strong whore." And Margery had also added her views of royal marital politics, indicating her opinion that a king should not marry one of his subjects.

In all of the cases examined so far, we ultimately lose sight of the women accused. The last we hear of most of them is the report that they are "in custody" or "in jail," and we can only assume that they were eventually released. A slightly different view is given in a document from early August 1535. Writing to Cromwell, Christopher Jenney, serjeant-at-law, reported the results of the York assizes. He indicated that there had been forty-two prisoners, among them two murderers, four other felons, and a monk, George Lasyngby, who had been found guilty of high treason.[46] Lasyngby was, in Jenney's opinion, a "willful fool and of small or no learning," and the monk had admitted his guilt. But guilt was not so clear in other cases: "there is more indicted of treason, but for that the words were to us so doubtful whether they made high treason or not we would not therefore proceed to the arraignment of them until your mastership and other of the king's council were made privy to the same for your further advice therein to be had."

In part, then, the problem seemed to be that justices weren't clear about what kinds of words were to be construed as treason under the new act. In part, though, the problem seemed to be that so many were accused; Jenney had arrived in York from the assizes at Hull on Sunday, and he needed to leave by Saturday, "for keeping our days and times of sitting in other places, albeit if we should but hear and examine all complaints by commission and otherwise that were had to do there, it had been needful for us to have tarried yet this four days at the least."

Such numbers of accused might account for why no judgments followed the rigorous investigations of so many women for what they had said. As Jenney commented about the York assizes, "I never saw so many complaints of women and of so small effect."

A letter to Cromwell from Richard Johnson and his wife, Alice, indicates something of what imprisonment might have been like for women being held pending further action in their cases.[47] Johnson identified himself as a "poor beadsman" from "the village of Buckstead beside Colchester in the county of Essex." He and his wife had been taken to Fulham by John Stokesley, the bishop of London, "about Shrovetide" (the three days—Sunday, Monday, and Tuesday—preceding Ash Wednesday), and had been kept there "until harvest following." They were held in "such extreme hunger and imprisonment" that "we were then almost famished insomuch that we would gladly [have] suffered death."

The king commanded Stokesley "to deliver" the two, but Johnson complained that the bishop had simply transferred them from Fulham to Colchester, where they were imprisoned again and where they were "worse treated . . . than before." About their detention in the prison Johnson wrote that, "if there came any good person of their charity to minister to us, they were so opprobriously said to that they durst not come no more at us." Johnson reminded Cromwell that there was "neither word nor deed that could be proved" against him and his wife. He begged to be delivered from the "cruel handling" of the bishop; in Johnson's words, "We in the most humblest wise beseeching your goodness of your tender pity that we might be fully set at liberty and to go home to our poor dwelling house and there to be let alone in peace."

Still, rumors and reports of rumors persisted. In a typically convoluted story Chapuys wrote to the emperor early in 1536 with a story that Gertrude Courtenay had told him, that the king had said that Anne used witchcraft to ensnare him. Despite the close call the marchioness had had over her involvement with Elizabeth Barton, she seems to have been unable to resist involving herself once more in dangerous talk. Chapuys also reported the more general gossip in court, that Henry would rid himself of his second wife and would marry his third.[48]

Meanwhile, in London the beadsman and curate William Cockes, of St. Olave's, Southwark, was accused of having spoken "uncourteous words" against the king.[49] But he had not only spoken against the king himself, he had incited "Green's wife to withstand . . . enacted matters," and he advised her to be obedient to the pope and not the king. Cockes denied the charges, saying that the strong language and "ruffling manner" of Green's wife caused people "to believe this matter to be of more gravity and weight than it is in very deed."

Sometimes women spoke out against issues aside from the king's marriages, of course. In York, for example, women's grievances included enclosures.[50] York civic records for 3 May 1536 recorded a plan to enclose the common of Knavesmire. The enclosure set off a serious riot on 15 May, with dikes and gates "riotously cast down and burnt." A number of men were investigated for their active participation in the "unlawful riot," but two women were also convicted for their part in the resistance. Isabell Lutton and Agnes Cook "spoke slanderous words of the . . . mayor and his brethren and banned [cursed] them with the ill evil."[51] All of the offenders—men and women, those who acted and those who spoke—seem to have suffered the same punishment: "it is agreed that the said offenders shall be committed unto the sheriff's prison and to be carried of the thewe [pillory-like apparatus] about this city three several days in example of like offenders."

Several months later, in August, the mayor of York called upon the "king's justices of peace" to investigate "diverse misdemeanors lately committed" in the city at night; someone had "slanderously" posted a series of "bills" intended "to be a great occasion to make debate, dissension, and variance within this city."[52] Trying to find out who was responsible for these bills occupied a great deal of energy; pages of examinations are recorded. A woman named Elizabeth Abney was suspected, and, although she denied any involvement—her husband, Thomas, a merchant, supported her—eventually her brother admitted that "as he is now remembered [he] wrote three of the said slanderous bills" for Elizabeth but that "his said sister made and of her malicious mind devised the several slanders contained in the said bills." Elizabeth finally confessed.

The assembled mayor, eleven aldermen, two sheriffs, and twenty-four members of the mayor's council judged Thomas Abney and his wife, Elizabeth, guilty "of the making and setting up of the said slanderous bills, by occasion whereof murder, variance, strife, and debate was very like to ensue among all the commonalty of the said city." Together with her husband, Elizabeth was sentenced to sitting backward on a horse, with a paper set on her head and another in her hands that read, "For setting up of slanderous bills and willful perjury, thus to be punished deserved have I." They would be led from the prison and paraded throughout the city and then banished: "neither the said Thomas Abney nor his said wife shall from thenceforth never inhabit nor dwell within the said city and suburbs of the same over and above fifteen days next to come, upon pain to be set of the pillory if that they hereafter do the contrary, and within the said time that they shall convey and have away forth of the city all their goods and cattle."

Instead of resisting the king's laws or disturbing the peace, still others of the king's subjects spread the rumor that Henry was dead. Maud Kebery was one of several accused of having claimed that Henry died and that Cromwell was keeping the death a secret: "one Maud Kebery . . . first did report the said words—she denied the same. . . . Her mother before her face said that she said she heard [Maud] say he was dead and then the said Maud confessed that she heard it spoken in the street of a woman and of whom she would not confess."[53]

More seriously, as the northern risings erupted during the late fall of 1536, Londoners expressed their support for the rebels and their antagonism to Cromwell. Among them was Margaret Williamson. In November she was sent to Maidstone jail for having sympathized with the northerners' threats to have Cromwell's head; "or this time twelve month," she had reportedly said, Cromwell's "head should be cut off, or else take her neck."[54]

Most of the women examined in 1537 did not attack the king's "enacted matters" or his third marriage. Instead, they attacked the king himself. One "Middleton's wife," for example, was examined about a scurrilous rhyme ("the which touched the King's Highness very sore") that was circulating in Halifax (West Yorkshire).[55] As it turned out, Middleton's wife wasn't the object of the investigation; rather, Sir Richard Tempest and his son-in-law John Lacy were. But Middleton's wife seems to have been the source of the rhyme that the two had helped in spreading, and so the investigators traced it back until they reached her.

What is fascinating about the "articles" that Sir Henry Saville recorded in this investigation is his attempt to transcribe the words of the speakers; in the dialogue Saville preserved we come closer to the voices of the speakers than in the usual third-person statements recorded by examiners. The "rhyme" itself isn't much. Tempest and Lacy had allegedly copied out only two lines: "An apple and a fair wench to dally withal / would please him very well." The problem for the investigators was to determine who the "him" referred to. Doctor Holdsworth, the vicar of Halifax, reported that he had heard the words from William Middleton, a yeoman. As one of the examiners in the investigation, Holdsworth asked Middleton, "Do ye remember very well the words that ye told me upon Saturday last?"

To which Middleton replied: "Yea, marry, do I! Howbeit I told the tale to you wrong, for I told my wife when I to home, how I showed the . . . rhyme that was made by Lacy of the king, and she said to me again that I told ye [a] very wrong tale, for yet it was by [about] the bishop of Canterbury." Not content with Middleton's response, Holdsworth sent his servant Christopher Walton "to drink and make good cheer with the said Middleton and his wife, and bade him spy a time and also hear this question: was the rhyme made against the king or the bishop of Canterbury?"

Walton in turn reported the conversation he had heard between the two:

> "Marry," said Middleton's wife, "it was made against the king and my Lord Privy Seal."
> "Dame, it is not so."
> Then she said to her husband, "Marry, it is so—for it was so made against the king and my Lord Privy Seal, by God, without fail."

There is no indication what Sir Henry Saville made of the muddled conversations he had so faithfully recorded.

The state papers preserve the report of another woman investigated later that year for what she had said. In August Sir John Porte wrote to Cromwell to report about the assizes in Stafford and Worcester.[56] About the cases against various people indicted for treason at Worcester he wrote: "Also were three priests and a woman in the prison for certain indiscreet words that they did speak as was alleged, and because the inquest by their evidence did nor could [not] find the same, they were delivered by proclamation."

Sometimes the "indiscreet words" of women got others, besides themselves, into trouble. In September 1537, for example, Margaret Towler's conversations were gathered as evidence by John de Vere, earl of Oxford, to be used against Thomas Neville, one of the brothers of John Neville, lord Latimer.[57] Oxford wrote to Cromwell with a series of depositions against Neville, at the same time warning Cromwell that Neville had no knowledge of the evidence being gathered against him.

Part of what is so fascinating in this record is that, once again, the attempt is made to quote the exact words of the conversation. In addition, there are also details about the places where the conversations took place, details that are omitted in most other surviving records. We also get a sense of how quickly and how far Margaret Towler traveled to spread her tales about Thomas Neville.

Margaret was a widow, the servant of the parson of Aldham (Essex), who was being held by Oxford. On a Wednesday Neville had arrived at the parsonage, saying, as Margaret reported his words to Oxford, "Mother Margaret, this is a pretty parsonage," and warning her to take good care of it. She left Neville and went into the kitchen. He followed her, and she then asked him, "Alas, Master Neville, shall my master be put to death wrongfully?"

Neville answered, "No . . . the king would not put him to death because he hath no lands to promote him withal."

"The king would not put a man to death wrongfully for a thousand pounds," Margaret objected.

"By the mass, but he would," Neville reportedly replied, and then he "went out the door."

By Thursday Margaret had traveled from Aldham to Earls Colne, where she had talked to John Shelton, a yeoman, and John Newton, a husbandman, "in John Sparrow's yard." There she told the two that on an earlier occasion she had said to Neville, "Alas, Master Neville, ye be woe of your brother." She had then heard Neville say, "at his own house as he lay on the bench in the parlour": "Yea, by the mass, so am I. But if I had the king here, he should never take man into the Tower more, for, by the mass, I trow he will not leave a man alive." Margaret said that, except for Neville's wife, she was the only one who had heard him say this. Although nothing more seems to have come of Oxford's investigations of Neville, this particular case, with Oxford's attempts to preserve the speakers' exact words and with his details of where and how conversations took place, is remarkably vivid.

Women could not only get others into trouble by speaking too freely, they could, and sometimes did, concoct evidence to use against others. This seems to be what happened in Newnton (Northamptonshire) in October 1537. Sir William Parr and Richard Throckmorton reported to Cromwell in November about their investigation of two men, John Newman and John Parke.[58] The two had gotten into trouble for "words spoken" against the king, but, as the investigation proceeded, it became more uncertain whether they had, after all, said what they were supposed to have said.

Newman was under suspicion of treason, Parke of misprision of treason for having concealed what he had heard Newman say. A number of people were examined, including the parson of Newnton, but the principal witness turned out to be one Margaret Pere. According to Margaret, she had heard Newman say, "It is pity that the king was ever crowned, for we have had more pilling and polling since [he] was crowned than ever we had before, and it is pity that he hath lived so long."

A witness named William Davy had originally confirmed what Margaret charged, but, by the time Parr and Throckmorton wrote, Davy had changed his story: "He rueth his confession . . . and saith that he never heard Newman speak no such words against the King's Highness, and that he confessed the same against him for malice and especially at the provocation, mischance, and labor of Margaret Pere, for [the] rancor and hatred she beareth to the said Newman." Although dutifully reporting the whole affair to Cromwell, Parr and Throckmorton concluded that "the said Margaret Pere maliciously contrived and forged to put [Newman and Parke] to vexation, and [there is] no such matter of truth nor words spoken nor mischie[f] intended against the King's Highness as she in the said bill hath alleged."

"Nevertheless," they wrote, "if it shall please the King's Majesty and your lordship to command us with any further matter either in this behalf or in any other thing, we shall endeavor ourselves to the uttermost of our power about the accomplishment of the same." Despite the lack of evidence against them, Newman and Parke were still in custody pending further word from Cromwell.

Although rumors about the king's death had circulated before, by the end of 1537 such reports had reached alarming proportions.[59] Many incidents were reported to Cromwell, the largest and most involved investigation conducted by Sir Walter Stonor at the end of December in Berkshire.[60] Sir Walter was responding to Cromwell's directive that "we should make diligent inquiry in these parts, what persons have lately noised and bruited that the King's Grace should be departed out of this life." The inquiry was drawing to a close, and Stonor outlined what he and his fellow commissioners understood as their charge in the matter: "by examinations taken of diverse persons whereby we might come to the knowledge of them that were the authors of the said matters or the chief spreaders of it, and how it is that the bruit and spreading of part of the said matter hath been done by the mischief and handling of such persons as we think it is meet for us to certify your lordship of it."

Although Stonor was sending all of the depositions to Cromwell, and although he reported that all of those examined had been punished so that "others by that example may beware of the like attempts hereafter," he was inquiring whether any further action was necessary. He also indicated that three people were being held in jail at Reading, presumably waiting word from Cromwell.

Among those Stonor had examined was Joan Boxworth, the daughter-in-law of John Boxworth, who had also been questioned.[61] Of the some twenty or so people who had been involved in spreading the rumor, she seems to have been the only one who went unpunished, though not because she was innocent. When examined, she admitted that she had heard the rumor, "in her own house of two strange men, the which men she remembereth not." She did remember what one of them, a fuller, had said: "in the said wind the greatest oak in England was fallen." Her father-in-law then told her, "it was meant that the king should be dead." Yet Stonor and his commissioners let Joan go: "And the said Joan being then great with child and looking every day her time, therefore she is respited without punishment."

For once we have a response to all of this. On 29 December Cromwell responded to Stonor to inform him of "the king's pleasure."[62] Not only were "the principal inventors and bruiters of the same to be duly punished" (among them Joan Boxworth's father-in-law, John), but the king directed Stonor to "continue your vigilance to harken whether any more of that sort will spring in those parts." If any more rumors were heard, Stonor and his commissioners were to apprehend those who spread them "and to see the same condignly punished after the same sort that in this affair is prescribed unto you." Their diligence would not go unrewarded: "your pains wherein, doubt you not, shall be considered accordingly."

While Stonor completed his investigations and waited for final word from Cromwell, Sir William Shelley reported only a few days later from Lewes (Sussex): "Friday all day we spent in examination of certain persons being accused."[63] He was holding all of the accused he had so far examined; they would remain in custody until the next meeting of the justices of the peace. But some he was still pursuing. One "Peter at Rith of Horsham," for example, "a very simple person," had reportedly heard "the tidings of the king's death" from "a poor woman, one Joan, the wife of Richard Betchet of Horsham, whom we as yet could not examine for shortness of time."

Along with rumors of the king's death there had also been some talk of the king's marriages; these reportedly came from "the wife of Thomas Audley, a victualler of Lewes, and she saith she heard them in her house by Edward Brown." Brown denied having said anything, and Shelley reported that "certain witnesses vouched by Audley's wife being examined do not testify with her, the remnant of the witnesses not yet examined." And, finally, one "Mistress Norris" had accused Nicholas Jenyns for seditious talk, this too to be further investigated.

Such words—rumors, insults, curses, scurrilous attacks—were dealt with in a number of ways. In addition to the 1534 Treason Act, the Succession Act of 1536 also provided for words to be construed as treason, specifically words that were spoken against the king's third marriage. Also in 1536 a proclamation was issued attacking "devilish and slanderous persons" who were spreading "slanderous, false, and detestable rumors, tales, and lies," particularly those that claimed new taxes would be levied by the king. The proclamation charged the king's loyal subjects to "apprehend all and every such person and persons that they can prove to have bruited or set forth any forged false rumors, tales, and lies": "they shall not only bring upon themselves the vengeance and indignation of God, to the peril and damnation of their souls, but also give us just cause to proceed against such rebels with our most royal power and force, to the utter destruction of them, their wives, and children."[64]

Circulars were also used in the ongoing campaign against dangerous talk, but the rumors reported with such frequency in late 1537 may in part be responsible for a revised charge issued to inferior courts early in 1538. On the long list of offenses to be particularly noted was the spreading of rumors by "tale-tellers and counterfeiters of news that import any hurt or damage to the king's person . . . or to move disorder."[65] Those who spread such "lying and slandering" were to be "abhorred and hated of any honest man": those spreading rumors "go about utterly to extirp love, concord, and quiet, whereby any commonwealth flourishes, and to sow in their place sedition, disorder, variance, and trouble." All those who heard such tales were urged to report them: "If there be or hath been any among you that hath reported or told any such news, by the oath that ye have made ye shall present his name, to whom, when and where he spake it."

Such action may have slowed the spread of rumors, but it did not halt them. On 1 January 1538 Cromwell received the news from Aylesford, in Kent, of a woman, "lately come from London," who had been spreading a rumor about the king's death.[66] When examined, she had also added rumors about increased taxes. She expressed no sorrow about the king's death: "Now we shall have a merry world." She was being held in Maidstone jail.

At this time Cranmer was also involved in investigating rumors of the king's death in Kent; he sent all the depositions he had taken to Cromwell, holding those he had examined pending Cromwell's instruction.[67] Among those being held was Agnes King, the wife of Thomas King. She had told examiners that Thomas Grant, "fisher," had come "to her door to sell fish and there he told her that . . . the King's Grace should be dead." Although she had warned Grant to be careful, telling him, "Take heed what you say—I will advise you for if it were so all the realm should repent it," she was among those still waiting for Cromwell's decision.

From March the state papers include a report from William Lucy, a Warwickshire justice of the peace.[68] Lucy encountered a new rumor altogether, and he had more than the usual difficulty in carrying out his investigation. Lucy heard reports about "one Phillips who did say that he heard that the Prince's Grace (whose life I beseech Jesus' Honor to continue to His pleasure and all our great comfort) should be departed." Lucy sent to the bailiff of the town where Phillips "spoke the words" to deliver Phillips to him immediately, but the bailiff "lay sick in his bed." Once the bailiff was well enough to leave his bed, he was delayed further by "so great abundance of rain" that the rising waters had prevented him from traveling.

When Lucy finally did examine Phillips, Phillips "confessed that he heard them of his wife, which also did hear them off another woman as she came from the market whom she had not seen before." When pressed about spreading the rumor himself, Phillips excused his conduct by saying that he had only "rehearsed" it just the one time, saying that, "if it could be proved that he ever spoke them before that time or since, he desired he might be hanged therefore."

Lucy described Phillips as a "sorrowful creature" and ordered only that he be "set . . . openly in the stocks in the churchyard" on the following Sunday.

A similar case was reported in the last week of March, when a woman named Agnes Davy was indicted at Ipswich. She was accused of having spread a rumor of the king's death in February, at Carleforth (Suffolk). According to the indictment against her, she had said the king was dead, that Prince Edward was close to death, and that "the king of Scots would enter the north parts of the realm, and the French king the south parts." Although indicted for these words, no further action seems to have been taken against her.[69]

Only one other report involving women survives from 1538 and it is from late September. It, too, concerns a rumor, but in some ways an even more troubling one.[70] In a long letter to Cromwell dated 20 September, William Fitzwilliam, earl of Southampton wrote about his meeting with "a poor man in lamentable wise saying that his wife was committed to prison in the west gate of Chichester." She had been imprisoned there for saying that "Sir Geoffrey Pole would have sent over the sea a band of men to his brother Cardinal Pole if . . . that he had not been taken before [for] other words."

Southampton wrote that the words had sounded to him like "high treason," and so he had set out "immediately" to investigate further. He had sent for the statements that had been taken. Since he thought the examining justice had been negligent in following up on the examinations, he was holding both the justice and the woman.

The woman was named Joan Sylkden of Walderton (Sussex), identified as "a spinster." She admitted having said that "if Sir Geoffrey Pole had continued unto March next coming that he would have made over to his brother, and further if my Lady of Salisbury had been a young woman as she was an old she had been burned." Joan, in turn, said she had heard these rumors from her mother, Alice Patchet. Both women, by their own confession, had repeated these tales to several others, and it is clear why Southampton suspected they were treasonous. Nevertheless, we hear nothing further of Joan or her mother. We do hear more of Sir Geoffrey Pole, however. Henry finally took action against the Pole, Neville, and Courtenay families. In late October Geoffrey Pole was arrested and examined in the Tower; although he would survive, his evidence was used against his brother. Henry Pole was tried for treason and executed on 9 December 1538.

As the decade of the 1530s drew to a close, the flood of rumors slowed to a trickle.[71] Only one report of a woman spreading rumors survives from 1539, this one involving Margaret Ede.[72] On 12 March Richard Covert and John Michell sent a letter to Cromwell informing him that they had in custody William Hole, of Horsham (Sussex). Hole was reported to have said that a tax of 15*d* was to be levied by the king for every wedding, christening, and burial, and, although Hole denied having said any such thing, he was being held by Covert and Michell.

Within days the rumor had been traced from Hole to Robert Wright, who in turn said he had heard the news from Margaret, the wife of John Ede. Covert and Michell wrote:

> whereupon the said Margaret was brought before us and examined thereupon, [and] said that true it is that she had [said] the same words as the said Wright had confessed. Whereupon she was demanded where she had [heard] these words. . . . She was at mass at a parish church called Ockley in the county of Sussex and there the priest being in the pulpit delivered diverse things.

Her claim to have heard such words from a priest in his pulpit might have resulted in further investigations, but Covert and Michell saw that Margaret was sixty years old and "lacking a great part of her hearing." They had committed her to ward, but they wrote that her husband was honest and that they had heard only good reports from her neighbors. She was to remain with the officers of the town of Horsham until further instructions were received.

Margaret Tyrell, the wife of William Tyrell, esquire, found herself in much more serious trouble, however, though there is very little detail about her case. In many ways it echoes that of Elizabeth Wood, and thus it makes a fitting end for our discussion of women's dangerous talk.

In the spring of 1540 Margaret Tyrell was condemned for her words: according to the act of attainder, she had "denied Prince Edward to be prince of England and next inheritable to the Crown."[73] There is no further information about her or her activities in the act condemning her, but a series of tantalizing notes shows that she had been under investigation for some time before she was finally attainted.

Margaret's words must have been spoken at some time in 1537, because in a list of his "remembrances," dated 24 November 1537, Cromwell had made a note for himself of an "examination of Tyrell's wife in the Tower." There is no further detail about when or how Margaret's dangerous talk concerning Prince Edward had come to Cromwell's attention, about when she had been taken into custody, or about what happened to her following her examination. But, in another set of remembrances compiled at the end of the month, Cromwell noted an "order to be taken for Tyrell's wife, a great offender," indicating that her examination must have produced results.[74]

By 5 December she was committed to the Tower, and a second examination must have followed because early in January of 1538 a list of Cromwell's remembrances makes note of yet another "examination of Tyrell's wife."[75] A list of prisoners compiled on 31 March 1538 indicates that Margaret Tyrell was still in the Tower.[76] She must have remained there until the spring of 1540, when she was attainted by Parliament. Margaret Tyrell was hanged, drawn, and quartered for her words denying Prince Edward.

If she were guilty of having said what she was charged with saying, it is clear that her words fell within the Treason Act. Interesting, however, is the fact that she was not charged with treason, nor was she tried; instead, like Elizabeth Barton, her case was handled in Parliament by means of an act of attainder. Of equal interest is her husband's fate. William Tyrell, a gentleman, had been tried and convicted for his treasonous words (among other things, he had said that the emperor and the French king would destroy both Henry and Prince Edward and that the king's assassins would "gain paradise"). Yet Margaret's husband was ultimately pardoned for what he had said. Prosecuted in 1541 for the words he uttered in 1536 and 1539, he was at last pardoned in March 1543—though David Gunston and Robert Harvey, who had been involved in the same talk and who had been prosecuted with Tyrell, were hanged, drawn, and quartered on 12 July 1541.[77]

What emerges from these reports is the extent to which all kinds of women from throughout the realm spoke out against the king, his marriages, his ministers, and his policies. In most cases what they said seems to have been recognized for what it was—foolish talk. While women's words might have been cause for concern, and while outspoken women might have been held pending further investigation or even punished by public humiliation, in most cases, engaging in scurrilous talk, gossiping freely, and spreading wild rumors seems not to have had serious results, even after the passage of the 1534 Treason Act. Women such as Margaret Chanseler, Margery Cowpland, and Joan Boxworth could be excused as drunk, out of their wits, or pregnant. In especially dangerous times, however, it might be judged expedient to remove women like Elizabeth Wood and Margaret Tyrell. Their dangerous talk did not distinguish itself by its malice or virulence but, rather, by its timing: they both talked too much and too freely during the time of the northern risings.

By the time the king's fifth marriage ended disastrously with the execution of Catherine Howard in 1542, rumors about Henry's marital career were again circulating, many of them to the effect that he would remarry his fourth wife, Anne of Cleves.[78] But only one woman's words were bothersome enough to evoke a response.[79] Jane Rattsey, a member of the household of Anne of Cleves, asked aloud the questions many people must have been asking themselves: "What a man is the king? How many wives will he have?" She was arrested and examined, but Henry had her discharged with only a warning. The king's matrimonial adventures were not yet over, but the pace of the drastic social, religious, and political changes of the 1530s had slowed, and the threat of rebellion had dissipated.[80]

SIX

Elizabeth Wood and the Dangers of Riot, Rebellion, and Conspiracy

Rumors that the king was dead and gossip that Anne Boleyn was a "strong whore" in themselves might not be dangerous, but, as the career of Elizabeth Barton demonstrated, words spoken against the king could encourage those who spoke them and those who heard them to more overt action. Such words might invite resistance to the suppression of religious houses. They might challenge the legitimacy of the king's heirs. They might inspire conspiracies. Or they might incite rebellion.

We have examined in some detail the political opinions expressed by Elizabeth Barton. Her predictions and warnings to the king ultimately led to her conviction for treason. We have also seen that women like Margaret Cheyne and Elizabeth Wood were convicted of treason for their involvement in, respectively, the Pilgrimage of Grace and the Walsingham conspiracy. But the dangers in speaking out did not silence women. Nor were women deterred from taking part in more active resistance to the king's policies by the dangers posed by such opposition.

Early in Henry's reign, women in London were involved in a variety of ways in the Evil May Day riots of 1517. The most extended account of the events leading up to this brief but explosive domestic disturbance is Edward Hall's.[1]

The Tudor chronicler paints a vivid picture of the tensions in London, which led to the riot. In part the tensions derived from economic factors: "the multitude of strangers was so great about London that the poor English could scarce get any living." In part the tensions arose from fear and resentment: the resident foreigners, Hall wrote, "were so proud that they disdained, mocked, and oppressed the Englishmen, which was the beginning of the grudge."[2]

According to Hall, "the Genoans, Frenchmen, and other strangers said and boasted themselves to be in such favor with the king and his council that they set naught by the rulers of the city." English merchants suffered because of the imports of the "merchant strangers," who brought silk, cloth of gold, wine, oil, iron, and "such other merchandise" that "no man almost buyeth of an Englishman." The result was economic hardship: Hall noted "how miserably the common artificers lived, and scarcely could get any work to find them, their wives, and children, for there were such a number of artificers strangers that took away all the living in manner."

As told by Hall, the foreigners in the city were not only monopolizing business; they disdained Londoners and flouted English law as well. Hall cited a number of incidents that contributed to the tensions in the city. One involved a dispute between a carpenter named Williamson and a Frenchmen over two stockdoves: Williamson had selected the pigeons and was about to pay for them when, in Hall's words, "a Frenchman took them out of his hand and said they were no meat for a carpenter."[3] The Frenchman, who had wanted to purchase the birds for the French ambassador, not only wound up with them, he also lodged a complaint with his ambassador, who in turn complained to the lord mayor, who in turn had the poor carpenter arrested. Even then the French ambassador wasn't satisfied; he petitioned the king for further punishment. But Sir John Baker learned of Williamson's imprisonment and went to plead for him to the ambassador, who reportedly replied, "By the body of God that the English knave should lose his life, for . . . no Englishman should deny [what] the Frenchmen required."

Another source of complaint involved a Frenchman who had killed an Englishman.[4] He was punished by banishment. While being led on his way, he carried a cross. Hall continued: "and then suddenly came a great sort of Frenchmen about him, and one of them said to the constable that led him, 'Sir, is this cross the price to kill an Englishman?' The constable was somewhat astonished and answered not. Then said another Frenchman, 'On that price we would be banished all, by the mass.' This saying was noted to be spoken spitefully."

One final story relayed by Hall involved a Lombard, Frances de Bard, who had "enticed a man's wife . . . to come to his chamber with her husband's plate."[5] When the husband learned of his wife's desertion, he had gone to the Lombard: "he demanded his wife, but answer was made he should not have her; then he demanded his plate, and in like manner answer was made that he should neither have plate nor wife." To add insult to injury: "And then the Lombard arrested the poor man for his wife's board while he kept her from her husband in his chamber." Hall summarized the result of all this: "This mock was much noted, and for these and many other oppressions done by them, there increased such a malice in the Englishmen's hearts that at the last it burst out."

Much of the enmity between Englishmen and foreigners is confirmed in the diplomatic reports of Sebastian Giustinian, Venetian ambassador in England. Along with Hall's account of the Evil May Day riots, Giustinian's letters provide the most coherent contemporary narrative of events.[6] Giustinian reported to the Seigniory, with some degree of smugness, that the enmity of the Londoners was directed primarily at the French, Florentines, and Genoese but not the Venetians, "as they have ever conducted themselves with equity and decorum."

Resentment eventually broke out into violence. A London citizen and broker named John Lincoln, "sore grudged at these matters," composed a bill of grievances just before Easter, 12 April. This bill was the subject of a sermon preached by a Doctor Beal on the Tuesday following Easter Sunday. As Giustinian reported:

> After Easter, a certain preacher, at the instigation of a citizen of London, preached as usual in the fields, where the whole city was in the habit of assembling with the magistrates. He abused the strangers in the town, and their manners and customs, alleging that they not only deprived the English of their industry and of the profits arising therefrom, but dishonored their dwellings by taking their wives and daughters. With this exasperating language and much more besides, he so irritated the populace that they threatened to cut the strangers to pieces and sack their houses on the first of May.[7]

Hall not only included much of the substance of Beal's sermon in his chronicle, he also noted the reaction in London: "Of this sermon many a light person took courage, and openly spake against strangers." Frances de Bard reacted quite differently; on hearing of the sermon, he and a number of his friends "jested and laughed how that Frances kept the Englishman's wife, saying that if they had the mayor's wife of London, they would keep her."

Violence erupted on 28 April, when, at the instigation of Lincoln, "diverse young men of the city assaulted the aliens as they passed by the streets, and some were stricken, and some were buffeted, and some thrown into the canal."[8] A few men were taken into custody and order restored, but tensions remained: "Then suddenly was a common secret rumor, and no man could tell how it began, than on May Day next the city would rebel and slay all aliens, in so much as diverse strangers fled out of the city."

Still, the rumor was not so "secret" that it failed to reach the mayor. He met with his aldermen on the evening of 29 April, at the same time sending word to Wolsey; Wolsey chanced to be meeting with some of the king's council, and they ordered a curfew for the city. The curfew did not prevent the riot, however, and servingmen, apprentices, watermen, and even a few priests were among the rioters. They ran through the city with "clubs and weapons," releasing prisoners from Newgate, throwing stones, bricks, bats, hot water, shoes, and boots, and sacking the houses of many foreigners. The king was notified, and peace was eventually restored.

Hundreds of rioting citizens were taken into custody and imprisoned in various jails in the city; Dr. Beal and John Lincoln, as instigators, were sent to the Tower. Proclamations were issued, and, although the rumors that preceded the riots seem to have been spread by men, the proclamation took particular aim at women's speech: "no women should come together to babble and talk, but all men should keep their wives in their houses."[9] The duke of Norfolk brought armed men into the city to keep order while the first batch of prisoners were tried for treason—attacking foreigners while the king was at peace with their princes had been deemed a treasonous breach of the peace of Christendom.

Some 278 people were among those arraigned before a commission of oyer and terminer at the Guildhall. Hall described the prisoners as "some men, some lads, some children of thirteen years," indicating that some of them were not men of the city but were, instead, husbandmen and laborers. As the prisoners were brought through the streets, Hall reported, "There was a great mourning of fathers and friends for their children and kinsfolk."[10]

Contemporary accounts differ on the number finally found guilty of high treason and adjudged "to be hanged, drawn, and quartered." Hall reported that thirteen were convicted. In a letter about the riots addressed to the Venetian Seigniory, Giustinian wrote that twelve had been convicted, but a few days later reported that twenty had been executed. Charles Wriothesley, in his brief account of the London riots and executions, wrote that eleven had been executed. Although the exact number of executions may be in doubt, there is no question that they followed swiftly, taking place between 5 and 7 May. Hall reported that there was no mercy shown to the guilty; they were, he said, "executed in most rigorous manner."

Sebastian Giustinian, meanwhile, reported that these executions had not ended the hostility against foreigners: "So great is the malignity . . . that what they are now unable to do for fear of death is done by their women, who evince immense hatred towards foreigners."[11] Giustinian was not specific about the ways women demonstrated their hatred, but, clearly, at least some London women had taken an active part in the riots. When Henry himself sat in judgment on the remainder of the prisoners at Westminster on 22 May, there appeared before him 400 men and 11 women.[12]

One curious aspect of the Evil May Day riots involves the reasons why Henry pardoned these remaining prisoners. They were paraded before the king with halters around their necks. In a letter written by Francesco Chieregato, papal nuncio to England, Henry pardoned these prisoners, otherwise destined for the gallows, because "our most serene and most compassionate queen, with tears in her eyes and on her bended knees, obtained their pardon from His Majesty, the act of grace being performed with great ceremony."[13] Chieregato's seems to be the only report that Queen Katherine secured the pardons; Hall indicated that the prisoners themselves cried "Mercy, Gracious Lord" and that, following Wolsey's advice and the pleas from the lords who had assembled at Westminster, the king pardoned them.[14] Other London chroniclers attribute the pardon variously to the pleas of the prisoners themselves, to Wolsey, or to the king's own judgment. Nevertheless, the story that Katherine sought the pardon, interceding on her knees for the prisoners, has proven irresistible to historians.[15]

Women were thus involved in the Evil May Day riots in a number of ways. At least some women must have actively participated in the rioting, since a handful appeared among the prisoners to be judged by Henry at Westminster. In addition to this active role, women, or at least one woman, could become an object of contention between the Londoners and the foreigners; the story of the woman who had deserted her husband for the Lombard Frances de Bard was widely known in London, and the Lombard and his fellows "jested and laughed" about it publicly in the king's gallery at Greenwich in the presence of a number of London merchants, the tale then being "reported about London." Those who heard it swore that they "would be revenged." Even after the peace of the city was restored, tensions remained, and, as Sebastian Giustinian reported, it was women who kept up the quarrel. What men were afraid to do "for fear of death" was done by women.

Just as women contributed by their actions to the Evil May Day riots, their words also played a part. Women's words could offer incitement to violence; the royal proclamation specifically addressed this potential of women's words, when it enjoined women from coming together "to babble and talk" and directed men to keep their wives at home. Yet it may also be that women's words, or at least one woman's words, could petition for peace. Queen Katherine continues even now to be credited for words that inspired the king's mercy when he pardoned the remaining rioters.

All of this occurred well before the king's political and religious reforms of the 1530s, however, but it did serve as a warning of how easily the king's subjects could be moved to sedition—of how little it might take for rumor to result in riot. The potential of words to spur violence was noted by Sir Thomas More, then undersheriff of London, who had investigated the riots and noted that the whole disturbance had been sparked by John Lincoln and two apprentices, who had "compassed between them" the rising.[16] For our purposes the Evil May Day riots also show that women could and did participate in civil disobedience, protesting, along with men, perceived or real injustice. The surviving accounts of the riots offer a wealth of information about how and why women were or could be involved.

An indication of what was to come during the remainder of the decade occurred in Oxford in 1530. There, while learned canonists and theologians debated the king's divorce, opposition from the town contributed to the difficulties of the discussions. The women of Oxford reportedly stoned John Longland, bishop of Lincoln, for his efforts to secure an opinion on Henry's behalf.[17]

Even more tantalizing than this brief reference to the women of Oxford is the single surviving account of a mob action that reportedly took place in early October 1531. The only mention of this attack by women on Anne Boleyn is found in a letter received from France by the French ambassador in Venice.[18] The "advices from France" is dated 24 November:

> It is said that more than seven weeks ago a mob of from seven to eight thousand women of London went out of the town to seize Boleyn's daughter, the sweetheart of the king of England, who was supping at a villa [una casa di piacere] on a river, the king not being with her; and having received notice of this, she escaped by crossing the river in a boat. The women had intended to kill her; and amongst the mob were many men, disguised as women. Nor has any great demonstration been made about this, because it was a thing done by women.[19]

There is no other mention of this "thing done by women" in the state papers, so such a mob of women may never have attempted to grab Anne Boleyn and kill her. But, even as rumor and gossip, it corroborates the particular antipathy of women noted by other contemporary reporters, including Chapuys. The account also suggests that, even if Henry's government declined to make "any great demonstration" about the affair because it was "a thing done by women," it was clearly a thing that at least one contemporary observer thought could and would be done by women.

Numerous reports document women's participation in such "mob" action throughout the decade. A riot involving women occurred in Norfolk in 1532, for example. Accounts of this demonstration are sketchy, but in the surviving writ Sir Thomas Audley, keeper of the Great Seal, directed a commission of oyer and terminer to investigate "a great riot and unlawful assembly of women" at Great Yarmouth, in Norfolk. The women had apparently rioted to show their opposition to Anne Boleyn.[20] But their protests were downplayed, at least in part, it seems, because it was thought that the riot "could not have been held without the connivance of their husbands."

Similarly, women were present among the crowds who protested the suppression of the monasteries. In Exeter a mob of women armed with spades and spikes reportedly attacked workmen who had been ordered to pull down the rood loft in a priory church. The women forced a workman to jump from the church's tower.[21] And in Northumberland, as the canons of Hexham defended their priory against the Dissolution commissioners, armed townsmen and townswomen surrounded the royal officers, who were forced to withdraw.[22]

The specific reason for the 1537 rising of the commons against the king's commissioners in Somerset seems to have been less inspired by the king and questions of the succession than by economic hardship.[23] In early April, according to Wriothesley's chronicle, the king's commissioners had been sent into the county "for to take up corn," presumably under the king's right of purveyance. The riot that followed seemed to have no immediate political causes, then, but to have sprung from the more poignant and immediate reality that this requisition of grain took place when "the poor people" were already suffering from "the scarceness and dearth of grain."

The king's commissioners met with resistance, and those who participated in this initial resistance were put in ward. Then the disturbance escalated; in Wriothesley's account, "the people of the county began to rise and make an insurrection." The armed rioters, including women among them, were fairly quickly subdued, the "chief beginners thereof" taken into custody. By the end of the month a commission of oyer and terminer had condemned sixty for their sedition. Most of them were eventually pardoned, but at least a dozen were convicted and executed. Of those "hanged and quartered" one was a woman.[24]

Also convicted of high treason in the aftermath of rebellion was a woman named Agnes Presteman. Few details about her crime or her trial have survived, though the reason for her conviction is clear enough. In a reported dated 8 December 1538 the Council of the North reported to Henry the results of a number of oyer and terminer commissions.[25] Lord Latimer and other commissioners had been responsible for a session at York Castle, held on 3 December. According to the Council's report, "[Latimer and the other commissioners] have right well and diligently applied themselves to serve Your Majesty in all your affairs there, at which time there were four persons condemned for high treason, that is to say Henry Presteman and Agnes, his mother, for recepting of John Presteman excepted out of your gracious general pardon." The Council's letter includes no further details, indicating that the identity of John Presteman and the reason why he was excluded from the general pardon would have been clear to the king. They are less clear to us, but it's possible to sketch at least something of the picture.

Following the January risings in the north instigated by Francis Bigod, the king had issued a general pardon. On 20 July 1537 Norfolk had written to Cromwell, enclosing a list of names of those who were to be "excepted out" of this pardon.[26] On that list were two men named John Presteman: John Presteman of "Lyllesdale Hall" (perhaps for Lilleshall, Staffordshire?) and John Presteman, son of William Presteman of Helmsley, North Yorkshire. No reasons are given for why Norfolk believed the men should be excluded from the pardon. But, if we look back at the statement Sir John Bulmer wrote out after he had been charged with treason, we find that he claimed to have made a thorough search of various "treasonous bills" that had been circulating at the time of Bigod's rising.[27] One of those who had shown Sir John such a bill was a man whom he identified as "one Presteman."

According to Bulmer's statement, this Presteman had come from the commons with the bill "to see as I liked it." The substance of the bill, as Sir John recalled it, was that "men should pay no gersums [fines], and that they should ever have with them the old lord or the new." This was the bill to which Sir John had responded, "when two dogs fight for a bone, the third will take it up; for this will make the gentlemen and the commons fall forth, and the king shall take up the matter."[28]

The man Bulmer had named as "one Presteman" is identified no further, but it may well be that this was John Presteman, later excepted from the general pardon—the John Presteman who was then "recepted," or harbored, by Agnes Presteman and her son Henry. The relationship between Agnes and her son to John isn't stated in the surviving documents—he could have been husband and father or son and brother or even, perhaps, some more distant relation, though, given the risks involved, the closer relationships seem more likely. In any case, harboring John Presteman resulted in a conviction of high treason, and Agnes and her son Henry were among the last to be judged guilty of treason in the aftermath of the northern risings. Although there is no surviving account of their execution, we might suspect that, in the uneasy quiet in the northern counties after the rebellions were put down, the sentence was carried out.

Women were also named when Walter Hungerford, lord Hungerford, was attainted for treason in 1540.[29] In June of that year he was condemned by an act of Parliament for a number of offenses. The "abominable vice of buggery" was one of the charges against him, certainly the most unusual, and that "crime" alone may have been enough to attaint him for treason. In addition, though, he was charged with having been involved with Sir Hugh Woodes, identified as a chaplain, a Dr. Mawdelyn, and "one Mother Roche," all of whom had been asked "to conjure" for Hungerford "and show how long the king should live."[30] According to the French ambassador, magic was involved in this treasonous conspiracy: Hungerford was attainted *d'avoir usé d'art magique et invocation des dyables*.[31] Lord Hungerford was beheaded at Tyburn on 28 July 1540, following the execution of his friend Thomas Cromwell.

London chroniclers took note of Hungerford's death. Hall wrote that at the time of his execution he "seemed to be very unquiet in mind and rather in a frenzy than otherwise." Wriothesley also noted the execution, indicating that Hungerford had been attainted for buggery, while Cromwell's treasons had been heresy, treason, felony, and extortion; the Grey Friars chronicler agreed with Wriothesley's account that Hungerford's "treason" had consisted of buggery.[32]

While Hungerford's crimes and execution are widely noted, we hear no more of Mother Roche or her conjuring.[33] The only reference to her occurs in the act of attainder passed against Hungerford, but there is no indication of what happened to the three conjurors who had been involved in predicting the time of the king's death.

The attainting of Hungerford did not end the investigation of his crimes, however. Another woman was also found to have been involved somehow in this treasonous conspiracy, one "Mother Huntley." On 15 June Sir Thomas Wriothesley, who had been Cromwell's secretary and who became secretary of state after his death, addressed a letter on behalf of the king's council from the palace of Westminster about "a certain old woman called Mother Huntley" whom he had recently examined.[34] Although the letter is not explicit, it seems that what Mother Huntley had said about Lord Hungerford had brought her to the council's attention. A "schedule" of her words was enclosed with the letter, and, although the letter is not altogether clear, it suggests that the woman herself had been sent along with the letter, accompanied by an urgent request that she be examined "upon such interrogatories as are contained in the said schedules and her depositions so taken." An immediate reply, under "sign and seal," was requested.

The enclosed schedule detailing Mother Huntley's involvement with Lord Hungerford has not survived, but, given the care Wriothesley seems to have taken with the examinations and depositions, his request for an addition examination of the woman, and the "speed and diligence" that he urged for the response, the information she had supplied must have been damaging. Unfortunately, we hear no more of her after this letter.

But we just might know something about her activities long before 1540. Some forty years earlier, around 1500, a chaplain named John Knight had been commanded by George Stanley, lord Strange, at the direction of Henry VII, to "go and make search in Southwark within the county of Surrey for one Alice, the wife of John Huntley."[35] According to Knight, whose story survives in a Chancery petition, Alice Huntley was being investigated because it was charged that she had "used and exercised the feats of witchcraft and sorcery against the law of the Church and of the King."

Knight had gone to Alice's Kent Street house, where he and Lord Strange's servants had "found diverse maumets [dolls or puppets] for witchcraft and enchantments, with other stuff buried and deeply hid under the earth, the which be ready to be showed." But in a strange turn of events Knight himself had been arrested following his investigation of Alice Huntley, his petition to Chancery the only surviving reference to the woman he had been sent to investigate for witchcraft and sorcery. Knight wrote from the Marshalsea prison, where he had been held for six days without bail, but he did not explain the reason for his arrest. We can only see that somehow his arrest was connected with his investigation of Alice Huntley.

While we can sympathize with the chaplain's plight—he was only doing what he had been directed to do—the reference to Alice Huntley is what is of interest to us here. It may only be coincidental, of course, but it is not impossible that Alice Huntley, widely noted for her "feats of witchcraft and sorcery" by 1500—so widely noted, in fact, that Henry VII himself had commanded men "to go and make search" for her—was the same "certain old woman named Mother Huntley" who had come to Sir Thomas Wriothesley's attention in 1540 for her involvement with Lord Hungerford. The woman may well have pursued her career in sorcery through the years, her reputation eventually involving her with Hungerford and his trio of conjurors.

One final example of a conspiracy to rebel was the Wakefield plot of 1541, which Anthony Fletcher attributes to "resentment at the punishments following the 1536 rising and the government's continuance of policies which were obnoxious to the north."[36] The plot involved a small group of gentry and clergy from Wakefield (Yorkshire), who planned to kill Robert Holgate, then president of the Council of the North, and seize Pontefract Castle. They intended to hold the castle until help arrived from Scotland. While the rebellion did not seem to have much popular support, fifty to one hundred people were involved. Among those taken into ward were Thomas Tattersall's wife, John Kent's wife, and one "Ryge's wife." The details of this "rather mysterious Yorkshire conspiracy" remain obscure, and it's not clear what part these women might have played. Of those involved, fourteen or fifteen were executed, but the women who had been taken into ward for their part in the conspiracy seem not to have been too seriously implicated, since one John Broke, applying for expenses to be paid, asks only for "15s 8d" for having carried the women to York and holding them there for three days.[37]

Conspiracies against the king, which broke out into armed rebellion, were relatively few in Henry's thirty-eight year reign. Early on the economic and social grievances that boiled over in the Evil May Day riots were confined to the city of London, the weapons of the rioters merely bricks, hot water, and shoes. An end was quickly made of the violence and the rioters.

But the political reforms of the 1530s resulted in much more dangerous protests and rebellions, chief among them the cluster of armed risings in the north in late 1536 and early 1537. Following quickly were the Walsingham conspiracy and the Taunton rebellion. In all of these disturbances women were actively and openly involved.

Although I have chosen here to focus on the activities of women not usually associated with political action, it should not be forgotten that during this same period noblewomen were also intimately involved in political faction and conspiracy. Recent studies of Anne Boleyn, for example, have shifted their focus from the ways she "bewitched" the king to analysis of her key role in factional politics.[38]

Women were also involved in 1538 when Henry, pressured by the threat of foreign invasion, eliminated the internal threat to his rule posed by the remaining nobles of the old Yorkist faction: Henry Pole, lord Montague; Henry Courtenay, marquis of Exeter; and Sir Edward Neville were beheaded on Tower Hill on 9 December 1538.[39] Lady Constance Pole, Montague's wife; Margaret Pole, countess of Salisbury and Pole's mother; and Gertrude Courtenay, marchioness of Exeter, were thoroughly investigated and repeatedly questioned about their own activities.[40] Courtenay's wife and the countess of Salisbury had been loyal to Queen Katherine, and both had been involved with Elizabeth Barton. Even after Barton's execution all three women had been involved in further dangerous talk about the king.

These women survived the executions of 1538. But Gertrude Courtenay remained in the Tower with her son, twelve years old. Margaret Pole, countess of Salisbury, also remained in custody, held first at Cowdray in Sussex by Wriothesley. Both women were attainted by Parliament in June 1539. The countess of Salisbury was then moved to the Tower. In April 1540 Gertrude Courtenay was pardoned and released, though her son remained behind. Margaret Pole remained in custody until 1541, when yet one more conspiracy, the Exeter conspiracy, resulted in her horrific execution. Sixty-eight years old, she was hacked to death on Tower Green on 27 May 1541.

None of this "White Rose" party had acted against the king. Even during the northern rebellions Exeter had marched to join Norfolk to suppress the risings. The evidence offered against them in 1538 consisted of what they had said to one another. They hadn't rebelled against Henry, but they had wished someone would. They hadn't conspired to kill the king, but they had wished he would die.

Although her life was far removed from those of Anne Boleyn or Margaret Pole, Elizabeth Wood was also executed for treason for what she said. For what they did, Agnes Presteman and an unnamed woman in Somerset lost their lives as well. And for what they had said or done, many other women were investigated, questioned, and imprisoned, their ultimate fate unknown. Privileged or obscure, drunk or sober, married or widowed, pregnant or not, old, young, deaf, angry, spiteful, confused, or crazy, women spoke out and took action.

SEVEN

Mabel Brigge and Her "Black Fast"

Early in February 1538 a thirty-two-year-old widow named Mabel Brigge was investigated for a strange crime.[1] According to her accusers, all from Holderness, in the East Riding of Yorkshire, Mabel had undertaken a "black fast," which, they claimed, had been "directed against" Henry VIII. The details of their stories varied considerably, but Mabel's accusers all agreed that her fast had been undertaken in order to cause the death of the king.

Although the fasting of a poor and obscure female servant does not now seem to offer much of a real threat to royal power and authority, Mabel Brigge and her fast were taken quite seriously by Henry VIII's Council of the North. The action against her was swift and decisive. She was first questioned about her fast on 5 February; on 11 March she was sent, along with her accusers, to York, where they were all examined for a second time. On 7 April 1538 the Council reported to Cromwell and Henry VIII the results of the Lenten assizes. Mabel Brigge had been convicted of treason for her "black fast to an abominable intent against" the king. She had been executed.

Of all the cases involving women we have so far encountered, none is quite so strange, or strangely moving, as the story of Mabel Brigge. When examined, she admitted that she had in fact been fasting, but she said that she had in no way threatened the king and that her fast had not been undertaken with any political intent. Despite her explanations, which were supported by the evidence of two other women, Mabel Brigge was convicted of treason.

The Council of the North's efforts to untangle the threads of Mabel's story began early in 1538. On 28 January a confession made by a woman named

Agnes Locker was recorded by the Council's examining justices and forwarded to the Council, then in Newcastle.[2] From surviving transcripts there is nothing to indicate just how the story had first come to the attention of the examiners but, clearly, reports of the events taking place in Holderness had reached them and moved them to action.

Agnes Locker began her confession by indicating that Mabel Brigge, a widow, had come with her two children to the Locker farm, Reysome Grange, the previous spring.[3] Mabel's unexpected arrival, probably at the end of April, had been followed "immediately" by a message from Mabel's former employer, a farmer named Nelson, who indicated to Agnes's husband John that, if Mabel could remain with the Lockers, Nelson would "see the costs of the said Mabel paid." The Lockers, husband and wife, must have agreed to this arrangement, for Mabel stayed with them—but she was not to remain long at Reysome Grange.

According to Agnes, she and her husband, John, had then observed that Mabel fasted the next Friday, Saturday, and Sunday, each day "till mass was done." The two questioned Mabel about her strange behavior. Mabel "made answer" that it was a "charitable" fast. The word *charitable* is a bit questionable here, since Agnes went on to testify that Mabel had said, "she fasted that never afore but for one man, and he broke his neck or it were all fasted, and so she trusted that they should do that had made all this business, and that was the king and this false duke that hath wrought all this woo in the world." The "business" and "this false duke" obviously referred to the investigations in Yorkshire being carried out by the Council of the North, under the direction of Thomas Howard, duke of Norfolk.

Questioning Mabel further, Agnes's husband, John, asked her "why she fasted so." Agnes Locker told her examiners that Mabel had claimed that she had been hired for the fast by Isabel Buck, the wife of William Buck. Agnes surely intended to clear her own family from any involvement with Mabel's activities, for she was quick to state that her husband, John, had said "'Fie on her,' and put her [Mabel] forth of his house." John went to see Isabel Buck immediately thereafter. Still according to Agnes, Isabel admitted to John that she had hired Mabel, and she agreed to return with him to the Locker house, where he supposedly confronted both women; he was, Agnes testified, "angry and rebuked them."

Isabel Buck then went home to own husband, William, to whom she had "declared all the matter." Buck then went to Locker, warning him, "I pray you be good, and what ye will after me, I shall give it you, so [let] this matter go no further."

But the matter had gone further. Continuing her story to the examiners, Agnes Locker said her husband had wanted to find out why Isabel had commissioned Mabel to fast. Isabel had told the two Lockers that the fast had been undertaken at the direction of the chantry priest of Holmpton, Thomas Marshall. According to Agnes, Isabel's husband, William, had come once more to the Lockers' farm, this time with his father, "old Buck," and that the two had "prayed him [Locker] to be good and let [prevent] this matter to be opened abroad." The Bucks had then offered a bribe of sorts; Agnes said Isabel had given her husband John three shillings and two yards of cloth, presumably to keep the matter quiet.

Finishing her confession, Agnes told her examiners that, when Mabel left the Lockers' farm, she went to William Fisher, who lived in Welwick, where she undertook another fast, "calling it the 'black fast.'" When this second fast was ended, Agnes reported that Mabel had said, "Now I have ended this fast, and all Holderness may pray for Buck's wife and me." When Agnes's confession was "disclosed," Sir Ralph Ellercar, acting for the Council of the North, was sent to Holderness "to examine and attach all and every the persons suspect of and in the premises." He gathered all those involved in the web of suspicion: John and Agnes Locker; William and Isabel Buck; Sir Ralph Bell, vicar of Hollym; Sir Thomas Marshall, chantry priest of Holmpton; William Fisher of Welwick; and Mabel Brigge herself. They were examined by Ellercar and six others over the course of three days, from 4 to 6 February. Their surviving evidence provides a great deal of detail about Mabel Brigge and her fast—and a great deal of confusion and contradiction.

William Fisher, described as a husbandman, fifty-four years old, was the first to be examined by Ellercar, and his statement continues Agnes Locker's tale about what had happened the previous spring.[4] Fisher picked up the narrative of Mabel's story after she had left the Locker farm. Having been "put forth" from Reysome Grange, Mabel had gone to Fisher in Welwick. While living in Welwick, Mabel had undertaken a second fast, this one lasting about six weeks. Then "about Michaelmas last" (29 September) Fisher testified that John Locker came to him in Welwick and asked him to go to the vicar Ralph Bell to "record" Mabel's fasting. If Mabel's six-week fast had been completed by the time Locker met with Fisher, she must have begun her fast by mid-August at the very latest.

On ending this second fast, according to Fisher's evidence, Mabel said, "All Holderness was bound to pray for her and one other wife, and that was one William Buck's wife of Holmpton." Obviously eager to clear himself of any suspicion that he had condoned Mabel's activities, William claimed he had beaten Mabel "with a staff" and "put her away from him and would suffer her no longer to tarry." He also suggested that Mabel was a thief: "he had money taken forth of his purse which lay locked in an ark [chest] and he, supposing the said Mabel had his money, did ask her for it, and she answered and said, 'The devil and he know who had it, for she had none.'"

These two documents—the "confession" of Agnes Locker and the deposition of William Fisher—illustrate the difficulties in sorting out just what had gone on in Holderness. There is, first, the question about how many fasts had taken place. The Lockers seem to have witnessed one fast, which began at their farm in Holmpton right after Mabel's arrival. This fast had commenced on a Friday, had continued through Saturday and Sunday, and was described as "St. Trinian's fast":

> she did take at the Friday at nine three morsels of bread and sups of water, and so much again at the Saturday at nine, and no more meat nor drink [until] the high mass was done upon the Sunday. . . . She must be the first in the church of the Sunday in the morning and the last in the church after mass, and . . . she might not neither . . . speak to any man or woman whatsoever they did say unto her.[5]

Mabel seems to have undertaken a second fast after she had moved on to Fisher's farm in Welwick, this one called the "black fast." This second fast had taken place on successive days over the course of five or six weeks. According to Fisher's description, Mabel fasted on Tuesday during the first week, on Wednesday during the second week, on Thursday during the third week, and so on. John Locker must have heard about this second fast and then gone to Fisher's farm in Welwick. Even though we might conclude that Mabel had fasted twice, the examinations don't make this absolutely clear, nor do they specify which of the fasts was the one under investigation. And, as the investigation proceeded, just how many fasts had gone on, and just who had been fasting when, became even more unclear.

A second source of difficulty is in sorting out the sequence of events. The questioning of Mabel Brigge and her accusers took place over the course of the few days between 28 January and 6 February 1538. The meetings and fasts that they were all questioned about had taken place in 1537. To some extent confusion about the sequence of events is complicated for the modern reader because the events are dated by religious feasts and saints' days cited in the testimony. To a greater extent, though, the confusion stems from the obvious difficulty of the examinants themselves in pinpointing the exact days when the events they remembered had occurred.

Mabel's arrival at the Locker farm, in Holmpton, Holderness, had taken place in the spring of 1537, about a week before "Cross Days" (3 May), probably at the end of April, then. Agnes Locker testified that Mabel had begun her fast immediately after her arrival at their farm. The Lockers' testimony implies that Mabel's activities took place over three successive days, on Friday, Saturday, and Sunday, and that they had dismissed her on the following Monday. If that were the case, Mabel had spent less than a week with the Lockers. It may be, however, that the examining justices weren't clear enough yet on the details of the fasting; Mabel's fast might have taken place over three successive weeks, which would have kept her with the Lockers well into May.

In any case the Lockers claimed that, after they had witnessed Mabel's fasting, they had immediately dismissed her, and she had then gone to Fisher's farm in Welwick. While in Welwick, she had started a second fast. According to William Fisher, this fast had taken place over the course of six weeks. By the end of September John Locker heard about this second fast and made his way to Fisher's farm and "desired him to go to the vicar of Hollym to record the fasting" of Mabel. Fisher did this and also beat and dismissed Mabel.

This is the rough outline of events, though all of those examined disagreed about a number of specifics—not least of which about "the intent" of Mabel's fasts—and about just when Mabel had been asked to fast and when she had left Reysome Grange to go to Fisher in Welwick.

Tackled next by the examiners on 4 February was Isabel Buck, the wife of William Buck, described as being fifty years old.[6] Her testimony confuses the sequence of events, because she claims she was unaware of anything unusual in Holmpton until "about St. John Baptist's day" (24 June), when Agnes Locker had come to her with the information that Mabel Brigge had "slandered" her. (If the Lockers' chronology of events is correct, they dismissed Mabel long before the end of June.)

Setting aside questions of chronology for the moment, we learn from Isabel Buck that Agnes had told her that Mabel claimed to have been hired by Isabel "to fast St. Trinian fast for a wreck-taking of the King's Highness's Grace and the duke of Norfolk." Isabel told her examiners that she had been angry at Agnes Locker's report. Confronting Mabel, Isabel asked "why she so did report by her." Mabel then denied telling Agnes Locker any such story: "she said she fasted for money that the said Isabel had away seven years afore that."

Still according to Isabel, John Locker hadn't come to the Bucks with his questions about Mabel Brigge until Michaelmas, 29 September. As Isabel Buck recalled the sequence of events surrounding Mabel Brigge's fasting, that was when Locker first told William Buck about the fast supposedly commissioned by his wife and directed against the king and Norfolk. Isabel said that her own husband had responded, "If it can so be proved, then clearly I forsake my wife." But, according to Isabel, Locker had said, "It is not so, I dare well say, and therefore I would with my will it should cease and go no further in this matter."

Next deposed by the examiners was Ralph Bell, aged sixty, the vicar of Hollym.[7] In his examination, which took place on 5 February, Bell said that John and Agnes Locker had first come to him with questions about fasting around Michaelmas. He confused an already confusing situation when he conflated the two kinds of fasts Mabel had supposedly undertaken, saying that the Lockers had, while at confession, "secretly declared and opened their minds unto me, saying that Mabel Brigge did fast a fast called black fast or St. Trinian's fast" at their farm. The fast had been intended to "consume and shorten" the reign of the king. Then, "about St. Katharine's day last" (25 November), the Lockers had returned "at sundry times," telling him that Isabel Buck "would not let them be in quietness nor rest, and that she was the occasion and provoker of the said Mabel to fast."

John Locker, thirty-four years old, was also questioned on 5 February.[8] His evidence added more specific details about Mabel's fasts to the investigation. He described the first fast Mabel had undertaken, the one that took place while she was at his farm. He seemed eager to absolve himself of any complicity in her actions; he said that she had fasted on Friday, Saturday, and Sunday, and he insisted that he had dismissed her on Monday, after he learned that Isabel Buck had paid her a peck of wheat and some linen cloth "to fast the said fast to the intent that God should send to the unhappy king and duke a mischief." On learning this, he said he went immediately to Isabel Buck. He said she admitted the truth of Mabel's claim but entreated John Locker "to be good" to her. Locker testified that he had replied, "if she had been good to herself, he would have been good." All this confirmed the story his wife told.

Still on that same Monday, Locker said he had gone to Ralph Bell, the vicar of Hollym, who told him he knew nothing about the fast, which Isabel Buck claimed had been undertaken at the urging of Bell, "her ghostly father." Then, Locker said, the Bucks and Thomas Marshall, chantry priest, had searched him out. Locker claimed that Marshall had said "he was but a simple person, and that the fast that the said Buck's wife caused to be fasted for her, she had taken that fast upon her seven years since." This part of Locker's evidence was very different than his wife's recounting of events.

According to Locker, he dismissed Mabel on that same hectic Monday. Then, around 1 August, he heard that Mabel was planning to fast for six weeks. He concluded his evidence by saying he then went immediately to William Fisher so that they could report Mabel to Ralph Bell, the vicar of Hollym.

Locker's account of the events of the preceding spring indicated that he had dismissed Mabel Brigge before the end of April and had gone to William Fisher's farm around 1 August. This not only contradicts Isabel Buck's statement but also the vicar Ralph Bell's account of events and William Fisher's recollections of when Locker had visited his farm with his concerns about Mabel's fasting.

Locker's examination was followed by that of William Buck. Buck, fifty years old, deposed first that his wife had inquired of Thomas Marshall, the chantry priest, about whether it "might stand with the laws of the Church that Mabel Brigge might fast for her, forasmuch she [Isabel] was faint and not able to stand it herself." The priest, Buck said, indicated that the church laws would allow it and that he himself "would abide by it." Buck said that he knew his wife had hired Mabel to fast for her, but he claimed that he hadn't known "for what intent or purpose" Mabel had fasted.

Thomas Marshall confirmed that he had been consulted by Isabel Buck about a St. Trinian's fast, but his testimony surely didn't clarify the events for his examiners. Instead, Marshall testified that he had discussed with her a St. Trinian's fast that someone—it's not clear who—had undertaken some seven years earlier. Marshall added also that Isabel Buck begged him to go with her to the Lockers' farm at Reysome Grange. There the Lockers told the priest that Mabel Brigge had said she fasted "for mischief." Marshall claimed to have said to Isabel and the Lockers, "That is evil-favored sayings that ye do make." In another self-justifying claim, he said that he told them, "I know I shall say the truth whensoever it shall be called." Thomas Marshall must have intended his statement to the examiners to be this statement "of truth," but it surely didn't help clarify what had gone on in Holderness.

For one thing there is no clear connection between Marshall's claims that Isabel had asked him about a St. Trinian fast made seven years before and his statement that Mabel had been involved in a fast. Further complicating matters was that he was not very clear about just who had made this earlier fast; from his statement he might have meant that he himself had made this fast or that seven years before Isabel Buck had fasted a St. Trinian fast.

Mabel was also questioned on 5 February.[9] She is identified in the surviving record as "of Hollym," which may have been her home before she was widowed and taken on by Nelson, the farmer she worked for before arriving at the house of John Locker. Under examination something of her emotional state is revealed. On Trinity Sunday (27 May) of the preceding year Mabel claimed to have met Isabel Buck while she was on her way to church. Isabel had asked "how she did," to which Mabel responded "full weakly." The widow had added that "her child that her living hang by was taken from her."

What Mabel meant isn't clear from her statement. Perhaps she meant that her own child had recently died; she had arrived at Reysome Grange in April with two children. Or she might have meant that a child for whose care she was responsible had been taken from her. (No one in the case ever specifies what Mabel's duties as "servant" were on any of the farms where she had been employed.) Isabel Buck responded to Mabel's plaintive comment by asking her to "fast St. Trinian's fast for her." Mabel told her examiners that she had asked "to what intent" the fast was to be undertaken. She said Isabel had told her that she had lost some money; if Mabel would fast for her, she would give her "a peck of wheat and half a yard cloth." Mabel agreed to fast for Isabel: "she fasted the said fast, trusting in God and St. Trinian that the said money should be found again."

Mabel then turned suspicion to the Lockers. She admitted that John Locker had asked her about her fast; learning that Mabel was attempting to help Isabel find lost money, he had, Mabel said, replied "that Buck and his wife had enough, and that they might help both you and me." If Mabel would "say she hired you to fast to that intent that God should take a vengeance of the king," Locker proposed giving her two shillings himself and getting for her the five shillings that Nelson (her former employer) still owed her.

What is important here is that Mabel claimed she was first approached by Isabel Buck about fasting for her on Trinity Sunday (27 May), long after the time that the Lockers said she began her first fast and long after the time the Lockers claimed to have dismissed her. Isabel Buck testified that Agnes Locker first came to her late in June (John the Baptist's Day, 24 June) to tell her about Mabel's claim that she was hired by Isabel to fast for her.

On 6 February one final witness was examined, a widow named Elizabeth Broune. Her deposition was taken before a different group of questioners, but was signed by Ellercar and the other six examining justices, who had been inquiring into the case.[10] Broune's testimony seems to confirm something of what Mabel had confessed the day before. According to her deposition, Elizabeth Broune said she had been traveling from Holmpton to Welwick the previous spring or summer, some time between Whitsunday (20 May 1537) and Lammas (1 August). As she passed William Buck's house, Isabel "called her" and asked her to tell Mabel, then in Welwick, to "fast no more for her," adding that "she had lost forth of her bosom certain money, and for to come to knowledge thereof again the said Mabel did fast." When Elizabeth Broune gave Mabel the message from Isabel, Mabel replied "that she had done with her fast, and that she would fast for herself."

Elizabeth Broune seems to have been the one impartial witness to all that had gone on the previous spring, and, as such, her evidence seems to support the claim of both Mabel Brigge and Isabel Buck that the fasting arrangement had been undertaken in order to recover lost money and that it had occurred later than the Lockers claimed. The fast Elizabeth Broune knew about, however, was the fast Mabel had undertaken in Welwick rather than the one in Holmpton, and her story seems to have been dismissed by the investigators, since she is not among those later shifted to York and reexamined.

Charges and countercharges must have flown thick and fast among those tangled in this net. The depositions of all those examined about the fasting and its "intent" reveal that the Lockers and the Bucks were pitted against each other in the resulting conflict over Mabel's activities. It's hard to avoid the suspicion that there had been animosity in Holmpton between these neighbors long before Mabel's arrival on the scene. The Bucks were older, in their fifties, the Lockers both in their thirties. John Locker revealed certain jealousy about his neighbors, indicating that the Bucks had so much that they didn't need any help in recovering lost money.

Following their examinations Mabel Brigge and her accusers were all sent to York for further investigations.[11] John Uvedale wrote from York to the Council of the North on 11 March, indicating that they had all been kept "in ward severally in three sundry prisons" but that they "were brought this present day to York." There, he reported, each one was again examined, "of new" and "apart" from the others, Uvedale reporting that the deponents had all "acknowledged and affirmed all such depositions as heretofore they have confessed."

Uvedale recorded some further information that had come from this second set of examinations. Agnes Locker said that Isabel Buck feared greatly for her husband; she "languished and made great sorrow." She added that, before they had all been taken into custody, Isabel Buck had met with Mabel Brigge in a stable at the Bucks' home; the two women "swore hand in hand, foot upon foot, and kissed upon the same, that the same Mabel should never disclose or discover the same fast." Mabel Brigge added further information that revealed something of the existing animosities in Holderness, which might have led to the series of recriminations that entangled them all: "if the said Buck would have been surety for the said Locker for 7 *l* for kine [cows] unto one John Wright of Holderness, all this business should not have been."

Still, the action taken against Mabel Brigge was swift and decisive. On 7 April the Council of the North reported to Cromwell and Henry VIII the results of the Lenten assizes.[12] Mabel Brigge had been convicted of treason for her "black fast to an abominable intent against Your Highness and the duke of Norfolk." She had been executed for her crime.

Isabel Buck had been convicted as well, though the Council reported that she was "reprieved by the justices unto your pleasure be further known for such causes as the justices will show Your Grace at their repair unto your presence." William Buck and Thomas Marshall had both been found guilty of misprision, "for concealment of the said fast."

What are we to make of all this?

Apart from the confusion of the story, Mabel Brigge's case is remarkable for its drama and its detail. Of all the cases involving women we have reviewed, none is so well documented as Mabel's. Even so, it remains completely baffling. After all the witnesses had been examined, not much at all seemed certain except that at some point in the spring of 1537 Mabel Brigge embarked on a fast of some sort for someone and to some end.

Also reasonably certain was that, after the conflicts between the Lockers and the Bucks over the fasting had broken out in Holmpton, Mabel was dismissed by the Lockers and traveled to Welwick to take up residence there with William Fisher. Elizabeth Broune testified that Isabel Buck had spoken to her about carrying a message, halting Mabel's fast, to the widow when she was in Welwick; Elizabeth Broune remembered having carried this message to Mabel some time during the summer of 1537—between the end of May (Whitsunday, 25 May) and the beginning of August (Lammas, 1 August).

Unwilling to leave Mabel alone and having heard reports of a second fast, the black fast, John Locker had also traveled from Holmpton to Welwick. According to William Fisher, Locker arrived there "about Michaelmas last" (29 September) to persuade him to go to the vicar to record the details of Mabel's fasting. This date fits with Elizabeth Broune's recollections of events; if Mabel's fast in Welwick had occurred over the course of five or six weeks, she could well have embarked on her fasting during the summer months of 1537, just as Elizabeth Broune had deposed.

Ralph Bell, vicar of Hollym, confirmed that the Lockers had told him about Mabel's fasting around Michaelmas; they had also complained to him "about St. Katharine's day last" (25 November) that Isabel Buck was harrassing them about the incident, keeping them from "quietness" and "rest."

But, aside from these few events about which there seemed to be no question, many contradictions remained—and many questions remained unanswered. Striking is that Mabel arrived so unexpectedly at the Lockers' farm in Holmpton. She had been sent to them from a farmer named Nelson. His message that he would pay for her to work at the Lockers seems strange, though even John Locker, with his inexhaustible energy and his almost obsessive pursuit of Mabel, doesn't indicate why she had left Nelson's farm so suddenly or why it was that Nelson had sent Mabel to the Lockers.

Mabel's "crime" is also unusual. Her fasting was so remarkable that it had drawn the attention of her neighbors even before charges that she was fasting "against" the king were made. No suggestion is made in the surviving records that, while fasting was the kind of behavior that often attracted interest and comment, it was a somewhat unusual kind of *criminal* behavior.

Remarkably, several other references to a black fast exist. The earliest comes in 1517 from Lancashire, where a widow named Elizabeth Robinson was brought before Bowland jurors because she was accused of having publicly announced she was keeping a black fast to pray for vengeance against a man named Edmund Parker—who also happened to be one of the Bowland jurors.[13] She denied the charges and was instructed to clear herself by finding five neighbors to swear on her behalf. She did not appear with compurgators to support her oath and was therefore suspended from entering church.

Decades later, Visitation articles issued by Richard Barnes, the bishop of Durham, also mention a black fast. In 1576 Barnes issued an injunction against "any superstitious fasts as those of old," naming among the prohibited kinds of fast both St. Trinian's fast and what he called "the black fast."[14]

A third reference to a black fast survives, this one from as late as 1645, when a widow named Susan Marchant from Hintlesham (Suffolk) confessed that a devil came to her while she was milking a cow and singing a song.[15] Under examination, she also confessed to having three "imps"—one named Anthony, one named Will, and one named "Blackfast," whom she suckled. The imp named Blackfast had encouraged her to strike a cow lame.

All three of these references occur in cases investigated in ecclesiastical settings, however, while Mabel's fasting had involved her in a charge of treason. Before analyzing Mabel Brigge's treason any further, we should look more carefully into the nature of her "crime."

As the records just cited indicate, fasting was under the jurisdiction of English ecclesiastical courts well into the seventeenth century. As a religious practice, fasting was regulated by the ecclesiastical hierarchy, its use, abuse, or misuse to be investigated and corrected by the church's courts. The 1517 charges against Elizabeth Robinson indicate that fasting could be used as tool to cause physical harm to someone else, but ecclesiastical courts during Henry's reign were less often concerned about fasting as a means of causing harm than they were with parishioners ignoring the practice altogether. Throughout this period of political and religious uncertainty the practice of fasting was consistently reiterated as both orthodox and necessary, as were masses, "works of charity," and other acts of contrition.[16]

By the time of Elizabeth Tudor's reign, as Bishop Richard Barnes's injunctions indicate, ecclesiastical concern about fasting had not lessened but had, instead, come to focus on investigations of those accused of undertaking fasts that had been deemed unnecessary or of practicing specific kinds of fasts that had been abrogated.[17] But, even as the English Reformation progressed, interest in the act of fasting did not lessen, and accounts of "miraculous fasts" continued to be published long into the seventeenth century.[18]

Yet fasting was not only a religious practice, as the 1645 evidence about Susan Marchant's imp named Blackfast only faintly suggests. As an act, fasting was open to a variety of interpretations: it could be seen as a sign of sanctity, but it could also be a sign indicating that the person fasting was a witch.[19]

Much of the testimony about Mabel Brigge's fast does, in fact, suggest she might have been practicing some kind of witchcraft. Ecclesiastical courts frequently investigated charges that victims were being "wasted" or "consumed" by someone practicing magic against them. We have already noted the investigation of Alianor Dulyne, for example, who was accused in 1502 of using divination and of intending to kill her husband. Alianor Dulyne was examined by the Commissary of London; a dozen years earlier, in 1490, the same court had examined Johanna Benet for a similar maleficent act. Johanna had been charged with intending to harm a man with a wax candle. As the candle was consumed, it was charged, the man would waste away.[20] The case against Johanna Benet was not established, however, and the charges were suspended.

In the rather complicated case involving a woman named Tanglost, the bishop of St. David's believed himself to be the object of the same kind of sorcery. On first entering into his diocese, the bishop had been informed that a gentleman named Thomas Wyriott was involved in adultery. According to the bishop's information, Wyriott, "his wedded wife being alive, kept a woman called Tanglost," who was also married. The bishop attempted to discipline Wyriott, admonishing him "under the pain of censure . . . not to be adherent or company with the said Tanglost." But Wyriott and Tanglost chose to ignore the bishop, persisting in their relationship.

Two years later the prelate finally took Tanglost into ward, but Wyriott and "other riotous persons" broke into the castle where she was being held. Wyriott proceeded to "put away his wedded wife," who promptly died. Although Wyriott seems to have denied his wife any kind of support, her death wasn't attributed to his neglect: "the common voice and fame" was that Wyriott's wife "was destroyed with witchcraft by the means of the said Tanglost."

The bishop took Tanglost into ward once more and ultimately decided to banish her. Tanglost then went to Bristol, where she hired a woman named Margaret Hackett, "practiced in witchcraft," to destroy the bishop. The two returned to Wyriott's house, where, "in a chamber called Paradise Chamber," they made "two images of wax" to accomplish their goal. When Margaret was arrested and confessed, Tanglost hired another woman, one with "more cunning and experience," to make *three* wax images. Pursued by the bishop,

Tanglost fled once more to Bristol, where she was examined for heresy. Returned once more to the custody of the bishop of St. David's, Tanglost was again rescued by Wyriott and his friends. The harassed prelate petitioned the lord chancellor to order the case of Tanglost to the Court of Chancery.[21] Tanglost, meanwhile, answered that "the said bill is insufficient and uncertain . . . and only feigned of malice, and of no truth." She claimed she was "not guilty of any witchcraft, as by the said bill is supposed."[22]

While nothing more is recorded in the case of Tanglost, all of the examples cited show that practitioners were believed to be able to harm their victims by means of sorcery. In Mabel Brigge's case the Lockers had insisted that Mabel's fast had been undertaken to harm the king. While she denied these accusations, Mabel herself did admit that she had fasted in order to find Isabel Buck's lost money. This, too, sounds like she was practicing some sort of magic, which was often used to recover what had been lost.

As only one example, in 1499 Agnes Clerk claimed to have been given a holly stick by fairies. Her mother had taken the fairies' present to the curate of Ashfield, Suffolk, so that he could bless it. The two women intended to use the holly stick in order to find hidden treasure.[23]

Ecclesiastical courts in London dealt with many charges of witchcraft, among them several cases in which sorcery was used to recover lost goods. Such a case had been presented in 1476, for example, when Nazareth Jarbrey and Thomas Barley were examined for having used magic to recover stolen goods, and again in 1509, when Alice Ancetyr and Christopher Sandon were examined for the same reason.[24]

Such charges were still being made in 1554, when William Haslewood, a London clerk, was under examination in the same court for practicing "witchcraft or sorcery with a sieve and a pair of shears." Haslewood had lost his purse and remembered that, when he was a child, he had heard his mother say that when something was lost, using a sieve and a pair of shears would "bring to knowledge who had the thing lost." Haslewood had then hung the sieve "by the point of the shears and said these words: 'by Peter and Paul, he hath it,' naming the party whom he in that behalf suspected." Haslewood claimed never to have done such a thing before. He was assigned "penance thereon."[25]

Similar cases were recorded in York. The Archbishop's Court of Audience dealt with a number of presentments involving charges of sorcery arising out of the 1567 Visitation, among them one involving a woman known as Margaret Harper, who "taketh upon her to tell where things are that be gone or lost." Another involved John Skelton, a married man called an "enchanter," who was said to tell people "of their goods when they are stolen away, and where they are become."[26]

The aims of Mabel Brigge's fasts—both her intent as she described it (finding Isabel Buck's lost property) and her intent as the Lockers described it (harming the king)—sound very much as if she were, in fact, practicing magic. Moreover, in quite striking ways Mabel Brigge was exactly the kind of person who was most often believed to practice magic and to be regarded as a witch: she was female, she was poor, and she was alone.[27]

Before the passage of any witchcraft statute by Parliament, the practice of magic was most generally considered an ecclesiastical offense, liable to prosecution by church courts, as the examples we have examined illustrate.[28] But Mabel Brigge's offense was not referred to ecclesiastical examiners or to the local criminal jurisdiction. There is no indication in any of the surviving documents that her crime was a violation of ecclesiastical injunctions and no suggestion that she was under suspicion for witchcraft. Mabel's fast was clearly regarded as criminal—treasonous—behavior.

Why did she find herself before the Council of the North?

EIGHT

Mabel Brigge and Her Strange Behavior

Mabel Brigge's black fast was not the only unusual crime investigated by the government during the 1530s. Following the execution of Elizabeth Barton, many kinds of strange behavior were brought to the attention of Cromwell and, ultimately, the king.

In 1535, for example, Thomas, abbot of Abingdon, wrote to Cromwell that he had taken into custody a "suspect person," a priest, who had in his possession "certain books of conjurations."[1] According to the abbot, the priest's book contained "many conclusions" for "finding out of treasure hid" as well as for divining "many things." What seemed to disturb the abbot most, however, was that the priest's book also contained a number of illustrations ("figures") and, "amongst all, one the which hath a sword crossed over with a scepter." The abbot was writing to Cromwell for instructions, inquiring whether the priest should be sent to Oxford Castle or to Wallingford Castle.

In November 1537 Sir William Parr wrote to Cromwell about Henry Cowpar, a priest who had organized a series of "suspect" meetings.[2] Parr had concluded that such "secret" assemblies surely must have "an ill purpose and intention" and were apt to "contrive or forge things which might be contrary to . . . the king's peace." On investigating Cowpar and those who were attending the meetings he had arranged, Parr found that the group had been planning on conjuring to find treasure. The priest had been practicing more than "necromancy," however, for Parr discovered that he also had been making political predictions. Using an alphabetic prophecy, Cowpar claimed to have correctly predicted that Queen Anne would never be crowned and that "we should have a troublous world." Parr was writing to Cromwell for further instructions, and, while he waited, he indicated his plans to continue apprehending anyone who held secret assemblies.

Even more sinister, however, was the discovery in 1538 of a wax image unearthed in a London churchyard.[3] On 7 January a man named Fulk Vaughan was examined by Thomas Wriothesley (Cromwell's secretary), Paul Withipol (a London alderman), and Dr. Thomas Starkey (an influential humanist who had penned an attack on papal supremacy). Under examination Vaughan described the wax image as being "in the form of a young child with two pins thrust into it." Vaughan had taken the sheet the figure had been wrapped in to one Pole, a scrivener; the scrivener was himself a conjurer, and Vaughan inquired of him what the figure meant.

Pole replied, "Marry, . . . it was made to waste one," but he had criticized whoever had made the wax image, saying that he (or she) was "not his craft's master." For the magic to have worked properly, Pole said, the maker of the wax image should have put it "either in horse dung or in a dunghill." Pole's wife then appeared, interrupting any further discussion, but Vaughan told his three examiners that Pole had often spoken to him of "conjuring matters," claiming he could recover lost money. Even though Pole said that Cromwell had already taken conjuring books away from him, this obviously hadn't stopped the scrivener from continuing to practice magic.

A suggestion about how this story about a wax figure in the form of a child with pins sticking in it might have been interpreted comes from a second document from 1538, which also shows just how widely an incident could be reported.[4] In December a man named Richard Guercey confessed that, "being in the kitchen in Corpus Christi College [Oxford]," he had told the story of the wax image to one Sir Marshall. Instead of two pins, however, Guercey had heard that the "image of wax found in London way . . . had a knife sticking through his head or his heart." According to Guercey, the wax figure "represent[ed] the prince's person, and as that did consume, so likewise should the prince."

Any act, magic or otherwise, which intended "bodily harm" to the king, his queen, or "their heirs apparent" would clearly come under the provisions of the 1534 Treason Act, which defined as treason any attempt by "craft" or by imagination to cause such harm. Thus, Richard Guercey's story of the wax image and its intention to waste Henry's son Edward made its way into the state papers. This must surely have been the reason why Mabel Brigge's fast was investigated by the king's Council of the North and not by an ecclesiastical court, for the Lockers claimed that she had "fasted against" Henry. If true, surely it would have been a treasonable offense.

While these stories of conjuring clearly involve stories of strange behavior similar to Mabel's, they don't involve women whose actions seemed somehow suspect. But Mabel Brigge was not the only woman who had attracted attention for her strange behavior.

A brief report from Boston, Lincolnshire records the "articles against" a young woman named Mary Baynton, the daughter of Thomas Baynton of Bridlington (Yorkshire).[5] In Boston the eighteen-year-old Mary had been discovered wandering "in many houses . . . before diverse and sundry persons, as well men and women." She was telling people that she was the Princess Mary, Henry's daughter, "put forth into the broad world to shift for her living."

The report is undated, but it appears among the state papers for late September 1533, a critical period for Henry's daughter. Mary Baynton's tale certainly reflected the miseries of the princess. According to the "articles" recorded, Mary Baynton had said "that the French Queen [Mary Tudor, Henry's sister] was her aunt and her godmother, and upon a time the said French Queen . . . looked upon a book and said to her": 'Niece Mary, I am right sorry for you, for I hear that your fortune is very hard. Ye must go a-begging once in your life, either in your youth or in your age.' To which "Princess Mary" had replied, "therefore I take it upon me now in my youth, and I intend to go beyond the sea to mine uncle, the Emperor, as soon as I may get shipping."

Although she seems to have been arrested for having posed as the princess, Mary Baynton's story ends with this report of her wandering "in many houses" and talking to "diverse and sundry persons, as well men and women." Nothing more about Mary Baynton's story is known; nothing further appears in the state papers.

Mary Baynton's story has interested several historians.[6] In a note mentioning the young woman, Dodds and Dodds conclude that she had been received in Boston "with respect and sympathy," but there is nothing at all in the brief document that survives to indicate how she had been received or treated by those who heard her. Although the two historians note that no evidence suggests "that she had any accomplices," they nonetheless imply that accomplices must have existed, since Mary was "connected with Bridlington and Boston, which were two centres of . . . rebellion."

Keith Thomas also concludes that Mary's was a deliberate impersonation. He includes Mary Baynton with Lambert Simnel and Perkin Warbeck as "imposters masquerading as the representatives of some branch, real or imaginary, of the royal family." Mary is mentioned as well by David Loades, who also suggests her "impersonation" was a "calculated demonstration": "these were shrewd gibes, and do not suggest spontaneous adolescent fantasy."

But I am not sure we can conclude that Mary Baynton was manipulated by others in order to stir sympathy in the north for the princess and against the king. As we have seen in our discussion of Elizabeth Barton, in particular, and of dozens of other women, in general, ordinary women were well aware of the political situation and spoke out with "shrewd gibes" quite often—without having words placed in their mouths by more astute or informed accomplices. Certainly, Mary Baynton might have been deliberately used as a political tool, but there is nothing at all in the surviving document to suggest that such a conspiracy existed. It seems to me just as possible to conclude that she knew exactly what to say to attract attention or that she was truly suffering from delusions. That she seems to have gotten into no further trouble suggests that her three examiners, Nicholas Robson, Thomas Brown, and Robert Pulvertoft, concluded she was in fact *not* a part of some calculated demonstration. We might hope that she wound up safely back in Bridlington with her father, Thomas.

While we don't really know whether Mary Baynton's strange behavior was dangerous or pathetic, we can be sure of the terrible agony of nine women in Cumberland. These women were all widows, their husbands having been among the seventy-four rebels summarily condemned at Carlisle by the duke of Norfolk after the northern rebellions. Displaying the king's banner, the duke had sentenced the men under martial law, and they had been executed in their own villages, their bodies left hanging in ropes and chains as examples of the terrible fate that awaited armed rebels. But about two months later the bodies of some of the men were mysteriously cut down.

By early May a report of what happened had reached the king. Cromwell demanded an explanation from Norfolk, who defended himself by saying he had not been informed that the traitors' bodies had been taken down and buried: "I do perceive by your letter that ye would know whether such persons as were put to execution in Westmorland and Cumberland were taken down and buried by my commandment or not. Undoubtedly, my good lord, if I had consented thereunto, I would I had hanged by them, but on my troth it is eight or nine days past sith I heard first thereof."[7]

Anxious to clear himself, Norfolk wrote to the king on 16 May. The duke had received from Sir Thomas Curwen, sheriff of Cumberland, and Sir Thomas Wharton a series of "examinations of such as hath taken down part of your rebels where they were hanged."[8] The two had examined only nine suspects, and Norfolk reported that these were "all I can get knowledge of, and they be all women and not one man." Norfolk did not think much of the work of Curwen and Wharton: "I think Your Majesty hath not be[en] well served, and for my part, I think I have not been well handled not to have been advertised of so long time after it was done nor for no quick message that I have sent [could I get] better knowledge of the ill-doers."

Norfolk intended to pursue the matter further and requested further instruction from the king: "Most humbly beseeching Your Majesty to advise me of Your Highness's pleasure of what sort I shall punish such as come to my knowledge that have been offenders as well men as women, for I know not how sore by the law their offences will extend unto."

Although the examinations he forwarded to the king satisfied neither the duke himself nor Henry, they are moving testimony to action these few women of Cumberland had taken on behalf of their dead husbands. Altogether nine women had been examined, all of them living in and around Cockermouth: "Janet Jackson, late wife of John Jackson," "Christopher Smith's wife," "Richard Crage's wife," "John Wilson's wife," "Percival Hudson's wife," "Thomas Bell's wife," "John Fisher's wife," "John Buele's wife," and "John Peyrson's wife." Each had been questioned about "the loosing down of her husband" or "the cutting down of the gallows of her husband" or "the taking down of her husband hanged in chains" and then of the burial of the bodies.

None of the widows named a single man during her examination. Each insisted she had been helped only by other women: by "her mother-in-law," by "one Rodre's wife, widow of Embleton," by "a poor woman that she hired—she knoweth not her name," by "one Blandeman's wife called Bessie," by "two of her own daughters," by "diverse other women—their names she knoweth not," as only a few examples from the women's statements indicate. Together these women buried what remained of the bodies that had been left hanging for weeks.

The women did not know, or would not say, who had cut the bodies down, and this may have been part of what aroused Norfolk's suspicions that Curwen and Wharton had not pressed them very hard. Janet Jackson claimed that about "the cutting down she knoweth not." Christopher Smith's wife indicated "she knoweth not who took him down." Richard Crage's wife said "she knoweth not of his loosing forth of the chain." John Wilson's wife reported "she knoweth not of his taking down." Percival Hudson's wife said "she knew not of his taking down." John Fisher's wife also said "she knows not of his cutting down." John Buele's wife claimed she did "not know of the loosing down of her husband." John Peyrson's wife, too, denied knowing who had cut down the body of her husband: "she did not know of his loosing." Only Thomas Bell's wife said anything different. She took responsibility herself for having cut her husband down: "she in the daylight cut the rope he [was] hanging in with a thorncrook."

Having recovered their husbands' bodies, the women then tried to have them buried, and, if they could find no one to help them, they did the job themselves. Janet Jackson went with the women who had helped her to the churchyard at Cockermouth, and together the women buried the body as night fell. Christopher Smith's wife and the women who accompanied her buried "the said Smith" in the churchyard at Branthwaite "in the night." Richard Crage's wife had been accompanied by two women. They had asked a priest to bury Crage's body, but "the priest would not suffer him to be buried," so "in the night" the widow buried her husband's remains "in a dike."

John Wilson's wife and the four woman who helped her had taken "the said Wilson to Brigham church, and in the churchyard buried him upon the daylight." Percival Hudson's wife carried him on a cart to Torpenhow Church. The vicar there "would not suffer him to be buried," so Hudson's wife returned the body to where it had fallen when it was cut down. Three days later she retrieved the body once more, "and after that she buried [it] within the wall of Torpenhow churchyard in the night." Thomas Bell's wife buried her husband "at the day breaking" in Cockermouth churchyard. John Fisher's wife buried him, too, in the Cockermouth churchyard.

John Buele's wife said she had not known her husband's body had been cut down until he had lain "in the dike where he fell nine days." She then wound him in a sheet; eight days later she and the women who helped her carried the body to the church at Dearham, where they "buried him in the churchyard there in the night." John Peyrson's wife said she hadn't known of her husband's "loosing" either but that, after she learned of it, she had given "a sheet to one Bessie Matson to wind him in." He lay from Wednesday to Monday before she and several other women carried the body to the churchyard of Bridekirk "and in the daylight buried him."

These were the examinations Norfolk deemed insufficient. After reading them, I can imagine that Curwen and Wharton might not have had the heart to inquire any further. But Norfolk, Cromwell, and Henry pursued the matter vigorously. On 19 May Sir Thomas Curwen and Sir Thomas Wharton wrote once more to Norfolk, in response to a letter from him dated 11 May.[9] They reported that they had continued their investigations at Cockermouth, Penrith, and Carlisle. (In Westmorland, according to Curwen and Wharton, the earl of Cumberland was pursuing the cutting down of traitors' bodies there.) The letter to Norfolk was accompanied by "a brief remembrance" of another examination, one that had taken place the day before, 18 May. The same nine cases were under review, and Curwen and Wharton reported once more that the bodies had been buried by the men's widows. At this second examination, "in some cases" the women admitted to having cut down the bodies themselves. Crage's cousin and Buele's brother had admitted cutting down the bodies of those two men, but Curwen and Wharton indicated that the cousin and brother couldn't be pursued further, because they had already been "punished" for removing the bodies: "afterwards [they] died from the corruption of the bodies they cut down."[10]

Even so, the king still wasn't satisfied. On 22 May Cromwell wrote once more to Norfolk about the investigations:

> And as touching the depositions taken of certain women anent [concerning] the cutting down and burial of the traitors in Westmorland and Cumberland, surely having regard and respect to the evil example and perverse minds of the offenders, which is thought came not only of women's heads, but some men were the principal procurers, the King's Highness thinketh verily, that if the said depositions had been earnestly taken, the plainness of that matter might have been easily known. And therefore considering that such a misbehavior is not to be passed over without some convenient punishment, His Highness requireth you, according to your high wisdom and his trust, by all means possible to try and search out the principal doers and occasioners of the same, which once done, and they apprehended, punishment shall be devised for them according to the qualities of their offences.[11]

This is a chilling final note. We hear no more of the matter and no more about the nine women of Cumberland. Those who might have been questioned about similar cases in Penrith, Carlisle, and Westmorland remain unnamed, but the nine women in Cumberland were identified and had been questioned at least twice by the time Cromwell wrote on the king's behalf. What further attempts were made to "try" them are unknown, and what punishment meted out to them "according to the qualities of their offences" can only be guessed at. One significant point to note is that the king did not believe the women were solely responsible for what had gone on: the "thought," he said, "came not only of women's heads."

One further strange episode deserves attention before we return to the story of Mabel Brigge. In August 1538 a series of examinations were made in Salisbury. There a group of tradesmen and women—a chaplain, a fletcher, a singing man, a tailor, a painter, and a smith—were among those questioned about a story involving the king and a pilgrimage he would take to St. Michael's Mount.[12] The fact that it was a rumor about a pilgrimage that was being circulated is curious enough, but just as remarkable is the way this unusual behavior was quickly and thoroughly investigated.

The report of the rumor caused an explosion of activity in Salisbury, because the examinations, conducted by the mayor, Henry Coldston, were recorded on the very day that the rumor first became public. Coldston and his fellow examiners worked backwards from man to woman tracing the source of the story involving the king, an angel who appeared to him, his vision of the late Queen Jane, Portsmouth, and the king's pilgrimage to St. Michael's Mount.

Coldston began his investigation, dated 10 August, with Walter Williams, a fletcher, who said he had first heard about the king's pilgrimage at two o'clock that very afternoon from Sir Richard Hussey, a chaplain, who came to Williams "to mend his shafts." Hussey asked Williams if he had any news, and Williams said no. But Hussey did: "I heard, William, this hour that the King's Grace is gone to St. Michael's Mount on pilgrimage."

Williams replied that the story couldn't possibly be true—that anyone could travel to Portsmouth and find Henry there. But Hussey answered him, "There he will take shipping, as I heard." When Williams pressed him about where he had heard such a story, Hussey said he heard it from Thomas Selman as they had "sat together upon Alexander Weeks's stall."

Coldston questioned Selman next. Selman admitted that "about eleven of the clock afore noon" he had been sitting with Hussey at Weeks's stall and, when asked if he had any news, had said: "As I heard, ye shall hear. It was told me the King's Grace is at Portsmouth, and there will take shipping to go to St. Michael's Mount on pilgrimage." Selman added that he himself had heard the story at ten o'clock that morning, from a tailor named Philip Godfrey, whom he had met at the house of a woman named Jane Deloud.

Godfrey was examined next. Philip Godfrey said that he had first heard the rumor that morning at nine o'clock while he was at Jane Deloud's house, and he admitted having repeated it to Thomas Selman around ten. Jane Deloud was next deposed, and she named a group of men who came to her house on the morning of 10 August "to drink"; she heard "spoken among them that the king was at Portsmouth and that an angel did appear to His Grace that he should go on pilgrimage to St. Michael's Mount and offer a noble there upon pain of death." She added a new and fanciful detail to the story, one that no one else included: "and that Queen Jane did appear to His Grace and desired him to go on the same pilgrimage, but which of them spake it, she knoweth not."

Among the men who had been drinking at Jane Deloud's house were John Higgons, Thomas Vincent, John Hobbes, John Field, William Rile, and John Wilton. They all admitted having been drinking at Jane Deloud's, but they denied having heard anyone say anything "concerning Our Sovereign Lord the King." When Coldston questioned John Clark, a painter, he said he had talked about the story the day before, at 6:00 A.M., with the wife of John Ryppe. Clark was lodging with Ryppe. Ryppe's wife wasn't examined, but Ryppe was; he said he had been home from the time Clark got up until the time Clark went to work and that he hadn't witnessed any such conversation between his wife and his lodger.

Coldston then turned to John Hawkes, a smith. Hawkes testified that on 6 August he told the painter Clark the story about the pilgrimage. Hawkes himself heard the report from a widow named Isabel Nowell, who came to him on 24 July "to fetch fire" and said: "God save the king. I trust we shall go a-pilgrimage again, for I hear that His Grace will go a-pilgrimage to St. Michael's Mount."

Finally, Coldston questioned Isabel Nowell. She remembered her conversation with the smith Hawkes and that she had talked to him early on the morning of 24 July. She confirmed the details of their conversation and offered Coldston and his examiners the name of her source, Agnes Chacy, the wife of John Chacy; Agnes "told her all the whole matter above written." But there the investigation stopped.

Coldston and his fellow examiners didn't track down Agnes Chacy, and the ultimate source of the rumor was never found. Since no letter from Coldston about his investigation has survived, it's not clear whether he failed to find Agnes Chacy, decided the thread of the rumor wasn't dangerous enough to merit following any further, or simply ran out of energy to pursue the tale.

Like fasting, pilgrimages do not, at first glance, seem to be the kind of behavior that was politically motivated. But the Injunctions of 1536 issued by Cromwell had specifically attacked pilgrimage, an attack that became much sharper in the Injunctions of 1538.[13] Those examined in Salisbury were not only speculating about the king's pilgrimage but also seemed to be eager about the prospect of themselves going "a-pilgrimage again." Like fasting, then, the act of pilgrimage could be a kind of criminal behavior—and the flurry of rumors cause for a serious investigation. In spite of the dangerous temper of the times, however, nothing seems to have resulted from this investigation of men and women in Salisbury.[14]

But the case involving Mabel Brigge was pursued to the end. Her story, in fact, continued even after her execution. At the end of June in Kirkby Moorside (Yorkshire) a man named William Wood reported Robert Kirkby, priest, and Robert Lyon, parish clerk, for a dangerous conversation he had overheard.[15] According to Wood, he had been "occupied in his prayers" in the chapel when he heard priest Kirkby tell Robert Lyon, "I had as merry a night yesternight as I had this twelvemonth, declaring no further." To which remark the clerk Lyon responded: "I can tell you other news. The woman's prayer that was put to death at York hath light of one of them that we were talking upon the last week, for the king is dead." Kirkby reportedly expressed his satisfaction that Mabel Brigge's "prayer" had been answered:

"Vengeance must needs light upon him because he hath put so many men wrongfully to death." And so, it seems, at least one man might have believed that Mabel had been "put . . . wrongfully to death."

Unfortunately for Wood, his accusations weren't believed. Instead of getting the priest and the clerk into trouble, he wound up in trouble himself, becoming the subject of an investigation by the Council of the North. He was sent to York Castle and underwent a series of lengthy examinations, which revealed him to be a thoroughly disreputable troublemaker unable to hold onto steady employment.[16] And it was discovered that he had pestered Robert Lyons's daughter Bessie on an earlier occasion, after which the Lyons family had accused him publicly of being a thief. The priest Robert Kirkby had tried to make peace between Wood and the Lyons family, but Wood surely wanted to make trouble for Kirkby and Lyon.

For our purposes, though, it doesn't really matter whether Kirkby and Lyon actually said what Wood accused them of saying or not. What is significant is that the story of Mabel Brigge was known throughout Yorkshire and that her execution was connected with reports that the king had "put . . . wrongfully to death" at least some of those who had been accused of treason. Like Margaret Cheyne, whose execution had been talked about by a group of men gathered for breakfast, Mabel Brigge's fate was not ignored.

In fact, much about the case involving Mabel Brigge is reminiscent of the story of Margaret Cheyne, which began this book, and so, perhaps, Mabel's is a fitting end to our examination of the women who came to be involved, one way or another, in protesting the reforms of Henry VIII in the early sixteenth century.

Like Margaret Cheyne, Mabel Brigge was a woman without family support. She was a widow with two children, and no family members were examined, or even mentioned, during the investigation of her activities conducted by the Council of the North. Her story suggests that she had no connections of any kind and nowhere to turn. She had arrived at Reysome Grange unexpectedly, followed by a messenger from the farmer named Nelson indicating that he would pay the Lockers if they would take on Mabel.

After she was "put forth" from the Locker farm in Holmpton, she had gone to yet another situation with William Fisher in Welwick. When Locker persuaded Fisher to dismiss Mabel, Fisher beat her, and he also put her out. Where she went between the time that she left Fisher and the time that Ellercar arrested her is left unspecified in the record. Buffeted from place to place, Mabel Brigge seems to have had nowhere to turn for permanence or help.

Another interesting parallel between the stories of Mabel Brigge and Margaret Cheyne is that the official records make no mention of the children both women had. At the time she was taken into custody, Margaret had a baby just a few months old as well as three young daughters, and we are left wondering where these children were during the time of her imprisonment. We know nothing about them after her execution, except that they did survive.

Mabel Brigge also had children; two children accompanied her from Nelson's farm to the Lockers' Reysome Grange. William Fisher says nothing about any children having been with Mabel when she came to his farm in Welwick. Mabel herself mentioned one child during her examination, saying that "her child that her living hang by was taken from her," which perhaps meant that one of her two children had died. At least according to Mabel's testimony, Isabel Buck seems to have responded with some measure of sympathy to this remark, because Isabel responded by offering to hire Mabel to fast for her. But no further mention of Mabel Brigge's children is made by anyone else involved in the case.

Like Margaret Cheyne, Mabel Brigge seems also to have been caught up in a larger conflict. Margaret's husband, and probably Margaret herself, had been involved in the northern rebellions, while the "larger" conflict that involved Mabel Brigge seems to have been a feud in Holderness that pitted two families against each other. The Bucks were older, and their money seemed to have aroused jealousy in the Lockers. There was more than a little malice in the charges and countercharges that were recorded by investigators.

Everyone in Holderness agreed that Isabel Buck hired Mabel to fast for her, perhaps even to fast twice, once in Holmpton and then again in Welwick. Since Mabel seems from the records to have been taken on as a servant and then quickly dismissed without any wages having been paid her, she might well have been eager to fast for Isabel Buck in return for payment.

But, although everyone agreed that Mabel had been hired to fast, they disagreed about the intent of the fast: Mabel herself and Isabel Buck claimed the purpose had been to recover Isabel's lost money. Their explanations were confirmed by Elizabeth Broune, the only witness who was not connected either to the Lockers or to the Bucks but also the only witness who was not taken from Holderness to York for further examination. In fact, Mabel testified that it was John Locker who had first suggested that she accuse Isabel Buck of hiring her to fast "against" the king and thus get the Bucks into trouble. It was only the Lockers who claimed Mabel's fast had any political intention. It would be a mistake to assume that a woman would not undertake a fast for such a reason, but Mabel, Isabel Buck, and Elizabeth Broune denied any such intention.[17]

Whether she was arrested for her active involvement with the conspirators or simply for who she was, Margaret Cheyne was at least involved with those who had posed a real threat to Henry's government. But a small feud among farmers in Holderness was what ultimately involved Mabel Brigge in a treason case. Investigators took pages of depositions, but they never got a clear story. Maybe it just seemed easier to get rid of the problem than to solve it.

Just as many of the women involved in the Pilgrimage of Grace were never investigated, presumably because of their social status and strong family connections, so Isabel Buck's position and connections seem to have given her some measure of protection when Mabel's fasting was investigated by the Council of the North. Although she was convicted of treason along with the servant, Isabel was nevertheless reprieved, at least until Henry advised the Council about what action should be taken against her. We can't be sure that she was finally pardoned, but there is no record of any further action against her.[18]

As one final parallel with Margaret Cheyne, the story of Mabel Brigge and her crime spread quickly. In June the reports of her execution were the subject of conversation in Kirkby Moorside, and at least one man there spoke with some sympathy about her death.

A case such as the one involving Mabel Brigge has been overlooked by most historians, however, because it has seemed neither critical nor pivotal. It involved an obscure and poor woman whose execution seems hard to explain, for her strange behavior, even if it involved "compassing" or imagining the king's death, does not seem particularly threatening to Henry or his royal authority or to involve any offense of "real" political consequence. But it is a story that did not go unremarked in its own day; Mabel's contemporaries knew what had happened to her, and her death was an event of some significance to them.

Dangerous Talk and Strange Behavior

When I first began to consider investigating the ways in which women might have been involved in resistance to the reforms of Henry VIII, I was not sure that acts of *political* resistance could be distinguished, much less separated, from objections to the religious reforms also under way, yet I knew that the part women might have played in political protest was what was of most interest to me—and what was missing from even the most recent works of Tudor history. How did women respond to the issues raised by the king's Great Matter, to the king's succession problem, and to the assertion of royal supremacy, for example? If the clash between Henry VIII and the Church of Rome provoked the question "What is the state and how is it constructed," how did women respond to the answers supplied by king and Parliament?[1]

I was well aware that the line separating the political from the religious was never more blurred than during Henry's reign. Nevertheless, as I began to gather the stories I have told here, I found that, while I would have been hard-pressed to draw a line separating Tudor reform from Tudor Reformation, I could separate women whose protests were primarily about doctrine or dogma from women whose protests were more clearly about legitimate authority and right rule.[2]

Women such as Margaret Bowgas were charged with saying, "I believe in God, and he can do more good than Our Lady or any other saint"; Joan Baker claimed images were only a way for priests to make themselves rich; Alice Fonge, "like a heretic," denied that water "could save a human soul"; Mrs. Cowper read the Scriptures and was warned that the day would come when the bishop of

London would waste no more wood on heretics but would have them "tied together, sacked, and thrown into the Thames." Still other women, most notably Anne Askew, were arrested for heresy, tried, and found guilty, and burned at the stake.[3] These were very different than the words and actions of the women examined here.

In her analysis of London during the English Reformation, Susan Brigden paused to reflect about the role that women played during religious crises of the period that we have examined here. About the participation of women she wrote:

> Women were not silent in these congregations and were not only, nor even, following their husbands. Indeed, the authorities grew alarmed by the ardour with which London wives supported causes. . . . This female religious enthusiasm is usually to be glimpsed rather than counted. . . . We cannot know how many women converted others to an evangelical vocation and spurred them to action; how often the courage and zeal of women strengthened their husbands' faltering resolve. But we can guess.[4]

This comment was of interest to me as I began my investigations, and it might well be applied to the discussion of women's participation in Tudor politics. We cannot know just how many women involved themselves in politically motivated protest and resistance. But, after hearing the stories of women such as Margaret Cheyne, Elizabeth Barton, Elizabeth Wood, and Mabel Brigge, I would suggest that we can begin to do more than guess about the scope of their participation.

As I began to collect these stories, I realized that I approached the task with a number of assumptions about what I would find. As my investigations slowly progressed, I found that every one of my assumptions was challenged by what I discovered.

I assumed, for example, that the majority of women who became involved in political resistance would be more or less unwilling, or unwitting, participants. I assumed that Margaret Cheyne did not set out to involve herself with the rebels of the Pilgrimage of Grace, and I assumed that what was true of her would be true of most of other women as well. I believed that I would be narrating the stories of unfortunate women who had become victims. But, as soon as I began to gather more stories, I found I had to abandon my assumption. While some women, most notably Mabel Brigge, might have participated unwittingly in activities that were later constructed as political resistance, others—most notably Elizabeth Barton and Elizabeth Wood and surely

Margaret Cheyne—must have been aware of what they were saying and doing. As the stories collected here illustrate, women of all classes knew what was going on in court and Parliament, and they did not hesitate to make their opinions known. Nor did they hesitate to join in more active resistance, as their presence during the Pilgrimage of Grace and the Taunton rising attests.

I also assumed that, as with witchcraft accusations, the women who would be investigated and found guilty for their acts of political resistance would primarily be women alone, women who could be called "masterless women." Such was sometimes the case. The most obvious example is Elizabeth Barton, who was, as far as we can determine, a woman without any family at all, much less a father or a husband who could protect her or control her. At the same time that the Nun of Kent was being investigated for her predictions about the king's death, Mistress Amadas also found herself in trouble for her "prophetic" attacks on the king, but she had a husband to whom she could be returned, and she survived the investigation into her activities, while Elizabeth Barton did not. Mary Baynton, involved in what might have been judged a dangerous impersonation, could be safely returned to her Yorkshire father, Thomas Baynton. Mabel Brigge was a widow; having no husband or family, she was executed for treason. Isabel Buck, convicted of treason along with Mabel, seems on the other hand to have survived her ordeal, perhaps in part because she could be controlled by a husband (though one who also had been punished for his part in the fasting conspiracy), perhaps in larger part because the Bucks clearly had a wide range of local connections. Her father having been executed for treason, Margaret Cheyne had no family to whom she could turn for support, and, making the most of her isolation, Henry's government undertook a campaign to discredit her marriage to Sir John Bulmer as well. But, just as the pattern I expected to see began to emerge, I found Elizabeth Wood, the wife of a husbandman. Her marital status and the control a husband seemed to offer did not save her from execution for what she said in the aftermath of the Walsingham conspiracy.

I also assumed that women with some degree of social status—women with a vested interest in the world of high politics—would be more likely than other women to be involved with politically dangerous talk and strange behavior. Margaret Cheyne, whatever the circumstances of her birth, was connected to the powerful Stafford family, unarguably was married to at least one gentleman, William Cheyne, esquire, and probably was, despite official propaganda, married to Sir John Bulmer, a knight. But the women whose stories are included here come from a range of social classes, many from within the larger class of the "commons," from those who were the wives of civil servants to those who were the wives of husbandmen to those who were themselves landless laborers. Political comment and action were not limited to those who belonged to the nobility or the gentry or the well-to-do "middling" ranks of society: surprising numbers of very ordinary women were involved in politically oriented comment, action, and reaction.

Perhaps most significantly, I assumed that the kind of dangerous talk and strange behavior that women engaged in would be peculiarly female—that it would somehow be gendered activity. Gossip, for instance, is still stereotypically associated with "women's talk," while in the sixteenth century, "defamatory" words flew thick and fast between women, and charges that one woman had called another "whore" or "harlot" appear with overwhelming frequency in ecclesiastical court records.[5] Riot and rebellion, on the other hand, are most often associated with those who can and do bear arms, men.

But these assumptions were also challenged by the stories of the women I found. Just as often as women—even more often, as it turned out—men were accused of and investigated for gossip, for having engaged in scurrilous talk, idle tale telling, and spreading rumors, while, as we have seen, at least some women did participate in more active ways in riot and rebellion. And, although political prophecies were most often used by men as away of expressing their political opinions and desires, women could and did use them to express their own views. Strange behavior was equally suspect in men and women; men and women both were investigated, charged, and convicted for conjuring and impersonation and even for burying the bodies of loved ones or talking about pilgrimages.

While I also assumed that all cases of political protest and resistance would be dealt with summarily and harshly, such, after all, seems not to have been the case. Even after the disaster of Elizabeth Barton, most women were not executed for what had become capital offenses. They were investigated rigorously, but the cases that resulted in execution were clustered around the time of the Pilgrimage of Grace.[6] Whether those executed for treason during the traumatic years of 1536 and 1537 were punished for *real* acts of treason, as defined by law, is less clear—though a pragmatic view of their executions would suggest that their deterrent effect would have been just as valuable as the immediate effect of removing a very few guilty traitors.

Yet, even after I was forced to abandon my assumptions, I found I could not draw easy conclusions about the women who became involved in political protest and resistance. Or no easy conclusions but one: that women, many women, did engage in politically oriented comment, action, and reaction.

In early-sixteenth-century England women did not exercise formal political power. They did not sit in Parliament, hold office, act as justices, or head armies. Yet the sixteenth century was a period when women increasingly came to participate in political comment and protest throughout western Europe, and a number of recent works have begun to examine the significance of their activities. Historians have begun to reassess the ways in which women such as Katherine of Aragon, Anne Boleyn, and Catherine Parr participated in Tudor political and religious change, while, more recently, feminist historians have begun to assess the range of political activity by women of the nobility.

Such reexaminations have been made possible, at least in part, because historians have begun to expand their notions of political power to include what can be called "informal political power." This expansion has depended on are definition of the very notion of power itself. "Authority," or "power which is formally recognized and legitimated," has been separated from the concept of "power," which is "the ability to shape political events." Such a distinction has allowed for a reexamination of the roles of women in early sixteenth-century politics.[7] Even women like Katherine of Aragon and Anne Boleyn did not have authority, but even women like Margaret Cheyne and Elizabeth Barton could have power.

Trained in literature, I approached the task I set for myself here as a search for stories that were ignored or overlooked rather than as an attempt to calculate numbers or formulate statistical data.[8] I approached the documents I found with some reservation, aware that the representations of women's words and actions were transmitted solely through the eyes and the pens of others. The women investigated for their "dangerous talk and strange behavior" do not speak directly to us: their stories came to us filtered through the reports of fearful or malicious neighbors, through cautious letters of inquiry from anxious or frustrated investigators, through the official examinations recorded by the secretaries and notaries of the Crown. Under these circumstances, what kinds of stories would I find?

But I found that, despite the circumstances, the voices of other women have not been silenced. Women were present everywhere—in small towns, in the capital, in the midst of rebellion, and as part of conspiracies. And they were speaking out loud—to one another, to anyone who would listen, to the men who recorded their testimony. The documents that survive let us see where they were, who they were with, and what it was that incited their response.

To overlook these women and their stories is to deny their place in the popular reaction to the Tudor political reforms of the 1530s. At stake were not only problems of succession and of religious reformation but also much more fundamental problems of order and obedience. At issue were questions of authority, of legitimate power and its exercise, and of the right, or duty, of resistance to power used or abused.[9]

Women such as Margaret Cheyne, Elizabeth Barton, Elizabeth Wood, Mabel Brigge, and all the others whose stories we have heard may have been speaking sedition, or they may have been hapless victims tangled in a web of suspicion. But they played their part in reaction and resistance to royal power and in the negotiations undertaken to settle the confrontation. Their stories, their presence, and their voices, must be included in the narrative of the period.

NOTES

Introduction

1. Eric W. Ives, *Anne Boleyn* (Oxford, 1986); and Retha Warnicke, *The Rise and Fall of Anne Boleyn: Family Politics at the Court of Henry VIII* (Cambridge, 1989).
2. Barbara J. Harris, "Women and Politics in Early Tudor England," *The Historical Journal* 33 (1990), 359-60.

Chapter 1

1. Margaret Cheyne's story, which follows, can be pieced together by following documents now found in the state papers of Henry VIII (abstracted in *Letters and Papers, Foreign and Domestic, of the Reign of Henry VIII,* ed. J. S. Brewer et al., 21 vols. and *Addenda* [London, 1862-1932]; hereafter referred to as *LP)* and by supplementing these documents with contemporary London chronicles.

   Although her execution has been noted briefly by a number of historians, no account of her case has been the focus of any extended analysis. For a review of the comments on her fate by historians of Tudor England, see chapter 2.

   On the punishment meted out to those convicted of treason, see John Bellamy, *The Tudor Law of Treason: An Introduction* (London, 1979), especially chapter 5 ("To the Gallows and After"). The sentence read out to men convicted of treason is quoted by J. H. Baker, "Criminal Courts and Procedure at Common Law, 1550-1800," in *Crime in England, 1550-1800,* ed. James S. Cockburn (Princeton, NJ, 1977):

   > You are to be drawn upon a hurdle to the place of execution, and there you are to be hanged by the neck, and being alive cut down, and your privy-members to be cut off, and your bowels to be taken out of your belly and there burned, you being alive; and your head to be cut off, and your body to be divided into four quarters, and that your head and quarters be disposed of where his majesty shall think fit.

About the sentence for women convicted of treason, Baker continues, "By this horrific standard only, the judgment for women in high and petty treason was more favourable: 'to be burned with fire until you are dead'" (42). Although some degree of mercy might have motivated the kind of punishment meted out to women, Frances E. Dolan suggests a different reason for the form of women's punishment:

> Although nonnoble women could be whipped or hanged . . . no women of any class were ever disemboweled and quartered, or hanged in chains. . . . Explaining why women convicted of petty or high treason were burned at the stake, Sir Matthew Hale declares that "the other judgment"—that is, the severing and burning of the genitals, disemboweling, beheading, and quartering to which male traitors were subjected—"is *unseemly* for that sex." (Hale, *Historia Placitorum Coronae: The History of the Pleas of the Crown* [London, 1736]; qtd. in Dolan, "'Gentlemen, I have one thing more to say': Women on Scaffolds in England, 1563-1680," *Modern Philology*, 92 [1994], 166)

Dolan continues:

> I assume that Hale's concern is directed more at the executioners and spectators than the condemned. Understood as men's property, women's bodies played important roles in defining and securing masculine power, perpetuating gene-alogy, and transmitting inheritance; thus to open and display them on the scaffold would undermine masculine authority and privilege. The executioner would appear as a brutal rapist, the spectators as sadistic voyeurs. (166-67)

On the "modesty" and "public decency" of burning at the stake, see also Camille Naish, *Death Comes to the Maiden: Sex and Execution,* 1431-1933 (New York, 1991), chapter 1 ("Burials and Burnings: Modesty, Chivalry and Heresy"), esp. 8-9. A straightforward description of this "frightful" method of execution is on 22-23. Naish's second chapter, "Beheading: Nobility, Martyrdom, Matri-mony," discusses Anne Boleyn's execution at some length (42-50), with addi-tional comments on the beheading of Henry's fifth wife, Catherine Howard (50-52).

About the execution by burning of women convicted of treason, Bellamy writes:

> In theory the proper death for a female traitor was to be drawn to the place for execution and burned. The sentences passed on Anne Boleyn and Lady Jane Grey were that they should be burned, or beheaded, according to the prince's

pleasure, although eventually it was the latter which was decided on. There may not, in fact, in the period under review have been a single instance when a woman was burned for high treason. (207)

Although he mentions Margaret Cheyne once in his work (139), Bellamy must have missed her sentence and execution by burning for the crime of treason.

2. William D. Hamilton, ed., *A Chronicle of England during the Reigns of the Tudors, from A.D. 1485 to 1559, by Charles Wriothesley, Windsor Herald* (London, 1875), 1:63-64. Wriothesley's entry for 25 May 1537 reads:

> And, the 25 daye of Maye, beinge the Frydaye in Whytsonweke, Sir John Bolner, Sir Stephen Hamerton, knightes, were hanged and heddyd, Nicholas Tempeste, esquier, Docter Cokerell, preiste, Abbott condam [for quondam] of Fountens, and Docter Pykeringe, fryer, ware drawen from the Towre of London to Tyburne, and ther hanged, boweld, and quartered, and their hedes sett [on] London Bridge and diverse gates in London. (63-64)

On the sentences and executions of men convicted of high treason, see Bellamy, *Tudor Law of Treason;* and Baker, "Criminal Courts and Procedure." Another excellent source on treason law and cases of treason under Cromwell is G. R. Elton, *Policy and Policy: The Enforcement of the Reformation in the Age of Thomas Cromwell* (Cambridge, 1975), especially chapters 6 ("The Law of Treason"), 7 ("Treason Trials"), and 9 ("Victims and Victors").

3. Any discussion of the northern rebellions must start with the comprehensive work of Madeleine Hope Dodds and Ruth Dodds, *The Pilgrimage of Grace, 1536-1537, and the Exeter Conspiracy, 1538,* 2 vols. (Cambridge, 1915). In their precise and extensive chronicle of events they include a wealth of detail about all aspects of the rebellions.

Excellent summaries of events may be found in J. J. Scarisbrick, *Henry VIII* (Berkeley, CA, 1968), 338-46; G. R. Elton, *The New History of England,* vol. 2: *Reform and Reformation, England, 1509-1558* (London, 1977), 260-72; and John Guy, *Tudor England* (1988; rpt., Oxford, 1990), 149-53, who clarifies the overlapping risings as "three self-contained rebellions": the Lincolnshire rising, over by 18 October, the Pilgrimage of Grace proper, which lasted until December 1536, and a series of new revolts in the East Riding and northwest counties in January and February of 1537 (149). A concise and useful chronology appears in the *Historical Dictionary of Tudor England, 1485-1603,* listed under "Pilgrimage of Grace (1536-1537)."

Historians have speculated a great deal about the specific causes of the risings, variously suggesting a "neo-feudal conspiracy," social and economic discontents, conservative religious opposition to the reforms of Henry VIII, and the efforts of a "defeated court faction" to consolidate a new power base. Among the many accounts, see especially: A. G. Dickens, "Secular and Religious Motivation in the Pilgrimage of Grace," *Studies in Church History*, 4 (1967), 39-64; M. E. James, "Obedience and Dissent in Henrician England: The Lincolnshire Rebellion, 1536," *Past and Present*, 48 (1970), 3-78 (rpt. in *Society, Politics and Culture: Studies in Early Modern England* [Cambridge, 1986], 188-269); R. B. Smith, "The West Riding in the Pilgrimage of Grace," in *Land and Politics in the England of Henry VIII: The West Riding of Yorkshire, 1530-46* (Oxford, 1970), 165-212; Margaret Bowker, "Lincolnshire 1536: Heresy, Schism or Religious Discontent?" *Studies in Church History*, 9 (1972), 195-212; C. S. L. Davies, "Popular Religion and the Pilgrimage of Grace," in *Order and Disorder in Early Modern England, 1500-1700*, ed. Anthony Fletcher and John Stevenson (Cambridge, 1975), 58-91; Christopher Haigh, "Militant Resistance: The Pilgrimage of Grace," *Reformation and Resistance in Tudor Lancashire* (Cambridge, 1975), 118-38; G. R. Elton, "Politics and the Pilgrimage of Grace," in *After the Reformation: Essays in Honor of J. H. Hexter*, ed. Barbara Malament (Philadelphia, 1980), 20-56 (rpt. in *Studies in Tudor and Stuart Government* [Cambridge, 1983], 3:183-215); Scott M. Harrison, *The Pilgrimage of Grace in the Lake Counties, 1536-37* (London, 1981); C. S. L. Davies, "The Pilgrimage of Grace Reconsidered," in *Rebellion, Popular Protest and the Social Order in Early Modern England*, ed. Paul Slack (Cambridge, 1984), 16-38.

4.   The most readily accessible source for Bulmer's family history is the *International Genealogical Index, British Isles* (Church of Jesus Christ of the Latter Day Saints), hereafter referred to as *IGI*. I appreciate very much the help I received with this source from the volunteer staff of the Family History Center in Tacoma, Washington.

For additional important detail about Bulmer's family connections, see "The Petigre of Syr Willyam Bullmer, Knyght," in *Heraldic Visitation of the Northern Counties in 1530, by Thomas Tonge, Norroy King of Arms*, ed. W. H. D. Longstaffe (Durham, 1863), 25-26; "Pedigree of Bulmer of Wilton, Brancepeth, &c," in *The History and Antiquities of Cleveland, Comprising the Wapentake of East and West Langbargh, North Riding, County York*, ed. John Walker Ord (London, 1846), 385-86 (Ord's pedigree for the Bulmer family begins with Henry de Bulmer, living in 1066); and "Bulmer, of Wilton and Pinchinthorpe," in *The Visitation of Yorkshire, made in the Years 1584/85*, by Robert Glover, Somerset Herald . . . , ed. Joseph Foster (London, 1875), 193.

Even using such genealogies, it is sometimes difficult to know the relationships between branches of families. I have also relied on Dodds and Dodds,

Pilgrimage of Grace (vol. 1, chap. 3, "Affinity and Confederacy"), for details about Bulmer's relationships with various northern families.

5. It is certain that Edward Stafford, duke of Buckingham, had at least one illegitimate daughter. In 1520, for example, he was in the process of contracting a marriage for his "bastard daughter"; see note 7. Ord's "Pedigree of Bulmer" identifies Margaret as the duke of Buckingham's illegitimate daughter, an identification later accepted by Gerald Brenan and Edward Phillips Stratham in *The House of Howard* (London, 1907), 218 n. 3. The *IGI* also identifies Edward Stafford as Margaret's father and lists her among his children as "Margaret Stafford." The pedigree in Foster, however, is unique in naming Margaret as the daughter of Henry Stafford (not further identified by Foster), most likely Edward Stafford's brother Henry, earl of Wiltshire from 1509 to 1523. (Foster surely could not mean Henry Stafford, second duke of Buckingham [Edward Stafford's father], who died in 1483, or Henry Stafford [Edward Stafford's son], born in 1501, nor the Henry Stafford born about 1513 who is identified as Margaret's [also illegitimate] brother.)

    No name is cited in any contemporary source for the woman who was the mother of Stafford's illegitimate daughter (the *IGI* identifies the mother of "Margaret Stafford" simply as "Mrs. Edward Stafford"). Barbara J. Harris, *Edward Stafford, Third Duke of Buckingham, 1478-1521* (Stanford, CA 1986), suggests that Margaret Geddynge, a gentlewoman and member of Buckingham's household from as early as 1499, may have had a long-standing sexual involvement with Stafford (46-47). It is tempting to conclude she was Margaret Cheyne's mother.

6. For William Bulmer's allegiance to Buckingham—and Henry VIII's anger and suspicion—see Harris, *Edward Stafford,* 167-68, 180-86.

7. Details about Margaret's marriage to William Cheyne, such as when it might have taken place, are not known, nor is any information about the identity of William Cheyne himself certain. The *IGI* indicates only that Margaret was married first to William Cheyne, who had been born in 1509; no date is suggested for this first marriage. The King's Bench indictment against Margaret Cheyne, meanwhile, identified William Cheyne as "late of London, esquire," suggesting not only that he was dead and that he had been a resident of London but also that he was a gentleman. A "William Cheyney" does figure at least once in the state papers; in November 1510 the king granted custody of two London tenements to one William Cheyne for twelve years; if Margaret's husband was born in 1509, the William Cheyne named in the 1510 grant was probably not the William Cheyne she married but might have been a relative, even a father. The *IGI* and the *Dictionary of National Biography (DNB)* list several William Cheynes old enough to have been this London man as well as numerous William

Cheynes from the fifteenth century. A William Cheyne was recorder of London in the fourteenth century, for example (see Helena M. Chew and William Kellaway, *London Assize of Nuisance, 1301-1431* [London, 1973], 158-63).

Edward Stafford's marital arrangements for his "bastard daughter" had involved the purchase of the wardship and marriage of Thomas Fitzgerald (British Library MS Cotton Titus B.i, fol. 182, abstracted in *LP* III.1, 1070; and *LP* III.1, 1285), an arrangement still pending in 1521 at the time Buckingham was attainted for treason and executed. Thomas Fitzgerald was the son of Gerald Fitzgerald, earl of Kildare. If the illegitimate daughter for whom he had been intending this match were indeed Margaret (she would have been around ten or eleven in 1521), Stafford's disgrace and execution must have nullified this match. On Buckingham's relationship with Thomas Fitzgerald, see also Helen Miller, *Henry VIII and the English Nobility* (New York, 1986), 47.

Margaret's marriage to William Cheyne would thus have occurred at some time after Buckingham's execution in 1521. (Since Margaret was born about 1511 *[IGI]*, a later date is more reasonable though not necessary. Sir John Bulmer and his first wife, Anne Bigod, had been married when they were young; by 1530, when Sir John himself was only about forty years old, five of the six children of this first marriage, born between 1510 and 1518, were already married. Sir John's brother William was known to have married when both he and his wife Elizabeth were about eleven years old.)

8. The pedigrees disagree on the legitimacy of the daughters born to Sir John Bulmer and Margaret. Ord notes that three daughters, "Anne," "Maria," and "Francisca," were born "ante nupt" (386). Foster's pedigree records Frances and "Maria" as "natus ante matrimonium," while Anne was "nata post matrimonium" (193).

Foster's pedigree is supported by the information in the *IGI*, which records Martha (not Mary) born about 1531 in Wilton and Frances born about 1533. Anne Bulmer's birth is dated about 1535.

9. No dates for Margaret Cheyne and John Bulmer's marriage are included in Ord or Foster, but the *IGI* notes the date as about 1534 and indicates that they were married at Wilton. Dodds and Dodds indicate that Sir John and Margaret had married by 1536 (*Pilgrimage of Grace*, 1:39).

Evers's letter is abstracted in *LP* XII.1, 66.

10. Sir William Bulmer's letter is found in *LP* XII.1, 236.

Although not including a date, Ord's "Pedigree of Bulmer" does indicate Sir John had married Margaret as his second wife and records the birth of their son John as legitimate as well.

11. *LP* XII.1, 6. This document has been transcribed in full by Mary Bateson, "The Pilgrimage of Grace," *EHR*, 5 (1890), 330-43; according to the statement made by Robert Aske,

there was a certan nombre of bothe partes appoynted to enter, comyn togeder at Doncastre brig, whereof, of the north was appoynted the Lord Latymer, the Lord Lumley, the Lord Darcy, Sir Robert Constable, the said Sir Thomas Hilton, Sir Ralf Ellerker, Sir John Bulmer, Robert Bowes, Robert Chaloner, and other certayn knightes. (337)

Specific details about Bulmer's activities during the rebellions are found throughout the two-volume narrative of Dodds and Dodds, *Pilgrimage of Grace*.

12. *LP* XI, 1135(2). The state papers also preserve a letter from the prior to Sir John, dated 13 December, informing him that "several of the brethren are using themselves very unreliously to the great inquietation of him and other brethren" and asking Sir John's help in dealing with them (*LP* XI, 1295).

13. *LP* XII.1, 1184.

14. *LP* XII.1, 1408.

15. All original documents are cited by their state papers designation and followed by their *LP* reference: SP 1/119, fols. 63-64 (*LP* XII.1, 1083). The transcriptions are my own.

16. SP 1/119, fols. 65-69 (*LP* XII.1, 1084). Lord John Lumley's son and heir, George Lumley, had been arrested in January for his part in Bigod's rising. In March, then, when Bulmer and Lumley were contemplating further rebellion, George Lumley was being held in the Tower "with very little hope of obtaining mercy from the King," according to Dodds and Dodds (*Pilgrimage of Grace*, 2:159). Although Bulmer and George Lumley would die for their part in rebellion, Lord John Lumley was not arrested. According to Dodds and Dodds:

> The simplicity of George Lumley's conduct might have pleaded for him in more favourable circumstances, but where there was little hope of justice there was none at all of mercy. The King had a particular reason for his death. It had seemingly been decided that the government dared not attempt to arrest Lord Lumley, but he could be made to suffer for his offences through his son. (2:199)

17. On the procedures of investigation into charges of treason, see Bellamy, *Tudor Law of Treason*, chap. 3 ("Apprehension, Examination, and Indictment"), and chap. 4 ("Trial"). Very helpful information on the procedures of accusation and trial is also to be found in John Bellamy, *Crime and Public Order in England in the Later Middle Ages* (Toronto, 1973), especially chapter 5 ("Accusation and Trial"); and Michael R. Weisser, *Crime and Punishment in Early Modern Europe* (Atlantic Highlands, NJ 1979).

An excellent survey of methods of prosecution, modes of trial, criminal jurisdiction, and felony trials, though for a slightly later period, is Baker,

"Criminal Courts and Procedure," 15-48. Baker includes many references to the earlier sixteenth century.

18. SP 1/118, fols. 84-85 (*LP* XII.1, 870).

19. SP 1/118, fols. 127-28 (*LP* XII.1, 902).

20. SP 1/118, fols. 152-54 (*LP* XII.1, 918).

21. SP 1/121, fols. 209-34 (*LP* XII.2, 181); printed by Henry Ellis, "An Account of the Charges of Certain Prisoner in the Tower," *Archaeologia,* 18 (1817), 294-97.

22. *LP* XII.1, 1142.

23. SP 1/119, fols. 63-64 (*LP* XII.1, 1083).

24. A Herefordshire man had used the same words in December 1536, when he said "it is an old saying that two dogs striveth for a bone and the third dog shall come and take the bone away." He explained that by this he had meant that "the northern men and the Scots were the two dogs and the king the third dog" (SP 1/112, fol. 257; qtd. in *LP* XI, 1328).

25. For all of the following, see SP 1/119, fols. 65-69 (*LP* XII.1, 1084). Watts clearly feared he himself could be charged with misprision of treason. According to Bellamy: "It was the duty of everyone to report suspected treason. Not to do so had itself been declared treasonous at least as early as the thirteenth century" (*Tudor Law of Treason,* 83).

26. SP 1/119, fol. 70 (*LP* XII.1, 1085).

27. On the process of pretrial examination, see Bellamy, *Tudor Law of Treason,* 104-9. For an example of what such interrogatories would have been like, see the questions drawn up for an examination of Sir Geoffrey Pole in 1538 (*LP* XIII.2, 695[3]).

28. Sir John's is the first in a long series of abstracts of depositions taken from the northern rebels: SP 1/119, fols. 73-87 (*LP* XII.1, 1087). Sir John's statement occupies folio 73. These documents are terribly mutilated and heavily emended in *LP.*

29. SP 1/119, fol. 74 (*LP* XII.1, 1087). On the "crafting of a narrative" in documentary evidence, see Natalie Zeamon Davis, *Fiction in the Archives: Pardon Tales and their Tellers in Sixteenth-Century France* (Stanford, CA 1987). In exploring the multiple authorship of letters of pardon and remission, Davis notes that each such document had "at least two persons, and often more, involved in its composition": the "notaries or secretaries," the "clerks that did much of the actual writing," and, of course, the "first author of the story . . . the supplicant" (15-18). In chapter 3, "Bloodshed and the Woman's Voice," Davis focuses specifically on how women's pardon stories were shaped by those who recorded them as well as those who dictated them.

Davis's concept of "multiple authorship" is significant for our purposes here, since the documents I include in this study also involve several voices in addition to that of the woman being examined: the women's stories are always mediated by men, the examiners and secretaries who record them, for example. Unlike her husband, Sir John Bulmer, who had the opportunity of writing his own story with his own hand, Margaret Cheyne could only respond to questions asked of her, her responses then transmitted by the notary John ap Rhys.

30. SP 1/119, fol. 75 (*LP* XII.1, 1087). *LP* attributes the second statement in the series of depositions to Sir John Bulmer, emending the abstract headed "Sir Joh" to "Sir Joh[n Bulmer]; clearly this evidence represents a statement by Sir John Watts, however, and not a second statement by Sir John Bulmer.

31. The chaplain's deposition has been combined in the state papers record with that of Margaret Cheyne; whoever has transcribed the document in *LP* has failed to include a note indicating the statement was taken from Sir William Stainous. This omission may be due to the badly damaged state of the original state paper document.

32. *LP* XII.1, 1207. On the drawing of indictments, see Bellamy, *Tudor Law of Treason,* 125-29.

33. KB 8/10/3 (*LP* XII.1, 1227). Nicholas Tempest, esquire, James Cockerell, the former prior of Guisborough, William Thirsk, the former abbot of Fountains Abbey, and John Pickering, of Bridlington—all executed at Tyburn with Sir John Bulmer—were tried on the same day, along with William Wood, the prior of Bridlington, Adam Sedbar, the abbot of Jervaux, and John Pickering, of Lythe, a priest, who seems to have been arrested and convicted solely because he was Sir Francis Bigod's chaplain.

34. In addition to the executions noted at the outset of this chapter, Sir Thomas Percy, Sir Francis Bigod, George Lumley, and two monks—Adam Sedbar, abbot of Jervaux, and William Wood, prior of Bridlington—were executed at Tyburn on 2 June. Lord Thomas Darcy was beheaded on Tower Hill the same day. Lord John Hussey remained in the Tower; the king wanted him to be executed in Lincoln. Sir Robert Constable and Robert Aske also remained in the Tower; on 12 June Henry decided that Constable should be hanged at Hull in chains until he died and that Aske should suffer the same fate at York. All three condemned men left the Tower on 28 June in the custody of Sir Thomas Wentworth. According to Dodds and Dodds (*Pilgrimage of Grace,* 2:220), at Huntingdon they were handed over by Wentworth to Sir William Parr. Parr took them to Lincoln, where Hussey was put in the charge of Charles Brandon, the duke of Suffolk. Parr continued on with Constable and Aske to Hull, where the two condemned men were handed over to Norfolk. The exact date of Hussey's execution is not recorded. Constable's execution took place on 6 July at Beverly Gate in Hull; Aske died on 12 July in York on Clifford Tower.

35. Most of the works listed in note 3 address in some way the relative guilt or innocence of those charged (as well as suggesting something of their varying

motives for rebellion), and their authors have speculated to some extent about others involved in the rebellions who were not charged. The most extensive treatment is Dodds and Dodds (*Pilgrimage of Grace,* 2:183-213), the later works providing important new assessments and valuable reinterpretations. The detail in Dodds and Dodds, nevertheless, remains unsurpassed.

36.   On hearsay evidence, see Bellamy, *Tudor Law of Treason,* 157-58; and Baker, "Criminal Courts and Procedure," 39.

37.   On the procedures of treason trials, see Bellamy, *Tudor Law of Treason,* 132-81. A description of the offering of evidence is on 147-51; especially important was the introduction of examinations and confessions at the trial. Bellamy claims that no witnesses were needed at treason trials (152-60), only the written examinations and other evidence; Elton, however, indicates that at least one witness was required, though he notes that "it would seem as a rule the government did not like to proceed on so slender a basis" (308). See also the entry "Common Law" in *Historical Dictionary of Tudor England;* and Baker, "Criminal Courts and Procedure."

38.   25 Henry VIII, c. 22; 26 Henry VIII, c. 13; 28 Henry, c. 7.

39.   For the 1352 act (25 Edward III, st. 5, c. 2; A. Luders et al., eds., *Statutes of the Realm* [London, 1810-24], 1:319), see S. B. Chrimes and A. L. Brown, *Select Documents of English Constitutional History,* 1307-1485 (London, 1961), 76.

   The 1534 Succession Act first defined *writing or deed* as treason, and *word* to be misprision; treason by word was added in the 1534 Treason Act. See Isobel D. Thornley, "Treason by Words in the Fifteenth Century," *EHR,* 32 (1917), 556-61; G. R. Elton, "The Law of Treason in the Early Reformation," *The Historical Journal,* 11 (1968), 211-36; and, for an extended analysis of the evolution of the treasons acts in the 1530s, Elton, *Policy and Police,* 265-78, 285-92; and Bellamy, *Tudor Law of Treason.*

40.   The 1534 Treason Act reads:

> yf any person or personnes . . . do malicyously wyshe will or desyre by wordes or writinge, or by crafte ymagen invente practyse or attempte, any bodely harme to be donne or commytted to the Kynges moste royall personne, the Quenes, or their heires apparaunt, or to depryve theym or any of theym of the dignite title or name of their royall estates, or sclaunderouysly & malyciously publishe & pronounce, by expresse writinge or wordes, that the Kynge oure Soverayn Lorde shulde be heretyke, scismatike, Tiraunt ynfidell or Usurper of the Crowne . . . then everie suche parsonne and personnes so offendinge . . . theyr aydours counsaylours consentours and abettoures, beynge thereof lawfully convicte accordinge to the Lawes and Customes of this Realme, shalbe adjuged traytours. . . . (26 Henry VIII, c. 13; *Statutes of the Realm,* 3:508)

41. Women's roles in the private sphere, the home, are often distinguished from men's roles in public life. But a useful analysis of "the fluid boundaries between the domestic and political spheres" during the sixteenth century is found in Frances E. Dolan, *Dangerous Familiars: Representations of Domestic Crime in England, 1550-1700* (Ithaca, NY, 1994), especially chapters 1-3.

42. Although those accused of treason did not usually have the help of legal counsel at their trial (Bellamy, *Tudor Law of Treason,* 142; Baker, "Criminal Courts and Procedure," 36-37), they could often challenge the prosecution, and were sometimes successful in their objections (Bellamy, *Tudor Law of Treason,* 150-52, 158-62). For only one contemporary example, see the account of Lord Dacre's trial for treason in Thomas B. Howell, *A Complete Collection of State Trials and Proceedings for High Treason . . .* (London, 1816), 1:407-8.

     It wasn't only someone of Lord Dacre's status who could use legal technicalities when accused of a crime; Elton writes, "a good many of those known to have used legal technicalities to escape the consequences of their deeds were insignificant and poor" ("Crime and the Historian," intro., *Crime in England,* 11).

Chapter 2

1. Roger Bigelow Merriman, *Life and Letters of Thomas Cromwell* (1902; rpt., Oxford, 1968), vol. 2, letter 189 (also in *Letters and Papers, Foreign and Domestic, of the Reign of Henry VIII,* ed. J. S. Brewer et al., 21 vols. and *Addenda* [London, 1862-1932], XII.1, 1272; hereafter referred to as *LP*).

2. British Library MS Harley 282, fol. 203 (*LP* XII.2, 41).

3. BL MS Harley 282, fol. 205 (*LP* XII.2, 228).

4. SP 1/123, fols. 120-23 (*LP,* XII.2, 357).

5. *Chronicle of the Grey Friars of London,* ed. John G. Nichols (London, 1852), 40-41. The Franciscan house was near Newgate.

     About the compiler of the *Chronicle of the Grey Friars,* Nichols writes:

     > It is towards the end of the reign of Henry the Eighth that this chronicle begins to have a character of its own. The writer had a watchful regard to the religious changes of the times, and he naturally recorded those in particular which occurred within the sphere of his personal observation, in the city of London. . . . He appears to have retained possession of the book after the dissolution of the house of the Grey Friars. . . . It is therefore not to the Grey Friars as a body,

or to the attention and accuracy of their successive registrars, that we have to attribute the chief historical value that exists in the following pages; but rather to the individual merit of him whom we may fairly regard as the last of the London Franciscans. (ix-x)

6.   Edward Hall, *The Triumphant Reigne of Kyng Henry the VIII . . .* , ed. Charles Whibley, 2 vols. (London, 1904), 2:279. Hall was born about 1498 or 1499 and died in 1547. In addition to his career as a lawyer, Hall was a member of Parliament (by 1542) and, interestingly, a witness to the confession of Anne Askew (20 March 1544). His chronicle, first printed in 1542, begins with the accession of Henry IV and concludes with the death of Henry VIII *(Dictionary of National Biography;* hereafter referred to as *DNB).*

7.   William D. Hamilton, ed., *A Chronicle of England during the Reigns of the Tudors, from A.D. 1485 to 1559, by Charles Wriothesley, Windsor Herald* (London [Camden Society], 1875), 1:64. Wriothesley's entry for 25 May 1537 reads: "And the same daye Margaret Cheyney, other wife to Bolmer called, was drawen after them from the Tower of London into Smythfyld, and there brent, according to hir judgment, God pardon her sowle, being the Frydaye in Whytson weeke; she was a very fayre creature and a bewtyfull."

Wriothesley was probably born in 1508 and died in 1562. His cousin was Thomas Wriothesley, first earl of Southampton *(DNB).* His chronicle contains many eyewitness accounts of important events during the 1530s, the trial of Anne Boleyn to name only one. Wriothesley seems to take particular note of all executions taking place in London, those of convicted heretics and criminals as well as those of traitors. He also records with some relish other bloody occurrences: "This year [1540], the ninth day of April, being Friday, one Turk's wife, a fishmonger dwelling at the Red Lion against Saint Magnus Church, slew herself with a knife" (1:114-15); "This year [1541], the 21 of December, a shoemaker's wife of St. Martin's parish beside St. Anthony's, rode about the city with a paper on her head which feigned herself to labor with child, and had flayed a cat and conveyed it privily on her body, and said it was her child, which cat was hanged on her body before her breast as she rode, and 2 quick cats also" (1:132); and "This year [1542], the 17th of March, was boiled in Smithfield one Margaret Davie, a maiden, which had poisoned 3 households that she dwelled in, one being her master's, which died of the same; and one Darington and his wife, which also she dwelled with in Coleman Street, which died of the same; and also one Tinley's wife, which died also of the same" (1:134-35).

The "London Chronicle in the Times of King Henry VII and King Henry VIII," ed. Clarence Hopper, in *Camden Miscellany IV* (London, 1859) also briefly mentions Margaret Cheyne's execution (11); no mention of Margaret Cheyne is made in the accounts of the Pilgrimage of Grace and the executions that followed in "A London Chronicle, 1523-1555," ed. Charles C. Kingsford, in *Camden Miscellany XII* (London, 1910), 13-14; "Chronicle of the Years 1532-1537, Written by a Monk of St. Augustine's Canterbury," ed. John G. Nichols in *Narratives of the Days of the Reformation* (London, 1859), 284-85; or *Chronicle of King Henry VIII of England . . . Written in Spanish,* ed. Martin A. S. Hume (London, 1889), 33-36. In his compilation of London chronicles John Stowe notes the rebellion and the execution of those convicted of treason, including a reference to "Margaret Cheyney otherwise Ladye Boylmer" (*A Summarie of the Chronicles . . . 1575* (London, 1575 [STC 23325]), 440.

8. James A. Froude, *History of England from the Fall of Wolsey to the Defeat of the Spanish Armada,* 12 vols. (London, 1893), 3:35. Froude also concluded, "the world went its light way, thinking no more of Lady Bulmer than if she had been a mere Protestant heretic." (Burning at the stake was the penalty for all those—men and women—convicted of heresy, while, as we have seen, it was the legal penalty for women convicted of treason but not the penalty usually exacted.) Despite Froude's assertions, reports in the state papers as well as contemporary chronicle accounts indicate that "the world" knew quite well that Margaret Cheyne had been burned at the stake for treason, not for heresy.

9. A. F. Pollard, *Henry VIII* (London, 1902); J. D. Mackie, *The Oxford History of England,* vol. 7: *The Earlier Tudors, 1485-1558* (Oxford, 1952), 392; G. R. Elton, *New History of England,* vol. 2: *Reform and Reformation: England 1509-1558* (London, 1977), 262; John Guy, *Tudor England* (Oxford, 1986), 151.

10. Madeleine Hope Dodds and Ruth Dodds, *The Pilgrimage of Grace, 1536-1537, and the Exeter Conspiracy, 1538,* 2 vols. (Cambridge, 1915), 2:215-16.

11. On the dangers of disorderly women and of the increasing legal subjection of wives to their husbands "as a guarantee of the obedience of both men and women to the . . . centralizing state," see Natalie Zemon Davis, "Women on Top," *Society and Culture in Early Modern France: Eight Essays* (Stanford, CA, 1975), 124-151, 310-15 nn. Davis also considers the legal status of a woman in regard to crime. Because of her nature, she was "not responsible for her actions; her husband was responsible, for she was subject to him": "In England, in most felonious acts by a married woman to which her husband could be shown to be privy or at which he was present, the wife could not be held entirely culpable. If indicted, she might be acquitted or receive a lesser sentence than he for the same crime" (146).

On the legal status of wives, see also the very insightful summary in Frances E. Dolan, *Dangerous Familiars: Representations of Domestic Crime in England, 1550-1700* (Ithaca, NY, 1994), especially 26-31. See also John K. Yost, "The Value of Married Life for the Social Order in the Early English Renaissance," *Societas: A Review of Social History,* 6 (1976), 25-39.

12. In addition to the analysis found in the sources cited in chapter 1 (nn. 3, 35), see, for example, David D. Knowles, *The Religious Orders in England* (Cambridge, 1961), 3:333-35, for his views on the guilt of those executed.

13. Many recent studies explore the theatricality of public executions and the display of power and authority represented on the scaffold; see, as a foundational work, Michel Foucault, *Discipline and Punish: The Birth of the Prison,* trans. Alan Sheridan (New York, 1977). Among those who have extended the "history of repression" is Pieter Spierenburg, who "attempts to construct a 'counter-paradigm' to Foucault's" in *The Spectacle of Suffering, Executions and the Evolution of Repression: From a Preindustrial Metropolis to the European Experience* (Cambridge, 1984); especially useful are his chapters on "The Stagers: the Authorities and the Dramatization of Executions" and "The Watchers: Spectators at the Scaffold." See also Douglas Hay, "Property, Authority and the Criminal Law," in *Albion's Fatal Tree: Crime and Society in Eighteenth-Century England,* ed. Peter L. Hay et al. (New York, 1975), 17-64; Randall McGowen, "The Body and Punishment," *Journal of Modern History,* 59 (1987), 651-66; and Thomas W. Laqueur, "Crowds, Carnival and the State in English Executions, 1604-1868," in *The First Modern Society: Essays in English History in Honour of Lawrence Stone,* ed. A. L. Beier et al. (Cambridge, 1989), 305-55.

Focusing on the issues of gender and execution are Camille Naish, *Death Comes to the Maiden: Sex and Execution, 1431-1933* (New York, 1991); and E. J. Burford and Sandra Shulman, *Of Bridles and Burnings: The Punishment of Women* (New York, 1992). In *Witchcraze: A New History of the European Witch Hunts* (San Francisco, CA, 1994), Anne Llewellyn Barstow makes clear both the particular violence and the powerful symbolic value of death by burning at the stake:

> The ultimate form of torture was to be burned alive, and the most horrifying symbol of some men's power over all women and over some other men was public execution at the stake.
>
> That this torture was carried out in the presence of large crowds often numbering in the thousands gave it a ritual meaning beyond that of simple punishment. As a public purging of evil, it declared that the land was rid of demonic enemies and that not a trace of their hated presence remained. Once the condemned had been reduced to ashes, those very ashes would be thrown to the wind or scattered over moving water. (143)

About the burning of witches, Barstow writes, "Strangely, little can be found in the trial records or eyewitness accounts about the culmination of the trials: the carrying out of the death sentence is seldom described, and almost never in detail" (149).

This silence about the actual executions in witchcraft documents contrasts with the very graphic descriptions of the burning executions of convicted heretics, which survive in great numbers, most obviously in John Foxe's *The Acts and Monuments of John Foxe,* ed. George Townsend, 8 vols. (1837-41; rpt., New York, 1965); see, for example, Foxe's description of the burning of the Marian martyrs, among them Latimer, Ridley, and Cranmer. But, Frances Dolan notes, while Foxe describes the burnings of men in sometimes gruesome detail, he is reticent on the deaths of female martyrs. Dolan suggests why: "the accounts of women's execution do not emphasize that spectacle but the moral self-assertion it could occasion" ("'Gentlemen, I have one thing more to say': Women on Scaffolds in England, 1563-1680," *Modern Philology,* 92 [1994], 168"). Her analysis of Foxe's account of Anne Askew's burning (and of the accounts of the public executions of several other women, both literary and criminal) suggests several reasons for the suppression of the suffering of the female body. On burning at the stake as a method of execution for women observing "due decency in the face of high treason," see also Naish's chapter "Burials and Burnings" in *Death Comes to the Maiden.*

14. *LP* XI, 688 (4).
15. *LP* XI, 560, 562.
16. Scott M. Harrison, *The Pilgrimage of Grace in the Lake Counties, 1537-38* (London, 1981), 96. Harrison concludes, "If one accepts an estimate for the total population of the region of approximately seventy thousand in 1536, the fact that over one-third of the inhabitants were active rebels indicates a high level of involvement."
17. *LP* XI, 970. Kendall was sent to the Tower. A bill for high treason against him, along with twelve other prisoners, was presented at the court of Lincoln of 5 March; on 26 March he was tried at the Guildhall and found guilty. He was executed at Tyburn on 29 March.
18. The letter is printed in *State Papers of the Reign of Henry VIII* (London, 1831), 1:498-505.
19. Wriothesley, *Chronicle of England,* 1:61. For a more detailed account of this rebellion, see chapter 6.

    Frances Dolan ("Women on Scaffolds") indicates that no women were hanged and quartered (166), but Wriothesley's account here, if it is accurate, suggests an exception. A second instance of hanging and quartering a woman, involving Margaret Tyrell, is discussed in chapter 5.
20. SP 1/112, fol. 38 (*LP* XI, 1195). On the treason of Sir Rhys ap Griffith, see chapter 4.
21. On the extent of Hussey's "guilt," see Dodds and Dodds, *Pilgrimage of Grace,* 1:21-22, 2:195-96.

22. I am quoting here from the abstract printed in *LP* XI, 10; the same document is also printed as *LP* VII, 1025. While the word *nought* could conceivably been intended to mean "nothing" (her words were unimportant), it's more likely that *nought* is to be understood in the sense I have suggested here, as "wicked" or "evil."

23. BL MS Cotton Otho C.x, fol. 254 (*LP* XI, 222).

24. SP 1/109, fols. 70-74 (*LP* XI, 852); and SP 1/110, fols. 151-55 (*LP* XI, 969).

25. *LP* XII.1, 1087.

26. E 36/119, fol. 82 (*LP* XII.1, 976); and E 36/119, fol. 83 (*LP* XII.1, 981).

27. For details of the Stapleton family, consult the Stapleton family pedigree in Joseph Foster, *Pedigrees of the County Families of Yorkshire* (London, 1874), vol. 1. Information on the Stapleton family is also in Dodds and Dodds, *Pilgrimage of Grace*, 1:57-58.

      As only one more indication of how interconnected these families were, not only was Christopher Stapleton's first wife a member of the Aske family; his son Brian married Margery, daughter of Sir John Constable of Halsham (Yorkshire).

28. For the entire deposition, see *LP* XII.1, 392. For the original of Elizabeth Stapleton's words, see E 36/118, fol. 74.

29. *LP* XII.1, 392.

30. SP 1/123, fols. 27-31 (*LP* XII.2, 291). On Norfolk's continuing investigations into the source of this letter, see also *LP* XII.2, 741, 850.

31. *LP* XII.2, 356.

32. *LP* XII.2, 733.

33. *LP* XII.2, 828.

34. This is from Chapuy's 1 July 1536 letter to the Emperor Charles V (*LP* XI, 7).

35. Dodds and Dodds, 2:215-16.

36. SP 1/129, fols. 136-37 (*LP* XIII.1, 365).

37. Gerald Brenan and Edward Phillips Stratham, *The House of Howard* (London, 1907) noted the execution of "the hapless Lady Bulmer," who "heard her character foully (and, as has since been shown, lyingly) attacked by the King's lawyers" (218 n. 3). Unfortunately, they provide no reference to indicate the source of their information that the attacks on her character were "lyingly" made.

38. For all of this, see Foster, *Visitation of Yorkshire*, 193; for the date of John Bulmer's death, see International Genealogical Index, British Isles *(IGI)*.

39. KB 8/10/2 (*LP* XII.1, 1227).

40. *LP* XII.2, 850.

41. *LP* XIII.1, 627.

42. Wriothesley, *Chronicle of England,* 1:63.

43. Details about Ralph Bulmer's restoration are found in Ord, 386. The pedigree in Foster (*Visitation of Yorkshire,* 193) confirms the restoration of Ralph Bulmer

but gives no date. No historians of the Pilgrimage of Grace have noted Ralph Bulmer's survival or his eventual regaining of his attainted father's property. Dodds and Dodds, in fact, indicate that his fate is unknown: "He [Ralph Bulmer] was still imprisoned there [in the Tower] in the following year and it is not certain when, if ever, he was released" (*Pilgrimage of Grace,* 2:202).

The *IGI* misidentifies Sir John Bulmer's eldest son as "John" but correctly indicates his marriage in 1531 to Ann Tempest and gives the date of 1558 for his death.

44. Even if Margaret were the daughter of Henry Stafford instead of Edward Stafford (see chap. 1), her Stafford connections would remain the same.

45. The second duke of Buckingham's political career is most familiar from Shakespeare's version *(Richard III).* After being declared a traitor by Richard, Buckingham was captured, beheaded, and his estates confiscated. (For an accessible summary, see *DNB.*)

46. *LP* III, 128. For the third duke's treason, see Harris, *Edward Stafford;* and Mortimer Levine, "The Fall of Edward, Duke of Buckingham," in *Tudor Men and Institutions: Studies in English Law and Government,* ed. Arthur J. Slavin (Baton Rouge, LA, 1972), 32-48.

Margaret Cheyne's connections to traitors are almost uncanny. If Buckingham had completed his arrangements for marrying his "bastard daughter" to his ward Thomas Fitzgerald, Margaret would have married the son of Gerald Fitzgerald, earl of Kildare, whose "treasonable negotiations" caused Henry to hold him in the Tower a number of times; he died there in 1534. Thomas Fitzgerald himself, meanwhile, was involved in rebellion in Ireland; he was executed for treason at Tyburn on 3 February 1537 (see *DNB*).

47. Harris, *Edward Stafford,* 167; and Levine, "Fall of Edward," 37.

48. On this, see Dodds and Dodds, *Pilgrimage of Grace,* 1:37-38; and Harris, *Edward Stafford,* 167-68, 180-86.

49. *LP* III, 1284.

50. Helen Miller, *Henry VIII and the English Nobility* (New York, 1986), 46-47.

51. See Barbara J. Harris, "Marriage Sixteenth-Century Style: Elizabeth Stafford and the Third Duke of Norfolk," *Journal of Social History,* 15 (1982), 371-82.

Many of Elizabeth Stafford's letters to the king and Cromwell are printed in *Letters of Royal and Illustrious Ladies of Great Britain, from the Commencement of the Twelfth Century to the Close of the Reign of Queen Mary,* ed. Mary Anne Everett Wood (London, 1846), vols. 2-3.

52. Miller, *Henry VIII and the English Nobility,* 47.

53. For details about Norfolk's actions against Margaret and Sir John, see chapter 1.

54. Harris, "Marriage," 375.

55. Ibid., 379.

56. Two recent articles have focused on the role of privileged women in Tudor politics: Barbara J. Harris, "Women and Politics in Early Tudor England," *The Historical Journal,* 33 (1990), 259-81; and Barbara A. Hanawalt, "Lady Honor Lisle's Networks of Influence," in *Women and Power in the Middle Ages,* ed. Mary Erler and Maryanne Kowaleski (Athens, GA, 1988), 188-212. For a less sanguine view of women's political roles, see Mortimer Levine, "The Place of Women in Tudor Government," in *Tudor Rule and Tudor Revolution: Essays for G. R. Elton from His American Friends,* ed. Delloyd J. Guth and John McKenna (Cambridge, MA, 1982), 109-23.

On women and Renaissance political theory, see Ian Maclean, *The Renaissance Notion of Woman: A Study in the Fortunes of Scholasticism and Medical Science in European Intellectual Life* (1980; rpt., Cambridge, 1988); Hanna Fenichel Pitkin, *Fortune Is a Woman: Gender and Politics in the Thought of Niccolò Machiavelli* (Berkeley, CA, 1984); and Constance Jordan, *Renaissance Feminism: Literary Texts and Political Models* (Ithaca, NY, 1990).

57. The refrain in Sir Thomas Wyatt's poem written on the occasion of Anne Boleyn's execution (K. Muir and P. Thomson, *Poems of Sir Thomas Wyatt* [Liverpool, 1969], 187).

Chapter 3

1. The many documents relating to Elizabeth Barton preserved in the state papers are all abstracted in *Letters and Papers, Foreign and Domestic, of the Reign of Henry VIII,* ed. J. S. Brewer et al., 21 vols. and *Addenda* (London, 1862-1932), hereafter referred to as *LP:* from 1528, *LP*IV(2), 4806 (SP 1/50, fols. 161-62); from 1532, *LP*V, 1698 (SP 1/73, fols. 27-28); from 1533, *LP*VI, 835 (SP 1/77, fols. 237-38), 869 (BL MS Harley 6148, fol. 28), 887 (SP 1/78, fols. 26-27), 967 (SP 1/78, fol. 119), 1148 (SP 1/79, fols. 73-74), 1149 (SP 1/79, fols. 75-76), 1194 (BL MS Cotton Titus B.i, fol. 489), 1333 (SP 1/80, fol. 16), 1336 (SP 1/80, fol. 21), 1369 (SP 1/80, fols. 51-52), 1370 (E 36/143, fol. 29), 1371, 1381 (BL MS Cotton Titus B.i, fol. 453), 1382 (BL MS Cotton Titus, B.i, fol. 464), 1419, 1422 (SP 1/80, fols. 105-6), 1433 (SP 3/12, fol. 126), 1438 (BL MS Additional 27447, fol. 75), 1445, 1460, 1464 (BL MS Cotton Cleopatra E.iv, fols. 94-95), 1465 (SP 1/80, fols. 124-25), 1466 (BL MS Cotton Cleopatra E.iv, fols. 87-90), 1467 (BL MS Cotton Cleopatra E.vi, fol. 154), 1468 (SP 1/80, fols. 126-46), 1469 (BL MS Cotton Cleopatra E.iv, fol. 81), 1470 (BL MS Cotton Cleopatra E.iv, fol. 91), 1471 (BL MS Cotton Cleopatra E.iv, fol. 98); 1512 (BL MS Cotton Cleopatra E.iv, fol. 96), 1519 (BL MS Harley 6148, fol. 5), 1546 (SP 1/81, fols.

6-7); from 1534, *LP*VII 17 (SP 1/82, fols. 15-16), 48 (BL MS Cotton Titus B.i, fol. 427, 428), 52 (BL MS Cotton Titus B.i, fol. 430), 61 (SP 1/82, fol. 74), 70 (25 HVIII, c. 12), 72 (SP 1/82, fols. 85-97), 138 (SP 1/82, fol. 150), 139 (SP 1/82, fol. 151), 192 (BL MS Cotton Cleopatra E.iv, fol. 97), 238 (BL MS Cotton Cleopatra E.iv, fols. 101-4), 287, 288 (SP 1/82, fols. 254-57), 289 (BL MS Cotton Cleopatra E.vi, fol. 149), 290 (SP 1/82, fols. 258-59), 303 (SP 1/82, 270-71); from 1539, *LP* XIV.2, 402 (SP 1/154, 72); from 1543, *LP* XVIII.2, 546; and *LP* Addendum 1.2, 1632 (SP 1/244, fol. 194).

2. Edward Hall, *The Triumphant Reigne of Kyng Henry VIII. . . ,* ed. Charles Whibley. (London, 1904), 2:259.

On the form of scaffold speeches, see Lacey Baldwin Smith, "English Treason Trials and Confessions in the Sixteenth Century," *Journal of the History of Ideas,* 15 (1954), 471-97; J. A. Sharpe, "'Last Dying Speeches': Religion, Ideology and Public Execution in Seventeenth-Century England," *Past and Present,* no. 17 (1985), 144-67; and, focusing on women, Frances E. Dolan, "'Gentlemen, I have one thing more to say': Women on Scaffolds in England, 1563-1680," *Modern Philology,* 92 (1994), 157-78.

The events of Elizabeth Barton's life have been told and retold. An entry appears in the *Catholic Encyclopedia,* a much longer and far less balanced biographical entry appears in the *Dictionary of National Biography (DNB),* and an entry also appears in the recent *Historical Dictionary of Tudor England, 1485-1603.*

Among the standard Tudor histories we surveyed in relation to Margaret Cheyne, James A. Froude (*History of England from the Fall of Wolsey to the Defeat of the Spanish Armada,* 12 vols. [London, 1893]), for example, discusses Elizabeth Barton's case in some detail (vol. 1, "The Story of the Nun of Kent," 312-26 and vol. 2, "The Nun of Kent," 51-59, "The Nun and the Five Monks Brought to Trial," 65-66, "Attainder of the Nun and Her Accomplices," 90-91, "The Bill of Attainder is Passed," 94-95, and "The Execution of the Nun," 95-96). Her case is more briefly mentioned in J. D. Mackie (*The Oxford History of England,* vol. 7: *The Earlier Tudors, 1485-1558* [Oxford, 1952], 361-62); G. R. Elton (*New History of England,* vol. 2: *Reform and Reformation: England 1509-1558* [London, 1977], 180-81, 292); and John Guy (*Tudor England* [Oxford, 1986], 138-39, 457).

Interesting discussions of her case are also to be found in such diverse sources as David Knowles, *The Religious Orders in England,* vol. 3 (Cambridge, 1959), chapter 15, "Elizabeth Barton"; G. R. Elton, *Policy and Police: The Enforcement of the Reformation in the Age of Thomas Cromwell* (Cambridge, 1972); Peter Clarke, *English Provincial Society from the Reformation to the Revolution: Religion, Politics and Society in Kent, 1500-1640* (Hassocks, England,

1977), 32-35; John Bellamy, *The Tudor Law of Treason: An Introduction* (Toronto, 1979); Retha M. Warnicke, *Women of the English Renaissance and Reformation* (Westport, CT, 1983), 68-69; Susan Brigden, *London and the Reformation* (Oxford, 1989), 214-15; and Patricia Crawford, *Women and Religion in England, 1500-1700* (New York, 1993), 28-29, 108.

Separate essays on various aspects of Elizabeth Barton's story include A. Denton Cheney, "The Holy Maid of Kent," *Transactions of the Royal Historical Society*, 18 (1904), 107-29; and E. J. Devereux, "Elizabeth Barton and Tudor Censorship," *Bulletin of John Rylands Library*, 49 (1966), 91-106. Elizabeth Barton is the subject of a fairly recent full-length biography, Alan Neame's *The Holy Maid of Kent: The Life of Elizabeth Barton, 1506-1534* (London, 1971), a valuable if overwrought hagiography. Neame's narrative is exhaustive: he traces each of those accused with Elizabeth Barton as well as the woman herself. His collection of original documents in the case is superb, and his transcriptions of those texts are extraordinarily helpful. But Neame's position as "a direct descendant of the man in whose house the Holy Maid of Kent saw her first visions and uttered her earliest prophecy" ("Acknowledgments") indicates something of the aim of his study—to defend Elizabeth Barton as a visionary and a martyr. Equally problematic are the accounts of Elizabeth Barton in Adam Hamilton, O. S. B., *The Angel of Syon: The Life and Martyrdom of Blessed Richard Reynolds, Bridgettine Monk of Syon, Martyred at Tyburn, May 5, 1535* (London, 1905); and Alfred Winnifrith, *The Fair Maids of Kent by a Man of Kent* (Folkestone, Kent, 1921), chapter 7. A balanced account is J. R. McKee's *Dame Elizabeth Barton, O. S. B., the Holy Maid of Kent* (London, 1925).

3.   There has been some confusion among historians about the number of men executed on 20 April 1534. Six men were condemned with Elizabeth Barton—the five executed plus Richard Master, the rector of Aldington, Elizabeth Barton's home parish in Kent. Master was subsequently pardoned. Some historians assume that Hugh Rich, an Observant Friar, actually died in prison, but that was not the case. On this see Richard Rex, "The Execution of the Holy Maid of Kent," *The Bulletin of the Institute of Historical Research*, 64 (1991), 216-20.

4.   25 Henry VIII, c. 12 (A. Luders et al., *Statutes of the Realm* [London, 1810-24], 3:446-51).

5.   The contemporary pamphlet *A Marvelous Work of Late Done at Court-of-Strete* was written and published by Edward Thwaites in 1527. Thwaites was attainted of treason for his relationship with Elizabeth Barton and forced to take part in her public penance, but ultimately he was pardoned. No copy of his pamphlet has survived (see Devereux, "Elizabeth Barton and Tudor Censorship," 94-95), though William Lambarde preserved at least some of the text of Thwaites's

pamphlet in *A Perambulation of Kent: Conteining the Description, Hystorie, and Customes of That Shire* (1570; rpt. London, 1826):

> For not long since, it chaunced mee to see a little Pamphlet, conteining foure and twentie leaves, penned by Edward Thwaytes, or I wote not by what doltish dreamer, prynted by Robert Redman, intituled A maruelous worke of late done at Court of Streete in Kent, and published (as it pretendeth) to the devout people of that time for their spirituall consolation: in which I found the very first beginning, to have beene as followeth. (170)

The story of Elizabeth Barton is found in Lambarde, *Perambulation of Kent*, 170-75. The date of Elizabeth Barton's birth is confirmed as 1506 by a Latin account of her life preserved among the state papers related to the investigation of her prophecies; see *LP* VI, 1468[6].

6. In one letter addressed to her in 1532, Elizabeth Barton's correspondent informed her that her "sister" was well. In this letter, Elizabeth herself is addressed by her correspondent as "My lover, my sister, my earthly comfort," *sister* in this instance used in the spiritual and religious sense. Given the way the letter reads, it is possible that, in referring to the health of Elizabeth's "sister," the writer means a biological sister, but the exact nature of the relationship cannot be determined; for the full text, see SP 1/73, fols. 27-28 (*LP* 5, 1698[2]).

   Lists of her associates and contacts are found, for example, in SP 1/81, fols. 126-28 (LP VI, 1468[1]).

7. Edward Thwaites, as preserved in Lambarde, *Perambulation of Kent*, 170-71.

8. The report of Master to Warham is mentioned both in the public sermon preached against Elizabeth Barton on 23 November 1533 (L. E. Whatmore, "The Sermon against the Holy Maid of Kent and Her Adherents . . . " *English Historical Review*, 58 [1943], 463-75) and in the act of attainder passed by Parliament (with its clear position on the falsity of her visions): "And one Richard Maister, clerke, being parson of the seid parisshe of Aldyngton in the seid Countie of Kent, after that he had made to the late Archibisshop of Canterbury a farr larger report concernyng the hipocrisie, traunces, and speches of the seid Elizabeth than he colde justifie and abyde by."

9. From Whatmore, "Sermon," 465.

10. The commission is described to Cromwell by Thomas Goldwell in a letter written in late November 1533, as the investigation of Elizabeth Barton was concluding (BM MS Cotton Cleopatra E.iv, fol. 91; *LP* VI, 1470); Goldwell's lettter is printed in full in Thomas Wright, *Three Chapters of Letters Relating to the Suppression of Monasteries* (London, 1843), letter 7, 19-22.

11. Thwaites, as preserved in Lambarde, *Perambulation of Kent,* 173.

12. Cranmer's letter was written in December 1533 to Archdeacon Hawkins; it is printed in full in Henry Jenkyns, *The Remains of Thomas Cranmer, D.D., Archbishop of Canterbury* (Oxford, 1833), letter 84, 1:79-84. Cranmer seems to be relying on Thwaites's pamphlet for at least part of this account: "and a book [was] written of all the whole story thereof, and put into print, which ever since that time hath been commonly sold and gone abroad amonges all people" (80).

    The "Sermon" mentions Elizabeth Barton's "cure" and the subsequent publication of the account by Thwaites: "And after mass she kneeled afore the image of Our Lady of Court-of-Street and said then she was made perfectly whole. . . . And this is the great miracle that is so much spoken of in the said printed book" (466).

13. Whatmore, "Sermon," 466.

14. This pamphlet is no longer extant; see note 5.

15. Cranmer to Hawkins, printed in Jenkyns, *The Remains of Thomas Cranmer,* 1:80.

16. "And when they cry, 'Miracles, miracles' . . . either they are no miracles but they have feigned them . . . or else if there be miracles . . . then are they done of the devil (as the maid . . . of Kent)" (William Tyndale, *The Obedience of a Christian Man,* in *The Work of William Tyndale,* ed. G. E. Duffield [Philadelphia, 1965], 361-63).

17. SP 1/50, fols. 161-62 (*LP* IV.2, 4806).

18. Goldwell to Cromwell, in Wright, *Three Chapters of Letters,* 20.

19. For careful treatment of the events of the divorce, and excellent analysis, see J. J. Scarisbrick, *Henry VIII* (Berkeley, CA, 1968), 149-313.

20. On this, see Scarisbrick, *Henry VIII,* 154-55.

21. Warham's letter to Cromwell is SP 1/50, fols. 161-62 (*LP* IV.2, 4806).

22. Whatmore, "Sermon," 467; the substance of Elizabeth Barton's prophecies is also detailed in Goldwell's letter to Cromwell, in Wright, *Three Chapters of Letters,* 20.

23. Letter to Thomas Cromwell (BL MS Cotton Cleopatra E.iv, fols. 87-90; *LP* VI, 1466), printed in full by Wright, *Three Chapters of Letters,* letter 6, 14-19. This letter is from an unnamed informant who was reporting what he knew of "the whole story" of Elizabeth Barton's prophecies. The informant includes thirty-one items on his list.

24. Letter from Thomas More to Thomas Cromwell, March 1534 (*LP* VII, 287), printed in full in *The Correspondence of Sir Thomas More,* ed. Elizabeth F. Rogers (Princeton, 1947), letter 197, 481. More was named as an accessory in the bill of attainder drawn against Elizabeth Barton, and, if the bill had been passed with his name still included, he would have been guilty of misprision of treason. More's name was ultimately withdrawn from the bill, though he would be convicted of

treason for refusing the oath of supremacy in 1535; see T. B. Howell, *A Complete Collection of State Trials* (London, 1816), 1:385-96.

25. Letter from John Fisher to Henry VIII, 27 February 1534 (*LP* VII, 239), printed in Michael Macklen, *God Have Mercy: The Life of John Fisher of Rochester* (Ottawa, Canada 1968), 165-67. Like More, Fisher was named as an accessory in the bill of attainder presented to Parliament; his name remained on the bill, and he was attainted for misprision of treason. After refusing to take the oath of succession in 1534, he was again attainted for misprision of treason and then deprived of his bishopric (26 Henry VIII c. 3). For refusing the oath of Supremacy, he was tried for and convicted of treason in 1535; see Howell, *State Trials,* 1:395-408.

26. SP 1/80, fol. 138 (*LP* VI, 1468[5]).

27. Fisher to Henry VIII, printed in Macklen, *God Have Mercy,* 165-67.

28. More to Cromwell, in Rogers, *Correspondence of Sir Thomas More,* 480-88. The word *housewife* should be understood in its archaic, negative sense of "impertinent" or "worthless" woman.

   More calculated that it was "about eight or nine years" since he had first heard of Elizabeth Barton, thus indicating that she had come to his attention in 1525 or 1526, about the time, then, that she first became ill, began her prophetic career, and became a nun; if he is correct in remembering this date, then the roll of rudely rhymed prophecies he examined were probably the religious visions she had at that time. Some of the substance of her prophecies has been preserved in Lambarde. In addition, a fragment of verse is preserved in Whatmore, "Sermon," 472:

   > If thou the Sunday see not God in the face;
   > If thou die that week suddenly without confession,
   > Thou standest, man, in the way of damnation.

29. Letter to Thomas Cromwell, printed in Wright, *Three Chapters of Letters,* 14-15.

30. Ibid.

31. For the deposition, see SP 1/80, fol. 138 (*LP* VI, 1468[5]). The letter of this unnamed informant to Cromwell makes the meeting with the queen and her mother less sure, since it says Elizabeth claimed to have seen them "in spirit" standing in a garden; the informant goes on to say that Elizabeth saw that beside the queen stood "a lyttell devyll" that "put in hur [Anne's] mynd to say thus, 'Yow [the king] shall send my father unto themprowre [the emperor], and let hym shew the emprowre your mynd and conscience, and gyve hym these manny thowsand docates to have his good wyll, and thus it wulbe browght to passe'" (15). If this was something that Elizabeth Barton saw "in spirit," it shows that perhaps she was less politically aware than she was credited with being, since there

is little likelihood that Charles V could be bribed to support the king's divorce from Charles's own aunt, Katherine, and little likelihood that Anne Boleyn would have thought such a move could be successful.

32. 25 Henry VIII, c. 12 (*Statutes of the Realm,* 3:449).

33. For the deposition including Barton's claim, see SP 1/80, fol. 138 (*LP* VI, 1468[5]). This claim is made also in the letter on the nun's predictions received by Thomas Cromwell, in Wright, *Three Chapters of Letters,* 17.

    The *DNB* indicates Barton thrust herself into the king's presence in Canterbury, at his return from Calais, but this does not fit with the claims that Henry would have married Anne Boleyn in Calais if not for Elizabeth's prophecy to him before he crossed the Channel.

    Neame's highly dramatic version of this meeting is typical of his fictionalized account of critical events (see *Holy Maid of Kent,* 172-74).

34. More to Cromwell, in Rogers, *Correspondence of Sir Thomas More,* 480-88.

35. More to Elizabeth Barton, in Rogers, *Correspondence of Sir Thomas More,* letter 192, 464-66.

36. SP 1/82, fols. 258-59 (*LP* VII, 290).

37. For these meetings, see letter to Thomas Cromwell, in Wright, *Three Chapters of Letters,* 16. Both the public sermon preached against Elizabeth Barton and the act of attainder note her meetings with these papal representatives.

38. Cranmer to Hawkins, in Jenkyns, *Remains of Thomas Cranmer,* 1:80.

39. The first meeting of Elizabeth Barton and the marchioness of Exeter is reported by her waiting woman, Constance Bontayn, SP 1/138, fol. 210 (*LP* XIII.2, 802), and by Jasper Horsey, one of Exeter's men, SP 1/139, fols. 14-20 (*LP* XIII.2, 827[2]).

    Along with Henry Pole and Edward Neville, Henry Courtenay was executed by Henry VIII in 1538. In 1539, following the execution of her son, Lady Margaret Pole, countess of Salisbury, would be attainted for treason and held in the Tower until April 1541, when she was executed. Margaret Pole also saw Elizabeth Barton's prophecies. On the trials of the Poles, Neville, and Courtenay, see chapter 6.

    For examinations of Exeter, his wife, and their contacts, many of which mention the marchioness's meetings with Elizabeth Barton, see especially SP 1/138, fols. 158-59 (*LP* XIII.2, 765); SP 1/138, fols. 189-90 (*LP* XIII.2, 796); SP 1/138, fol. 210 (*LP* XIII.2, 802); SP 1/138, fols. 213-30 (*LP* XIII.2, 804[i-iii]); SP 1/139, fols. 14-20 (*LP* XIII.2, 827); SP 1/139, fols. 25-36 (*LP* XIII.2, 829); SP 1/139, fols. 37-75 (*LP* XIII.2, 830); SP 1/139, fols 76-80 (*LP* XIII.2, 831).

40. The second meeting was described in her confession by Elizabeth Barton: SP 1/80, fol. 142 (*LP* VI, 1468[7]).

41. The extensive lists of the contacts admitted by each of those arrested with Elizabeth Barton are found in SP 1/80, fols. 126-28 (*LP* VI, 1468[1-4]).

42. Quoted in Devereux, "Elizabeth Barton and Tudor Censorship," 99.

43. Cromwell's "remembrances" are abstracted in *LP* VI, 1194.

44. 25 Henry VIII c. 12 (*Statutes of the Realm*, 3:448); Whatmore, "Sermon," 474.

45. Cranmer to Cromwell, in Jenkyns, *Remains of Thomas Cranmer,* letter 90, 1:88-89.

46. See, for example, *Statues of the Realm,* 3:448 and Whatmore, "Sermon," 474.

47. More to Cromwell, in Rogers, *Correspondence of Sir Thomas More,* 481: "the bysshop of Canterburye that then was . . . sent vnto the Kinges Grace a roll of paper in which were wrytten certaine wordes of hers, that she had, as report was then made, at sundrye tymes spoken in her traunses; wheruppon it pleased the Kinges Grace to delyuer me the roll."

48. See *Statutes of the Realm,* 3:448 for the "heavenly letter" and Whatmore, "Sermon."

49. Cranmer to the prioress of St. Sepulchre's (*LP* VI, 869). Archbishop William Warham died in August 1532; Cranmer was consecrated on 30 March 1533.

50. Cromwell to Henry VIII (*LP,* VI, 887), printed by Roger B. Merriman, *The Life and Letters of Thomas Cromwell* (1902; rpt., Oxford, 1968), letter 52, 1:360-62.

51. The report to Cromwell is SP 1/78, fol. 119 (*LP* VI, 967).

52. See, for example, the letters from Christopher Hales, the king's attorney general, to Cromwell, dated 24 and 25 September (*LP* VI, 1148, 1149). Further reports of investigations sent to Cromwell include *LP* VI, 1333, 1336.

53. Cromwell's reports to the king and his "remembrances" about the investigation are found in *LP* VI, 1369, 1370, 1371, 1381, and 1382, covering the period from mid-September until the end of October.

54. Letter to Cromwell, in Wright, *Three Chapters of Letters,* 18.

55. Cranmer to Hawkins, in Jenkyns, *Remains of Thomas Cranmer,* 82.

56. Chapuys to Charles V (*LP* VI, 1419); the abbot of Hyde to Lady Lisle (LP VI, 1433); Lady Rutland to Sir William Paston (LP VI, 1438).

57. Chapuys to Charles V (*LP* VI, 1445).

58. Bellamy remarks that the act of attainder against Elizabeth Barton used the format and language of treason indictments in the King's Bench. He concludes, "it seems likely the act was based directly on the draft of an indictment, perhaps the one Cromwell noted he must draw for the offenders in treason and misprision concerning the Nun of Canterbury" (see Bellamy, *Tudor Law of Treason,* 28).

59. Salcot (also known as John Capon) was the abbot of Hyde and bishop-elect of Bangor. A draft of the charges against Elizabeth Barton and those attainted with her, along with a description of the crowd gathered for the public penance, is preserved in SP 1/82, fols. 85-86 (*LP* VII, 72[1]). A draft of the public sermon is preserved in SP 1/82, fols. 89-96 (*LP* VII, 72[3]), the entire speech printed by Whatmore ("Sermon").

60. SP 1/82, fol. 87 (*LP* VII, 72[2]).

61. Chapuys to Charles V (*LP* VI, 1460).

62. SP 1/80, fols. 126-46 (*LP* VI, 1468).

63. Cromwell's "remembrances," BL MS Cotton Titus B.i, fol. 430 (LP VII, 52): "to know what the king will have done with the nun and her accomplices."

64. 25 Henry VIII c. 12 (*Statutes of the Realm*, 3:451).

Chapter 4

1. Gertrude, marchioness of Exeter, to Henry VIII, BL MS Cotton Cleopatra E.iv, fols. 94-95 in *Letters and Papers, Foreign and Domestic, of the Reign of Henry VIII*, ed. J. S. Brewer et al., 21 vols. and *Addenda* (London, 1862-1932), VI, 1464; hereafter referred to as *LP*. This letter is printed in full in *Letters of Royal and Illustrious Ladies of Great Britain, from the Commencement of the Twelfth Century to the Close of the Reign of Queen Mary*, ed. Mary Anne Everett Wood (London, 1846), letter 44, 2:98-101.

2. Cromwell to Fisher (*LP* VII, 238); printed in Roger Bigelow Merriman, *Life and Letters of Thomas Cromwell*, 2 vols. (1902; rpt., Oxford, 1968), letter 68, 1:373-79.

3. More's long narrative to Cromwell (*LP* VII, 287) is printed in Elizabeth F. Rogers, ed., *The Correspondence of Sir Thomas More* (Princeton, 1947), letter 197, 480-88; his letter to Henry VIII (*LP* VII, 288) is printed on 488-91 (letter 198). More also wrote a long follow-up to Cromwell, thanking him for his "charitable labor" with the king on his behalf (letter 199, 491-501; abstracted in *LP* VII, 289).

4. Edward Hall, *The Triumphant Reign of Henry VIII . . .* , ed. Charles Whibley, 2 vols. (London, 1904), 2:244-45, 247-59. Elizabeth Barton's speech on the scaffold, as recorded by Hall, is printed at the beginning of chapter 3.

5. Charles Wriothesley, *A Chronicle of England during the Reigns of the Tudors, from A.D. 1485 to 1559 . . .* , ed. William D. Hamilton, 2 vols. (London [Camden Society], 1875), 1:23-24.

6. For the two anonymous London chronicles, see "London Chronicle during the Reigns of Henry VII and Henry VIII," ed. Clarence Hopper, in *The Camden Miscellany IV* (London, 1859), 9; and "A London Chronicle, 1523-1555," ed. Charles L. Kingsford in *The Camden Miscellany XII* (London, 1910), 8-9.

    Richard Hill's chronicle of events in London is printed as an appendix in *Songs, Carols, and Other Miscellaneous Poems, from the Balliol MS. 354, Richard Hill's Commonplace Book*, ed. Roman Dyboski (1908; rpt., London, 1937),

142-67. The quotation is from the *Chronicle of the Grey Friars of London,* ed. John G. Nichols (London [Camden Society], 1825), 37-38.

7. *Chronicle of King Henry VIII of England . . . Written in Spanish by an Unknown Hand,* ed. and trans. Martin A. Sharp Hume (London, 1889).

The story of Elizabeth Barton up until 1529, the time of Thomas Wolsey's death, is also omitted in the biography of Wolsey written by George Cavendish, *Thomas Wolsey, Late Cardinal, his Life and Death, Written by George Cavendish, his Gentleman-Usher,* ed. Roger Lockyer (London, 1973). Cavendish's *Life* was not impartial; Lockyer writes, "Sometimes out of loyalty to his master he [Cavendish] professes ignorance where it is likely that he knew the truth" (8). Although Cavendish omits all reference to the nun and her prophecies, he does include a comment Wolsey made, just before his death, about such predictions: "Now you may behold in this, how dark and obscure are riddles and prophecies. . . . Trust therefore, by mine advice, to no kind of dark riddles and prophecies, wherein ye may, as many have been, be deceived and brought to destruction" (167).

8. Thomas Goldwell to Cromwell (*LP* VI, 1470), in Thomas Wright, ed., *Three Chapters of Letters Relating to the Suppression of Monasteries* (London, 1843), 19-20.

9. Christopher Warener to Thomas Cromwell, SP 1/80, fol. 21 (*LP* VI, 1336).

10. See, for example, Goldwell's letter to Cromwell (18) and Cranmer's letter to Cromwell (in Henry Jenkyns, ed., *The Remains of Thomas Cranmer, D.D., Archbishop of Canterbury,* 4 vols. [Oxford, 1833], 1:81). Much of this is made also in the public sermon preached at St. Paul's Cross and in the formal act of attainder.

11. Thomas Cromwell to John Fisher, in Merriman, *Life and Letters of Thomas Cromwell,* letter 68, 1:373-79.

12. Thomas More to Thomas Cromwell, in Rogers, *Correspondence of Sir Thomas More,* letter 197, 480-88; the quoted comment is found on 485.

13. For Chapuys's first report, see *LP* VI, 1419; for the summary of the events in Westminster, see *LP,* VI, 1445.

14. Eleanor Manners, lady Rutland, to her father, Sir William Paston (*LP* VI, 1438).

15. *Chronicle of the Years 1532-1537, Written by a Monk of St. Augustine's, Canterbury,* ed. John G. Nichols, in *Narratives of the Days of the Reformation* (London, 1859), 280-81.

16. In addition to the sermon and the act itself, the government propagandist Richard Morison published an account of Elizabeth Barton as part of an "official" version of the divorce controversy and the executions of Fisher and More in *Apomaxis Calumniarum Convitiorumque,* printed in 1537 or 1538 (STC 18109).

17. My own comments about Elizabeth Barton, published in 1991, before I had investigated her case in any detail, are equally problematic: "Like today's rock stars and politicians, she seems to have had her 'career' managed by a careful handler, in this case a monk of Canterbury named Edward Bocking" (Sharon L. Jansen, *Political Protest and Prophecy under Henry VIII* [Suffolk, England 1991], 26).

18. J. J. Scarisbrick, *Henry VIII* (Berkeley, CA, 1968),323-24.

19. The case of Alianor Dulyne is printed in *A Series of Precedents and Proceedings in Criminal Causes, Extending from the year 1475 to 1640; Extracted from the Act-Books of Ecclesiastical Courts in the Diocese of London . . .*, ed. William H. Hale (London, 1847), 77: "Alienora Dulyn notatur quod ymaginavit quasdam artes divinatarias, ad interfleiendum [for "interficiendum"] maritum suum, et intoxicare voluit.

20. The cases of Johanna Hebe and Mabel Priors are from the *Liber Correctionis tempore Ricardi Parker, 1528*, printed in A. Percival Moore, "Proceedings of the Ecclesiastical Courts in the Archdeaconry of Leicester, 1516-1535," *Associated Architectural Societies, Reports and Papers*, 28, no. 2 (1905-6), 593-661. Johanna Hebe's case is found on 613, Priors's on 611. In *Religion and the Decline of Magic: Studies in Popular Beliefs in Sixteenth- and Seventeenth-Century England* (1971; rpt., London, 1980), Keith Thomas refers to Hebe's case (though without using her name), but he indicates she was summoned before the court for reporting apparitions of her father. That's not quite accurate, since she had been charged with assault; the information about the apparitions arose at the inquiry.

21. Brian L. Woodcock, *Medieval Ecclesiastical Courts in the Diocese of Canterbury* (Oxford, 1952), 81.

22. Printed in *The Fabric Rolls of York Minster, with an Appendix of Illustrative Documents* (Durham, 1859), 273. Beyond these accounts of divination, several cases of conjuring also appear in contemporary records. In 1535 a priest was reported for having a book of conjurations (SP 1/97, fols. 128-29 [*LP* IX, 551]), and the friar of Maydland was reported for necromancy (SP 1/99, fols. 67-68 [*LP* IX, 846]). In 1538 the discovery of a mysterious wax child caused quite a stir (see E 36/120, fol. 71 [*LP* XIII.1, 41]; and SP 1/141, fol. 67 [*LP* XIII.2, 1200]). For other reports of conjuring, see SP 1/126, fols. 177-78 (*LP* XII.2, 1102); and Henry Ellis, *Original Letters, Illustrative of English History*, 3rd ser., vol. 3 (London, 1846), letter 268. For further discussion of magic, see chapter 8.

23. From Sir Thomas More, *A Dialogue Concerning Heresies . . .* (1531), vol. 6 of *The Complete Works of St. Thomas More*, ed. Thomas M. C. Lawler et al. (New Haven, CT., 1981), 93.

24. More, *Dialogue Concerning Heresies*, 94. Anne Wentworth became a Franciscan nun at a convent just outside of Aldgate, London.

More reported another case of a young woman who was reputed for her religious visions (*Dialogue Concerning Heresies,* 87-88). Elizabeth, "the Holy Maid of Leominster" (Hereford), had appeared during the reign of Henry VII. As More told the story, "the prior brought privily a strange wench in to the church that said she was sent thither by God and would not lie out of the church." She was enclosed as an anchoress in the priory church: "she was grated within iron grates about in the rood loft." She was reputed to live without any food or water at all, "only angels' food." The people "not of the town only but also of the country about her" regarded her as "a very quick saint and daily sought so thick to see her that many that could not come near to her cried out loud, 'Holy Maiden Elizabeth, help me,'" and threw their offerings to her over the heads of the crowd.

In reality the prior delivered the "angels' food" to the "Holy Maid" by sleight of hand, and the two spent the nights together in the rood loft. She was taken into custody by the king's mother, who "tried" her; since the young woman could not do without food, "she was perceived for no saint and confessed all the matter." More thought the Holy Maid of Leominster should have been burned at the stake; instead, he reported, "I heard say she lived and fared well and was a common harlot at Calais many a fair day after, where she laughed at the matter full merrily."

Another case of fraud involving a young woman's visions is reported in a London chronicle for 1554, the second year of Queen Mary's reign:

> Upon Sunday, being the 15 day of July, 1554 . . . a young wench of the age of sixteen or seventeen years did open penance at Paul's Cross, standing upon a scaffold all the sermon time, and confessed her fault openly, that she being enticed by lewd counsel had counterfeited certain speeches in a house in Aldgate Street, about the which matter the people were wonderfully molested, some saying that it was a spirit that spoke in a wall, some one thing, some another. In this manner she used herself, and she lay in her bed and whistled in a strange whistle made for the nonce, then was there (as she confessed) six false knaves . . . which took upon themselves to interpret what the spirit spoke, expressing certain seditious words against the Queen's Highness. ("A London Chronicle, 1523-1555," 36-37)

Charles Wriothesley (2:117) also reports the story, naming the woman Elizabeth Crofte.

25. Thomas More to Thomas Cromwell (*LP* VII, 287); printed in Rogers, *Correspondence of Sir Thomas More,* letter 197, 480-88.

26. For a list of sources on political prophecy, see the appropriate section in the bibliography. For a detailed study of political prophecy during Henry's reign, see Jansen, *Political Protest.*

27. On prophecies and their use during Lancastrian-Yorkist civil wars and during the reign of Henry VII, see Jansen, *Political Protest.*

28. Summarizing the events of the 1530s is a daunting task, and I certainly will attempt no comprehensive discussion here. For this summary I have followed several standard accounts, including those of J. D. Mackie, *The Oxford History of England,* vol. 7: *The Earlier Tudors, 1485-1558* (Oxford, 1952); J. J. Scarisbrick, *Henry VIII;* G. R. Elton, *New History of England,* vol. 2: *Reform and Reformation: England 1509-1558* (London, 1977); and John Guy *Tudor England* (Oxford, 1986). On the disputes with Convocation, in addition to those works cited, see Christopher Haigh, *English Reformations: Religion, Politics, and Society under the Tudors* (Oxford, 1993), 105-15.

29. On the parliamentary actions of the decade, in addition to the works cited in note 28, see S. E. Lehmberg, *The Reformation Parliament, 1529-1536* (Cambridge, 1970). An excellent summary on the actions of the Reformation Parliament is found in the *Historical Dictionary of Tudor England.*

30. The best discussion of the government's efforts is in G. R. Elton, *Policy and Police: The Enforcement of the Reformation in the Age of Thomas Cromwell* (Cambridge, 1972).

31. An extraordinary number of reports about political prophecies surfaced during the decade of the 1530s. Documents in the state papers relating to political prophecies include: from 1530, *LP* IV.3, 6652 (SP 1/58, fols. 101-2); from 1532, *LP* V, 712 (SP 1/69, fols. 13-14), 1679 (SP 1/72, fols. 196-207); from 1533, *LP* VI, 257-58 (SP 1/75, fol. 38, 39); from 1534, *LP* VII, 923 (E 36/139), 1624 (SP 1/88, fol. 56); from 1535, *LP* VIII, 565 (SP 1/92, fols. 34-47), 567 (fols. 49-50), *LP* IX, 551 (SP 1/97, fols. 128-29); from 1536, *LP* X, appendix 10 (SP 1/81, fol. 175), 94 (SP 1/101, fols. 88-89), 121 (SP 1/101, fols. 114-15), 164 (SP 1/101, fols. 153-56), 614 (SP 1/103, fols. 76-77), 774 (SP 1/103, fols. 215-16), 1205 (SP 1/104[B], fol. 225), 1207 (SP 1/104(B), fol. 227), *LP* XI, 40, 791, 809 (SP 1/108, fol. 250), 970 (SP 1/110, fols. 156-62), 1260 (SP 1/112, fols. 169-74), *LP Addendum* I.1 1146; from 1537, *LP* XII.1, 318 (SP 1/115, fols. 175-77), 534 (SP 1/116, fols. 165-66), 841 (SP 1/118, fols. 1-8), 1023 (E 36/119, fol. 130), 1087 (SP 1/119, fols. 73-87), 1284 (SP 1/120, fols. 202-3), *LP* XII.2, 80 (BL MS Cotton Caligula B.i., fols. 130-31), 184 (SP 1/121, fol. 238), 602 (SP 1/124, fol. 132), 1212 (SP 1/127, fols. 63-67), 1231 (SP 1/127, fol. 97); from 1538, *LP* XIII.1, 107 (SP 1/128, fol. 124), 470 (SP 60/6, fols. 47-48); *LP* XIII.2, 1242 (E 36/120, fol. 58); from 1539, *LP* XIV.1, 178 (SP 1/142, fols 187-90), 186 (PRO 31/9, I, fol. 65), 232 (BL MS Cotton Caligula B.i., fol. 309), 241, 275 (SP 1/143, fols. 69-70), 806 (BL MS Cotton Titus B.i, fol. 271), 1027 (SP 60/8, fols. 35-38).

32. The state papers include extensive records and depositions, abstracted in *LP* III.1, 1284. The act attainting Buckingham is 14 and 15 Henry VIII, c. 20 (A. Luders

et al., eds., *Statutes of the Realm* [London, 1810-24], 3:246-58). For the most complete study of Buckingham and his fall, see Barbara J. Harris, *Edward Stafford, Third Duke of Buckingham, 1478-1521* (Stanford, CA, 1986). On Buckingham, see also chapters 1 and 2.

33. For the complete text of the indictment and a discussion of the prophecy in Griffith's arrest and conviction, see W. L. Williams, "A Welsh Insurrection," *Y Cymmrodor*, 16 (1903), 33-41. The act attainting Griffith is 23 Henry VIII, c. 34 (*Statutes of the Realm*, 3:415-16). For the activities of Katherine Howard, Sir Rhys ap Griffith's widow, during the Pilgrimage of Grace, see chapter 2.

34. On Sir Griffith's involvement with political prophecy, see also Jansen, *Political Protest*, 28-29. For "The Sayings of the Prophets," see 110-24 and S. L. Jansen, "'And he shall be called Edward': Sixteenth-Century Political Protest and Folger MS Loseley b.546," *English Literary Renaissance*, 23 (1993), 227-43, and 24 (1994), 699-714.

35. For the investigation of William Harlock, see SP 1/58, fols, 101-2 (*LP* IV.3, 6652); see also Jansen, *Political Protest*, 27-28.

36. For the investigation of William Neville, see E 163/10/21 (not found in *LP*), SP 1/69, fols. 13-14 (*LP* V, 712), SP 1/72, fols. 196-207 (*LP* V, 1679), SP 1/73, fols. 1-2 (*LP* V, 1680), SP 1/75, fol. 38 (*LP* VI, 257), SP 1/75, fol. 39 (*LP* VI, 258), SP 1/238, fol. 119 (*LP Addendum* I.1, 863); see also Jansen, *Political Protest*, 30-32; and Elton, *Policy and Police*, 50-57.

37. PRO 31/9, I, fol. 65 (*LP* XIV.1, 186). The document is found among the 1539 papers, but the prophecy was allegedly "showed and declared" in 1512; Cromwell was said to have known of this prophecy, recalling it particularly after Pole was created cardinal in Rome in December 1536 and later legate to England. See Merriman, *The Life and Letters of Thomas Cromwell*, 2:204-5.

38. Lockyer, *Thomas Wolsey*, 166-67.

39. *Calendar of Letters, Documents and State Papers Relating to the Negotiations between England and Spain Preserved in the Archives at Simancas and Elsewhere*, ed. G. A. Bergenroth et al., (London, 1862-1965), V.2, 54.

40. *LP* X, 911.

41. On John Amadas, see S. T. Bindoff, *The History of Parliament: The House of Commons, 1509-1558*, (London, 1982), 1:316-17. John Amadas (born by 1489 - d. 1554/55), of Court Gate, Tavistock, Devon, Eltham, Kent, and Launceston, Cornwall, was a member of a family that served the king in various capacities, primarily as goldsmiths. About John's father, William Amadas, Bindoff writes: he "made a career in the Household, where he rose to be one of the King's serjeants-at-arms"; John Amadas followed his father into the service of the Crown. He was married by 1519 and had one son and one daughter with his first wife (he remarried a woman named Elizabeth in 1542 or 1543). John Amadas represented Tavistock in the 1515 Parliament and,

according to Bindoff, "could have done so in others for which the name of the Tavistock members have been lost."

Another member of the family was Robert Amadas, and Elton (*Policy and Police,* 59-61) concludes that the woman investigated for prophecies in July 1533 was Robert Amadas's widow, apparently because the next document in the state papers (SP 1/78, fols. 64-65; *LP* VI, 924) is a record of account for the late Robert Amadas, which concludes, "Information of certain words spoken by Mistress Amadas as within appeareth." But Bindoff indicates that Robert Amadas's widow had been remarried the year before, in 1532 (*History of Parliament,* 1:317), thus making it unlikely that the woman specifically called "Mistress Amadas" in July 1533—who spoke so strongly about her unhappy marriage—was Robert Amadas's widow, recently remarried.

42. Her statement appears in BL MS Cotton Cleopatra E.iv, fols. 99-100 (*LP* VI, 923).

43. For the "moldwarp," or mole, see "The Prophecy of the Six Kings to Follow King John," in Rupert Taylor, *The Political Prophecy in England* (New York, 1911). Numerous prophecies use a dragon as a symbol, and the rising of a "dead man" is also a frequent motif. See Jansen, *Political Protest.*

44. Elizabeth Barton's prophecies, as reported in a letter to Thomas Cromwell; printed in Wright, *Three Chapters of Letters,* 18.

45. For John Dobson, vicar of Muston, and his prophecies, see SP 1/127, fols. 63-67 (*LP* XII.2, 1212). The contemporary version of "The Sayings of the Prophets" using alphabetic references is found in BL MS Lansdowne 762, fols. 48-50, while the priest Henry Cowpar and his prophecies are found in SP 1/126, fols. 177-78 (*LP* XII.2, 1102).

Perhaps the most familiar example of such alphabetic prophecies is found in Shakespeare's Richard III:

> And if King Edward be as true and just
> As I am subtle, false, and treacherous,
> This day should Clarence closely be mewed up,
> About a prophecy, which says that G
> Of Edward's heirs the murderer shall be. (I.i.36-40)

The ambivalence of such riddling predictions is the whole point of the scene, since Edward has unwittingly misconstrued *G* as George, duke of Clarence—missing its equal (and accurate) application to Richard, duke of Gloucester.

On alphabetic prophecy, see Taylor, *Political Prophecy,* 115; and Jansen, *Political Protest,* 110-16.

46. During the 1530s many were investigated for their involvement with political prophecy—and more than Elizabeth Barton were executed. See Jansen, *Political Protest,* for a complete discussion.

47. On Lucia da Narni, see Jodi Bilinkoff, "A Spanish Prophetess and Her Patrons: The Case of María de Santo Domingo," *Sixteenth Century Journal,* 23 (1992), 21-34.

48. On María de Santo Domingo, see Bilinkoff, "Spanish Prophetess." The Spanish prophetess is also mentioned in Ronald E. Surtz, *The Guitar of God: Gender, Power, and Authority in the Visionary World of Mother Juana de la Cruz, 1481-1534* (Philadelphia, 1990), but not in regard to her political predictions.

49. Bilinkoff, "Spanish Prophetess," 21.

50. On Sor María de la Visitación, see Richard L. Kagan, *Lucrecia's Dreams: Politics and Prophecy in Sixteenth-Century Spain* (Berkeley, CA, 1990), 6-7.

51. On Lucrecia de León, see Kagan, *Lucrecia's Dreams.*

52. For all this see Kagan, *Lucrecia's Dreams,* 124-28.

53. Ibid., 128.

54. On Lucrecia's trial and sentencing, see Kagan, *Lucrecia's Dreams,* 134-56. The Inquisition could not, in the end, carry out its sentence. No religious house would accept Lucrecia, since the young woman had had a daughter while in prison; the daughter was five years old by the time Lucrecia's trial was completed. After she left prison, Lucrecia and her child were placed temporarily in Toledo's Hospital of St. John the Baptist. Kagan speculates about what may have happened to Lucrecia after her stay there, but nothing is certain about her fate after she left St. John's.

     One additional name might be cited here. The case of the "Virgin of Venice," Madre Giovanna (b. 1496/97), is detailed by Marion Leathers Kuntz, "The Virgin of Venice and Concepts of the Millenium in Venice," in *The Politics of Gender in Early Modern Europe,* ed. Jean R. Brink, et al. (Kirksville, MO, 1989), 111-30. Although primarily a religious mystic with millenarian visions, the Virgin of Venice did make a number of predictions that involved the future of the city of Venice, which was to become a new Jerusalem and a new Rome. Kuntz writes that she had great influence over "wealthy Venetians" from the mid-1520s until the mid-1550s.

     See also Ottavia Niccoli, *Prophecy and People in Renaissance Italy,* trans. Lydia G. Cochrane (Princeton, NJ, 1990), for the connection between women and political prediction in Italy.

55. L. E. Whatmore, "The Sermon against the Holy Maid of Kent and Her Adherents . . . ," *English Historical Review,* 58 (1943), 465.

56. Thwaites, as preserved in William Lambarde, *A Peramabulation of Kent: Containing the Description, Hystorie, and Customes of That Shire* (1570; rpt., London, 1826), 174.

57. On women's choice of prophecy to express their views Keith Thomas writes: "the best hope of gaining an ear for female utterances was to represent them as the result of divine revelation. . . . [B]efore the Civil War, recourse to prophecy was the only means by which most women could hope to disseminate their opinions on public events" (*Religion and the Decline of Magic,* 163).

Of interest here as well is Patricia Crawford, *Women and Religion in England, 1500-1720* (New York, 1993), chapter 5 ("Dangerous Beliefs: Magic, Prophecy and Mysticism").

58. *Ecstasies: Deciphering the Witches' Sabbath,* trans. Raymond Rosenthal (New York, 1991), 10.

59. In its form Elizabeth Barton's speech differs in a few interesting particulars from the conventional pattern of scaffold confessions outlined by Lacey Baldwin Smith:

> Those about to suffer announced that they had come hither to die, and they were careful to point out to the surrounding multitude that they had been judged by the laws of the land and that they were content to accept the penalties which the law required. After granting the legality of their execution, they usually went on to hold themselves up as examples of the frightful fate in store for those who dared to sin against God and their king. Finally, they ended by requesting their audience to pray on their behalf that God and king would mercifully forgive them their trespasses and then, in a closing burst of loyalty, they expressed the hope that their gracious sovereign might long and happily reign over the kingdom in peace and tranquility. ("English Treason Trials and Confessions in the Sixteenth Century," *Journal of the History of Ideas,* 15 [1954], 476)

Noting a similar pattern in scaffold speeches in the seventeenth century, J. A. Sharpe concludes,

> The men and women whose executions we have noted were, for the most part, doing more than just accepting their fates. They were the willing central participants in a theatre of punishment, which offered not merely a spectacle, but also a reinforcement of certain values. When felons stood on the gallows and confessed their guilt not only for the offence for which they suffered death, but for a whole catalogue of wrongdoing, and expressed their true repentance for the same, they were helping to assert the legitimacy of the power which had brought them to their sad end. ("'Last Dying Speeches': Religion, Ideology and Public Execution in Seventeenth-Century England," *Past and Present,* no. 17 [1985], 156)

Even the executions of "lowly felons," Sharpe writes, were "attempts by the authorities to exert ideological control, to reassert certain values of obedience and conformity" (158). Crucial to the ceremony of execution was the scaffold speech, which represented the "active co-operation of the condemned" (162).

Given her life and career, Elizabeth Barton offers an important addition to Frances Dolan's essay about women on scaffolds: "For the female offender addressing a large audience—perhaps for the first and only time—from the scaffold, any speech, even one that affirmed the status quo and condemned herself, offered an opportunity to speak publicly that challenged powerful constraints on female self-assertion and volubility" ("'Gentlemen, I have one thing more to say': Women on Scaffolds in England, 1563-1680," *Modern Philology* 92 [1994], 69). Each of the condemned women Dolan examines uses the occasion of her execution to "challenge the church or courts that judge her and to show up the very men who are supposed to govern her, first through her transgressions, then through her self-assertions and counter-accusations" (177-78). But, having spoken out actively and publicly in her life, Elizabeth Barton, as we have seen, does not use the occasion of her last speech to challenge those who judged her; instead, she is forced to deny her power and authority at the time of her death, attributing her words and actions to the men who were about to die with her.

60. See Whatmore, "Sermon," 466; act of attainder, *Statutes of the Realm,* 3:448; Whatmore, "Sermon," 471.

61. *LP* VII, 192; printed in Wright, *Three Chapters of Letters,* letter 10, 26.

Chapter 5

1. As we have seen, the Succession Act had made words "to the prejudice, slander, disturbance and derogation" of Henry's second marriage misprision of treason. The new Treason Act had declared any desire or attempt—even spoken—to deprive the king, his wife, or his heir of their "dignities" or "title" treason; it was also treason to call the king "heretic, schismatic, tyrant, infidel, or usurper of the crown." See chapter 1.

2. SP 1/119, fol. 29 (in *Letters and Papers, Foreign and Domestic, of the Reign of Henry VIII,* ed. J. S. Brewer et al., 21 vols. and *Addenda* [London, 1862-1932], XI.1, 1045[1]; hereafter referred to as *LP*).

3. SP 1/119, fol. 30 (*LP* XI.1, 1045[2]).

4. SP 1/119, fol. 29 (*LP* XI.1, 1045[1]).

5. SP 1/119, fol. 30 (*LP* XI.1, 1046). The long entry for Sir Richard Gresham in the *Dictionary of National Biography (DNB)* indicates he was from an old Norfolk

family from the village of Gresham. Gresham had a variety of contacts with the court in general and with Cromwell in particular. Gresham had been elected sheriff of London in 1531, had become an alderman in 1536, and would be elected lord mayor of London on Michaelmas Day (29 September) 1537.

6. Documents referring to those investigated in Norfolk for expressing sympathy for the northern rebels include *LP* XII.1, 424; SP 1/121, fols. 31-33 (*LP* XII.2, 21); SP 1/121, fols. 70-73 (*LP* XII.2, 56); and *LP* XII.2, 150. An excellent summary of these disturbances and rumors in Norfolk is included in Madeleine Hope Dodds and Ruth Dodds, *The Pilgrimage of Grace, 1536-1537, and the Exeter Conspiracy, 1538,* 2 vols. (Cambridge, 1915), 2:174-75.

7. G. R. Elton, *Policy and Police: The Enforcement of the Reformation in the Age of Thomas Cromwell* (Cambridge, 1972), 144. Elton's story of the investigation into the plot is excellent (144-49); unlike Moreton (see n. 19), he spends at least a half-paragraph on Elizabeth Wood. For a discussion of the Walsingham plot, see also Christopher Haigh, *English Reformations: Religion, Politics, and Society under the Tudors* (Oxford, 1993), 149-51.

8. In the collection of extant documents on the Walsingham conspiracy, depositions taken from the Guisboroughs in Norfolk appear first, from George Guisborough (SP 1/119, fol. 33) and from William (fol. 34); depositions from Thomas Howse (fol. 35), Robert Hawker (fol. 36), and John Semble (fol. 36) follow (see abstracts in *LP* XI.1, 1056[1]). George Guisborough's examination in London is SP 1/119, fol. 37 (*LP* XI.1, 1056[2.i]).

9. SP 1/119, fol. 38 (*LP* XI.1, 1056[2.ii]). There is some confusion about the date the conspirators planned to rise. The deposition refers to "St. Helen's Day"; Elton, with no explanation, alters this to St. Eligius' Eve, 24 June (St. Eligius is probably better known as St. Eloi—Chaucer's Prioress's "strongest oath" was "by Seinte Loy"). Dodds and Dodds indicate the rising was planned for St. Helen's Day, 21 May, while Moreton (see n. 19) sets the date as 3 May, the Feast of the Invention of the Cross by Saint Helen. Elton does not say why he has dated the planned rising to St. Eligius's Eve. The date of 21 May, which Dodds and Dodds use, seems to be the day on which the Feast of Saint Helen is celebrated in the East (Saint Helen was Constantine's mother), but her feast day was celebrated on 18 August in western Europe. Moreton's date seems the most likely.

10. SP 1/119, fol. 51 (*LP* XI.1, 1063). While Heydon described them as "beggars," such a description does not seem justified, given their occupations.

11. SP 1/119, fols. 141-42 (*LP* XI.1, 1125).

12. SP 1/120, fol. 24 (*LP* XI.1, 1171). While being held in the castle, Rogerson tried to incite further rebellion (see abstracts of depositions taken from the prisoners, most of them accused felons, on 8 and 9 June, *LP* XII.2, 56, 68 [the originals of these documents are SP 1/121, fols. 70-73, 86-89]).

13. On 29 May Southwell wrote to Cromwell with notice that the Walsingham conspirators had been convicted. He enclosed lists of the prisoners and judgments against them, SP 1/120, fol. 226 (*LP* XII.1, 1300[2]); the controlment roll, which gives occupations, is KB 29/170, rot. 33. The indictments are found in KB 9/538/4-8.

14. Southwell sent a "memorandum of executions" to Cromwell, SP 1/120, fol. 227 (*LP* XII.1, 1300[3]).

15. Although Southwell's description of the condemned men's speeches is brief, their words seem to conform to the pattern described by Lacey Baldwin Smith, "English Treason Trials and Confessions in the Sixteenth Century," *Journal of the History of Ideas,* 15 (1954), 471-98.

16. SP 1/120, fols. 224-25 (*LP* XII.1, 1300[1]). No mention is made of the execution of Thomas Penne. Elton (*Policy and Police,* 148) indicates that "for reasons unknown" he was "left in gaol."

17. The charge appears in KB 29/170, rot. 33. Another brief glimpse of women's reactions to the conspiracy is to be found in a letter from Richard Southwell to Cromwell dated 2 June. Still in Norfolk looking into another case of "a person taken . . . for words," Southwell reported that, on hearing a report from Norwich after the assizes, "the wife of one of those to be executed fell down in a swoon, and so lay for an hour" (SP 1/121, fols. 199-24 [*LP* XII.2, 13]).

18. SP 1/120, fol. 228 (*LP* XII.1, 1301[1]).

19. C. E. Moreton, "The Walsingham Conspiracy," *Historical Research: The Bulletin of the Institute of Historical Research,* 60 (1987), 29-43. Something of the Walsingham conspiracy is also detailed in Dodds and Dodds, *Pilgrimage of Grace,* 2:175-79, with a reference to Elizabeth Wood on 177.

20. Heydon's "memorandum" of the report made by Bettes and Oakes on 28 May is SP 1/120, fol. 230 (*LP* XII.1, 1301[2]).

21. "Cloutshoes" are shoes studded with large-headed nails. The *OED* includes references that imply that cloutshoes could be used as weapons (a reference, for example, to a fifteenth-century Paston letter). Shoes and boots had been used as weapons in the Evil May Day riots of 1517; see chapter 6, below.

    It's interesting to note that Mistress Amadas (see chap. 4) also quoted a prophecy about the people's resistance with "clubs," indicating that, after the kingdom was "conquered by the Scots," the invaders would be driven out: "the clobs of Essex shall drive them forth again" (BL MS Cotton Cleopatra E.iv, fol. 99).

22. For the charge and subsequent conviction, see KB 29/170, rot. 33, and KB 9/538/13.

23. SP 1/120, fols. 246-47 (*LP* XII.1, 1316).

24. Edward Hall, *The Triumphant Reign of Henry VIII . . . ,* ed. Charles Whibley, 2 vols. (London, 1904), 2:145.

25. *LP* IV.3, 5702.

26.   Hall, *Triumphant Reign,* 2:155.

27.   George Cavendish, *Thomas Wolsey, Late Cardinal, his Life and Death, Written by George Cavendish, his Gentleman-Usher,* ed. Roger Lockyer (London, 1973), 66, 108.

28.   *Chronicle of King Henry VIII of England . . . Written in Spanish by an Unknown Hand,* ed. and trans. Martin A. Sharp Hume (London, 1889), 14.

29.   About the significance of such rumor and gossip, see Jan Vansina, *Oral Tradition as History* (Madison, WI, 1985):

> Hearsay or rumor is transmitted from ear to mouth. It . . . deals with news—indeed, with sensational news, since otherwise no rumor would build up. . . .
>
> Many rumors have a basis in fact, especially in a society without writing or mass media, where speech is the medium of information. . . .
>
> Rumor is the process by which a collective historical consciousness is built. The collective interpretations resulting from massive rumors lead to commonly accepted interpretations of events, nonevents, or sets of events. Hence a tradition based on rumor tells more about the mentality of the time of the happening than about the events themselves. (6)

(Vansina also comments on the "news" of prophecy, which can "pass into tradition . . . as glosses on the meaning of history" [7].)

Vansina is cited by Carole Levin in her article about Elizabeth Tudor's "self-representation" and popular reaction to the queen (often in the form of slander and gossip): "Power, Politics, and Sexuality: Images of Elizabeth I," in *The Politics of Gender in Early Modern Europe,* ed. Jean R. Brink et al. (Kirksville, MO, 1989), 95-110.

Levin cites several other very helpful analyses of the cultural significance of gossip: Max Gluckman, "Gossip and Scandal," *Current Anthropology,* 4 (1963), 307-16; Robert Paine, "What Is Gossip About? An Alternative Hypothesis," *Man,* n.s. 2 (1967), 278-85 (a typographical error in Levin's note misdates the article to 1976); Max Gluckman, "Psychological, Sociological and Anthropological Explanations of Witchcraft and Gossip: A Clarification," *Man,* n.s. 3 (1968), 20-34; and, more recently, Patricia Meyer Spacks, *Gossip* (Chicago, 1985). Spacks's first chapter, "Its Problematics," is particularly useful.

Spacks posits a range of gossip. At one "end of the continuum" is gossip that takes place "in private, at leisure, in a context of trust," which exists "only as a function of intimacy" (5). At the opposite extreme

> gossip manifests itself as distilled malice. It plays with reputations, circulating truths and half-truths and falsehoods about the activities, sometimes about the motives

and feelings, of others. Often it serves serious (possibly unconscious) purposes for the gossipers, whose manipulations of reputation can further political or social ambitions by damaging competitors or enemies, gratify envy and rage by diminishing another, generate an immediately satisfying sense of power, although the talkers acknowledge no such intent. Supplying a powerful weapon in the politics of large groups and small, gossip can effect incalculable harm.(4)

Spacks adds: "My characterization of the varieties of gossip raises the question of purpose. Gossip insists on its own frivolity. Even the most destructive gossip does not announce destructive intent; the talk's alleged 'idleness' protects its participants" (6). This very "idleness" and "frivolity" is exactly what is at issue in our discussion here, since such talk could be interpreted to construct treason after the 1534 Treason Act, its "idleness" and "frivolity," in this instance, not protecting its participants.

Spacks comments, too, about the often sexual nature of such talk: "Gossip, even when it avoids the [explicitly] sexual, bears about it a faint flavor of the erotic. (Of course, sexual activities and emotions supply the most familiar staple of gossip. . . .) The atmosphere of erotic titillation suggests gossip's implicit voyeurism. Surely everyone feels—although some suppress—the same prurient interest in others' privacies" (11).

In sum, Spacks's conclusions about the function of gossip are useful for the understanding the incidents that follow in our discussion: "As a mode of interpretation, gossip . . . helps people make sense of the past in light of the present, and of the present in relation to the past" (230).

30. Cavendish, *Life of Wolsey*, 127.

31. *Calendar of Letters, Documents and State Papers Relating to the Negotiations between England and Spain Preserved in the Archives at Simancas and Elsewhere,* ed. G. A. Bergenroth et al. (London, 1862-1965), IV.1, 302; hereafter referred to as *Calendar of State Papers, Spanish.*

32. *Calendar of State Papers, Spanish,* IV.2, 980.

33. *Calendar of State Papers and Manuscripts Relating to English Affairs Existing in the Archives and Collections of Venice and in Other Libraries in Northern Italy,* ed. J. Rawdon Brown et al. (London, 1864-1947), IV, 768; hereafter referred to as *Calendar of State Papers, Venetian.* Capello sent a number of dispatches describing the arrests of preachers who had publicly preached against the divorce (see, for example, letters 766, 767).

34. "A London Chronicle, 1523-1555," ed. Charles L. Kingsford, in *The Camden Miscellany XII* (London, 1910), 8.

35. On defamation as an ecclesiastical offense, see the very helpful discussion in Richard M. Wunderli, *London Church Courts and Society on the Eve of the*

Reformation (Cambridge, MA, 1981), 63-80. On women's accusations, Wunderli writes: "in the fifteenth century there were as many female plaintiffs as male. . . . After the turn of the sixteenth century numbers of male plaintiffs declined substantially. . . . Defendants in defamation suits, those who allegedly had imputed crimes to others, were also most often women; in some years the ratio of women to men was as high as three to one" (75-76).

On women and defamation, see also Laura Gowig, "Language, Power, and the Law: Women's Slander Litigation in Early Modern London," in *Women, Crime and the Courts,* ed. Jenny Kermode and Garthine Walker (Chapel Hill, NC, 1994), 26-47, and Carol Z. Wiener, "Sex Roles and Crime in Late Elizabethan Hertfordshire," *Journal of Social History,* 8 (1975), 38-60 (esp. 46-48).

On the use of *whore* and *harlot* as the most frequent words by which one woman defames another, see Wunderli, *London Church Courts,* 77-78; Gowig, "Language, Power, and the Law," 35-36; and Wiener, "Sex Roles," 48; as well as the printed visitations books and act-books for numerous examples.

Much has been written on women's "scolding" talk as well; see, for example, "Branks: Women Should Be Seen but Not Heard" and "Ducking Stool: The Shaming of the Shrew," in E. J. Burford and Sandra Shulman, *Of Bridles and Burnings: The Punishment of Women* (New York, 1992); and Lynda E. Boose, "Scolding Brides and Bridling Scolds: Taming the Woman's Unruly Member," *Shakespeare Quarterly,* 42 (1991), 179-213. Especially interesting is Boose's discussion on 194-212, beginning with her comment that, in the Tudor and Stuart periods, "an obsessive energy was invested in exerting control over the unruly woman—the woman who was exercising . . . her tongue under her own control rather than under the rule of a man."

Useful observations on women's gossip in the seventeenth century appear in Sara Heller Mendelson, *The Mental World of Stuart Women: Three Studies* (Amherst, MA, 1987).

Among the many reports of gossip, rumors, and threats in the state papers, see: from 1515, *LP* II.1, 147-48, 171, 325-26, 1259, 1313, 2733; from 1517, *LP* II.2, 3852; from 1518, *LP* II.2, 3951; from 1520, *LP* III.1, 995, 1003; from 1521, *LP* III.1, 1165, 1221, 1280, 1313-14, 1320, 1353, 1356, 1363; from 1523, *LP* III.2, 3082; from 1524, *LP* IV.1, 891; from 1525, *LP* IV.1, 1470-71; from 1526, *LP* IV.1, 2178, *LP* IV.2, 2450, 3230; from 1527, *LP* IV.2, 3530, 3703, 4012-13, 4040, 4140, 4252, 4309, 4501, 4669; from 1528, *LP,* IV.3, 5190; from 1532, *LP* V, 907 (SP 1/69, fols. 227-28); from 1533, *LP* VI, 873 (SP 1/78, fol. 20), 964 (SP 1/78, fols. 115-16), 1122 (SP 1/79, fol. 62), 1254 (SP 1/79, fol. 182); and from the Milanese envoy, *Calendar of State Papers, Venice,* IV, 632; from 1534, *LP* VII, 303, 454 (SP Fol. P, fol. 17), 480 (SP 1/83, fol. 91), 497 (SP 1/83, fols. 96-97), 559 (SP 1/83, fols. 184-85), 678 (SP 1/84, fol. 59), 802 (SP 1/84, fol. 172), 939

(SP 1/85, fol. 26-27), 973 (printed in Roger Bigelow Merriman, *Life and Letters of Thomas Cromwell,* 2 vols. [1902; rpt., Oxford, 1968], vol. 1, letter 76), 1020 (SP 1/85, fol. 93), 1440 (SP 1/87, fol. 38); from 1535, *LP* VIII, 39 (SP 1/89, fol. 22), 81 (SP 1/89, fol. 59), 278 (SP 1/90, fols. 184-85), 324 (SP 3/2, fol. 7), 480 (SP 1/91, fol. 176), 518 (SP 1/91, fol. 216), 565, 567, 609, 620 (SP 1/92, fol. 126), 624 (SP 1/92, fol. 127), 643 (SP 1/92, fol. 133), 727 (SP 1/92, fols. 187-88), 736 (SP 1/92, fols. 194-95), 737 (SP 1/92, fols. 197-97), 738 (SP 1/92, fols. 198-99), 771 (SP 3/14, fol. 20), 799 (SP 1/92, fols. 267-69), 802, 862 (SP 1/93, fols. 80-82), 893 (printed in Merriman, *Life and Letters of Thomas Cromwell,* vol. 1, letter 105), 949, 990 (SP 1/93, fol. 238), 1025, 1033, 1069, 1038; and Merriman, *Life and Letters of Thomas Cromwell,* vol. 2, letters 161, 168; from 1535, *LP* IX, 37, 46 (SP 1/95, fol. 49), 52 (SP 1/95, fol. 55), 74 (SP 1/95, fol. 76), 84 (SP 1/95, fols. 78-83), 136 (SP 1/95, fol. 137), 383 (SP 1/96, fols. 183-84), 404 (E 36/120, fol. 104), 491 (SP 1/97, fols. 72-74), 691 (SP 1/98, fol. 81), 786 (SP 1/99, fol. 9), 791 (SP 1/99, fol. 20), 864 (SP 1.99, fol. 77), 1123 (SP 1/100, fol. 80); from 1536, *LP* X, 49, 52 (SP 1/101, fol. 4), 77, 254, 272, 291, 693 (SP 1/103, fols. 141-44), 722 (SP 1/103, fols. 163-64); from 1536, *LP* XI, 140 (SP 1/105, fol. 109), 190 (SP 1/105, fol. 202), 196 (SP 1/105, fol. 211), 300 (SP 1/105, fols. 295-96), 301 (SP 1/106, fols. 1-2), 302 (SP 1/106, fols. 3-4), 354 (E 36/120, fol. 78), 393 (SP 1/106, fol. 97), 407 (SP 1/106, fols. 137-40), 417 (SP 1/106, fol. 142), 434 (SP 1/106, fols. 157-58), 464 (E 36/120, fol. 49), 486 (SP 1/106, fol. 191), 495, 878, 920 (SP 1/110, fols. 24-27), 1265 (SP 1/112, fols. 176-77), 1328 (SP 1/112, fols. 257-59), 1495 (SP 1/113, fols. 234-34); from 1537, *LP* XII.1, 62 (SP 1/114, fol. 73), 126 (SP 1/114, fol. 169), 298 (SP 1/115, fol. 141), 380 (E 36/119, fol. 48), 424 (SP 1/116, fols. 30-31), 508 (SP 1/116, fols. 119-24), 589 (SP 1/116, fols. 206-9), 685 (E 36/122, fol. 34), 775 (BL MS Cotton Caligula B.i, fol. 143), 784 (SP 1/117, fols. 192-95), 855 (BL MS Cotton Faustina, C.iii, fol. 455), 914 (E 36/119, fol. 125), 969 (SP 1/118, fols. 219-20), 976 (E 36/119, fol. 82), 990 (SP 1/118, fols. 231-334), 1147 (SP 1/119, fols. 184-97), 1212 (SP 1/120, fols. 100-4), 1259 (SP 1/120, fols. 169-70); from 1537, *LP* XII.2, 74 (SP 1/121, fols. 92-93), 339 (SP 1/123, fols. 91-92), 353 (SP 1/123, fol. 118), 530 (E 36/120, fol. 69), 741 (SP 1/125, fols. 21-22), 752 (SP 1/125, fols. 34-35), 764 (SP 1/125, fols. 46-51), 800 (SP 1/125, fols. 90-91), 912 (E 110/10, fol. 41), 918 (E 36/120, fol. 92), 1068 (SP 1/126, fols. 136-39), 1185 (SP 1/127, fol. 38), 1205 (SP 1/127, fol. 57), 1208[1] (SP 1/127, fols. 59-60), 1208[2] (E 36/120, fol. 57), 1220 (SP 1/127, fol. 81), 1252 (SP 1/127, fol. 120), 1298 (SP 1/127, fols. 170-71); from 1538, *LP* XIII.1, 7 (printed in Merriman, *Life and Letters of Thomas Cromwell,* vol. 2, letter 235), 16 (SP 1/128, fol. 20), 57 (SP 1/128, fol. 61), 58 (SP 1/128, fols. 62-63), 74 (SP 1/128, fols. 83-84), 533 (SP 1/130, fols. 78-79), 964 (SP 1/132, fols. 76-77), 996 (SP 3/2, fol. 121), 1346 (SP 1/134, fol. 131), 1370 (SP 1/134, fol. 157); and Merriman,

Life and Letters of Thomas Cromwell, vol. 2, letters 252, 274; *LP* XIII.2, 535 (SP 1/137, fols. 98-101), 555 (SP 1/137, fols. 131-34), 776 (SP 1/138, fols. 178-81; printed in Merriman, *Life and Letters of Thomas Cromwell,* vol. 2, letter 279), 964 (SP 1/140, fols. 16-17), 1090 (SP 1/140, fol. 125-26), 1175 (SP 1/140, fol. 118); from 1539, *LP* XIV.1, 178 (SP 1/142, fols. 187-90), 794, *LP* XIV.2, 11 (SP 1/153, fols. 5-6), 73 (SP 1/153, fols. 50-51), 102 (SP 1/153, fols. 74-75), 727 (SP ¾, 28; printed in Merriman, *Life and Letters of Thomas Cromwell,* vol. 2, letter 329); from 1540, *LP* XV, 252 (printed in Merriman, *Life and Letters of Thomas Cromwell,* vol. 2, letter 337); from 1541, *LP* XVI, 559 (SP 1/164, fols. 241-42); from 1542, *LP* XVII, 537; from 1543, *LP* XVIII.2, 546; from 1544, *LP,* XIX.2, 444[5]; from 1545, *LP,* XX.1, 282[25] (SP 60/12, fol. 33), 894 (SP 1/219, fol. 51).

This list is selective. Additional references are to be found in Christopher R. Duggan, "The Advent of Political Thought-Control in England: Seditious and Treasonable Speech, 1485-1547" (Ph.D. Diss., Northwestern University, 1993), particularly appendix 2 ("Seditious Word Cases under Henry VIII, 1509-30," 285-96) and appendix 3 ("Prosecutions for Verbal Treason, 1535-1547," 297-327).

36. SP 1/84, fol. 211 (*LP* VII, 840[1]).
37. SP 1/84, fols. 212-14 (*LP* VII, 840[2.i]).
38. SP 1/84, fol. 214 (*LP* VII, 840[2.ii]).
39. SP 1/85, fols. 199-202 (*LP* VI, 1175). There are two depositions, the first from John Brown, although he was only reporting what his wife had told him, the second from Alice herself.
40. SP 1/87, fol. 90 (*LP* VII, 1510).
41. SP 1/89, fol. 37 (*LP* VIII, 61).
42. SP 1/89, fol. 158 (*LP* VIII, 196)
43. The description of Anne as a "goggle-eyed whore" has certainly stuck; as Elton points out (*Policy and Police,* 137), it is a description that "has got into a good many textbooks." Unfortunately, despite Elton's comment that for this phrase Margaret Chanseler has "gained enduring fame," it's the *phrase* that has gained fame, not Margaret Chanseler; with the exception of Elton, historians have generally overlooked the woman who actually uttered the words.
44. The letter from Stonor is SP 1/93, fol. 42 (*LP* VIII, 844); the statements made by the witnesses are miscatalogued as SP 1/88, fol. 21 (*LP* VII, 1609, in which the misdating is noted).
45. SP 1/93, fol. 35 (*LP* VIII, 838); Cranmer's letter is only seven and a half lines long.
46. SP 1/95, fol. 38 (*LP* IX, 37[1]). Elton (*Policy and Police,* 211) discusses the monk of Jervaux, whose name he spells "George Lazenby."
47. SP 1/100, fol. 73 (*LP* IX, 1115).

48. *LP* X, 199, 282.
49. SP 1/106, fols. 3-4 (*LP* XI, 302).
50. Angelo Raine, ed., *York Civic Records* (York, 1945), 4:1-3. Women are often noted among the participants in enclosure riots. For one further example, see the extended case that pitted Henry Selby and the inhabitants of Thingden against John Mulsho (the documents cover the period 1509-38). Many of the documents are printed in *Select Cases before the King's Council in the Star Chamber, Commonly Called the Court of Star Chamber*, vol. 2: *A.D. 1509-1544*, ed. I. S. Leadham (London, 1911).
51. In *Religion and the Decline of Magic: Studies in Popular Beliefs in Sixteenth- and Seventeenth-Century England* (1971; rpt., London, 1980), Keith Thomas discusses such ritual cursing: "Helplessness in the face of their neighbours' hostility and the absence of any alternative means of redress made the ritual curse the resort of the poor and impotent" (608). In discussing Agnes Cook and Isabell Lutton, he concluded, "Cursing could thus be a substitute for political action."
    This particular resistance to enclosure was recorded in 1536; the state papers include an investigation into a series of "riots and unlawful assemblies" in Cumberland and Yorkshire the year before (SP 1/93, fols. 239-44 [*LP* VIII, 991, 992, 993]). There some "four score" tenants and freeholders, "the capital doers thereof," were indicted; "the cause and purpose of the aforesaid unlawful assemblies was only to pull down diverse enclosures." The "most notable offenders" were "committed to diverse wards" pending further investigation.
52. *York Civic Records*, 4:7-13. That wasn't the end of the "seditious and malicious words" spoken in York, however; in September another fracas broke out, with several townsmen accusing the mayor of being a "false perjured harlot and false knave," a man "false both to God and the king" (14-15). In October 1539 still more insulting words were spoken against the mayor, the men who spoke punished by spending three days and three nights in jail (43).
53. SP 1/106, fol. 142 (*LP* XI, 417).
54. Corporation of London Record Office, Repertory 9, fol. 222, as cited by Susan Brigden, *London and the Reformation* (Oxford, 1989), 252. Brigden notes as well several other reports of the support of Londoners for the northern rebels (152-53); for an additional contemporary report of "seditious rumors" in London, see *LP* XII.1, 62. For the northerners' threats against Cromwell, see, for example, *LP* XII.1, 199, 210.
55. SP 1/117, fols. 192-95 (*LP* XII.1, 784).
56. SP 1/124, fol. 34 (*LP* XII.2, 515).
57. SP 1/124, fols. 193-96 (*LP* XII.2, 665).
58. SP 1/126, fols. 136-39 (*LP* XII.2, 1068).

59. See, for example, SP 1/127, fols. 38, 57, 59-60, 81, 120, 170-71 (*LP*XII.2, 1185, 1205, 1208, 1220, 1252, 1298); for early 1539 see SP 1/128, fols. 20, 61, 62-63 (*LP*XIII.1, 16, 57, 58), SP 1/128, fol. 86, and BL MS Cotton appendix L, fols. 73-74 (*LP*XIII.1, 76). On the spread of this report, see Elton, *Policy and Police*, 73-78.

60. SP 1/127, fols. 123, 126-35 (*LP*XII.2, 1256).

61. The examination of Joan Boxworth is in SP 1/127, fol. 132.

62. BL MS Cotton Titus B.i, fol. 183 (*LP*XIII.1, 7); printed in Merriman, *Letters of Thomas Cromwell*, vol. 2, letter 235.

63. SP 1/127, fol. 161 (*LP*XII.2, 1282).

64. The Succession Act of 1536 is 28 Henry VIII, c. 7; see John Bellamy, *The Tudor Law of Treason: An Introduction* (London, 1979), 35-38. For the text of the 1536 proclamation "Ordering Punishment for Seditious Rumors . . . ," see Paul L. Hughes and James F. Larkin, *Tudor Royal Proclamations*, vol. 1: *The Early Tudors (1485-1553)* (New Haven, CT 1964), 244-45.

65. On the use of proclamation and circulars, see Elton, *Policy and Police*, 78-80. On the charge of 1538, see BL MS Additional 48047; quoted in part by Elton, *Policy and Police*, 46, and discussed 337-38.

    Propaganda was also employed in the government's campaign. See, for example, two pamphlets published by Richard Morison in 1536, both used in the campaign against the Pilgrimage of Grace but addressed as well to the dangers of sedition: "A Lamentation in Which Is Shown What Ruin and Destruction Cometh of Seditious Rebellion" and "A Remedy for Sedition Wherein Are Contained Many Things Concerning the True and Loyal Obeisance That Commons Owe unto Their Prince and Sovereign Lord the King," both printed by David S. Berkowitz in *Humanist Scholarship and Public Order* (Washington, DC, 1984).

66. For this I have used only the abstract in *LP*XIII.1, 6.

67. SP 1/128, fols. 86-87 (*LP*XIII.1, 76).

68. SP 1/130, fols. 81-83 (*LP*XIII.1, 543).

69. KB 9/545/85-86. According to Elton (*Policy and Police*, 74), the indictment was called by mandamus into the court of the King's Bench, "usually a proceeding intended to end in a quashing."

70. SP 1/136, fols. 200-203 (*LP*XIII.2, 392).

71. A report made by a woman to Cromwell appears in 1538. Anne Barneys from Norwich wrote to Cromwell about Richard Freeston, whom she accused of having "spoken words against the King's Grace and your lordship." At the time she heard him speak against the king, she had called Freeston a traitor, an accusation she repeated every time she met him since. She apologized for the delay in her report to Cromwell: "I would have reported it before this, but was great

with child, of which I have since been delivered" (SP 1,139, fol. 16 [*LP* XIII.2, 964]; qtd. from *LP*).

Women certainly could speak in the government's favor as well. During the investigation of the prior of Newburgh, one of the prior's tenants, Margaret Fulthorp, was examined. In conversation with the prior she had praised the duke of Norfolk, saying not only that he had served the king well but also that she wished he had come north even earlier, since Norfolk had served her and her husband a great deal of money by settling a dispute over rents in their favor (SP 1/126, fols. 23-30). The rather complicated investigation of the prior is summarized by Elton (*Policy and Police*, 333-35); in spite of the king's suspicions that the prior had a "cankered and malicious heart," the prior, who persisted in his absolute innocence, ultimately escaped conviction for treason.

72. SP 1/144, fol. 93 (*LP* XIV.1, 507).

73. The act of attainder for Margaret Tyrell is 32 HVIII c. 59 (*LP* XV, 498[57]). There are no detailed documents relating to Margaret Tyrell—no depositions or examinations, for example—only the act of attainder itself and brief reminders to himself made by Cromwell.

74. Cromwell's first note regarding Margaret Tyrell is found among his list of "remembrances" from November 1537, SP 1/126, fol. 155 (*LP* XII.2, 1122). The "order to be taken for Tyrell's wife" is BL MS Cotton Titus B.i, fol. 444 (*LP* XII.2, 1151). A nearly identical list is BL MS Cotton Titus B.i, fol. 439.

75. For the date of her imprisonment, see SP 1/130, fol. 212 (*LP* XIII.1, 627). The additional examination is noted in BL MS Cotton Titus B.i, fol. 472 (*LP* XIII.1, 187).

76. SP 1/130, fol. 212 (*LP* XIII.1, 627).

77. Tyrell's conviction is recorded in KB 27/1120, fol. 13. Privy Council notes from 7 July 1541 indicate that Tyrell "should be reprieved" (*LP* XVI, 973). There is no surviving detail about why Tyrell was reprieved but, in a letter to Francis I, the French ambassador in England theorized the reprieve was in order to "confront him [Tyrell] with some accomplices" (*LP* XVI, 1011). His pardon came in March 1543:

> William Tyrell, late of London, gentleman. Pardon of all treasons by him committed, of which he is or shall be attainted; the fact being that he stands indicted of diverse high treasons committed from 10 July 28 Henry VIII to 20 August 31 Henry VIII . . . also 4 August 18 Henry VIII, 12 November 29 Henry VIII (and at other times during the last three years), and 19 January 30 Henry VIII . . . of all which treasons the said William, Tuesday next after the three weeks of Holy Trinity 33 Henry VIII, was attainted at Westminster.

He was delated at Westminster on 4 March 1543 (*LP* XVIII.1, 346[9]).

78. For rumors about Anne of Cleves, see *LP* XVI, 1426, and *LP* XVII, 63, 124. Rumors that Anne of Cleves had borne Henry children emerged during the king's sixth (and final) marriage; see SP 1/219, fol. 49 (*LP* XXI.1, 894). It was also rumored in 1546 that Henry would once again have a new queen (*LP* XXI.1, 289, 1027).

79. SP 1/168, fol. 50 (*LP* XVI, 1407). Jane Rattsey was speaking to Elizabeth Bassett, another member of Anne's household.

80. In part the reduction of reports in the state papers may be the result of Cromwell's fall. At the time of his arrest his papers were seized. These papers account for the incredible wealth of detail for the years 1532-40.

Chapter 6

1. Edward Hall, *The Triumphant Reign of Henry VIII . . .*, ed. Charles Whibley, 2 vols. (London, 1904), 1:153-64. A relatively brief account is included in Charles Wriothesley, *A Chronicle of England during the Reigns of the Tudors, from A.D. 1485 to 1559*, ed. William D. Hamilton, 2 vols. (London [Camden Society], 1875), 1:11; *Chronicle of the Grey Friars of London*, ed. John G. Nichols (London [Camden Society], 1852), 30; and "A London Chronicle during the Reigns of Henry the Seventh and Henry the Eighth," ed. Clarence Hopper, in *The Camden Miscellany IV* (London, 1859), 7.

   See also *Letters and Papers, Foreign and Domestic, of the Reign of Henry VIII*, ed. J. S. Brewer et al., 21 vols. and *Addenda* (London, 1862-1932), II.2, 3233, 3244, 3259, 3367; hereafter referred to as *LP*.

   The Evil May Day riot figures in the opening scenes of the play of *Sir Thomas More* (see the discussion of this late-sixteenth-century representation of the riots by Peter Stallybrass, "The World Turned Upside Down: Inversion, Gender and the State" in *The Matter of Difference: Materialist Feminist Criticism of Shakespeare*, ed. Valerie Wayne [Ithaca, NY, 1991]), especially 211-14.

   Among Tudor historians, see J. D. Mackie, *The Oxford History of England*, vol. 7: *The Earlier Tudors, 1485-1558* (Oxford, 1952), 297-98, J. J. Scarisbrick, *Henry VIII* (Berkeley, CA, 1968), 67; not in John Guy, *Tudor England* (Oxford, 1986). A detailed account appears in Jasper Ridley, *Henry VIII* (London, 1984), 104-7. One of the best accounts is in Peter Gwyn, *The King's Cardinal* (London, 1990), 442-45. See also Susan Brigden, *London and the Reformation*, (Oxford, 1989), 129-33.

2. Hall, *Triumphant Reign*, 1:153-54.

3. Ibid., 1:154.

4. Ibid., 1:155.

5. Ibid., 1: 154-55.

6. For Sebastian Giustinian's reports, see *Calendar of State Papers and Manuscripts Relating to English Affairs Existing in the Archives and Collections of Venice and in Other Libraries in Northern Italy*, ed. J. Rawdon Brown et al. (London, 1864-1947), II, 879, 881, 883; hereafter referred to as *Calendar of State Papers, Venetian*. Giustinian's letters are abstracted in *LP* II.2, 3204, 3218, 3230. (Giustinian's letters have been collected by Rawdon Brown in *Four Years at the Court of Henry VIII: Selection of Despatches Written by the Venetian Ambassador, Sebastian Giustinian, and Addressed to the Signiory of Venice, January 12th 1515 to July 26th 1519*, 2 vols. [London, 1854].)

7. *Calendar of State Papers, Venetian*, II, 879.

8. Hall, *Triumphant Reign*, 1:157.

9. Ibid., 1:161.

10. Ibid.

11. *Calendar of State Papers, Venetian*, II, 879.

12. Hall, *Triumphant Reign*, 1:163.

13. Francesco Chieregato to Vigo de Campo San Pietro, 19 May, *Calendar of State Papers, Venetian*, II, 887.

14. Hall's report about Wolsey's role is supported by a letter dated 19 May from Nicholas Sagudino, Giustinian's secretary, to Alvise Foscari (*LP* II.2, 3259):

> on their [the prisoners] presenting themselves before His Majesty, the cardinal implored him aloud to pardon them, which the king said he would not by any means do; whereupon the said right reverend cardinal, turning towards the delinquents, announced the royal reply. . . . [T]he cardinal again besought His Majesty to grant them grace, some of the chief lords doing the like. So at length the king consented to pardon them, which was announced to these delinquents by said right reverend cardinal with tears in his eyes, and he made them a long discourse, urging them to lead good lives and comply with the royal will.

15. Scarisbrick *(Henry VIII)* includes it, for example, as does Ridley *(Henry VIII)*, who also quotes a ballad from Garrett Mattingly's *Catherine of Aragon* (1941; rpt., New York, 1990). According to Mattingly:

> The official version recorded that the 'prentices owed their lives to Henry's clemency and Wolsey's advice, but as the Londoners remembered it, it was Queen Catherine who . . . knelt before the king for the lives of the young men whose riot had spilled the blood of her Spanish countrymen.
>
>> For which, kind queen, with joyful heart

She heard their mothers' thanks and praise . . .
And lived beloved all her days.

Mattingly indicates the ballad was current a half century after the riots but gives no reference.

In *Divorced, Beheaded, Survived: A Feminist Reinterpretation of the Wives of Henry VIII* (Reading, MA, 1995) Karen Lindsey recounts the events of the Evil May Day riots (41-42), attributing the reprieve to *three* women, Queen Katherine, Mary Tudor ("the French queen"), and Margaret Tudor, queen of Scotland: "the three women rushed to Henry's chamber, throwing themselves at Henry's feet and begging him to spare the lives of the boys Norfolk had condemned to death." Their "spontaneous gesture" was reenacted as "a small piece" of the "sadistic farce" enacted by Henry and Wolsey at Westminster. Lindsey cites the nineteenth-century historian Agnes Strickland for this version of events (without indicating, however, which of Strickland's works this material comes from).

16. Sir Thomas More, *The Apology,* ed. J. B. Trapp, vol. 9 of *The Yale Edition of the Complete Works of St. Thomas More* (New Haven, CT, 1979), 156.

17. Haigh, *English Reformations: Religion, Politics, and Society under the Tudors* (Oxford, 1993), 100. For a summary of the dispute between the king and the university, see James McConica, ed., *The Collegiate University,* vol. 3 of *The History of the University of Oxford* (Oxford, 1986), 124-26. The letters from Henry to the university are abstracted in *LP* IV.3, 6303, 6308, 6320, and appendix 254; letters are printed in full by W. T. Mitchell in *Epistolae Academicae, 1508-1596* (Oxford, 1980), letters 187b, 191, 193, 194, 195a, 195b, 197a, 197b, 198.

18. *Calendar of State Papers, Venetian,* IV, 701.

19. I would also like to point out here the comment that "amongst the mob were many men, disguised as women." This suggests that it was more dangerous for men to act than for women, women presumably receiving less harsh treatment as a rule. The York civic records detailing the enclosure riots of 1536 indicate that some of the men involved in the disturbances had also disguised themselves in women's clothing. In the "confession" of Alexander Mason, a smith, aged forty years, he admits that he was involved in the casting down of the gates "in his own proper person" but accused Ralph Walker, a shoemaker, of being there "in women's clothing with a muffel [covering] over his face" (Angelo Raine, ed., *York Civic Records* [York, 1945], 4:3).

20. *LP* V, 1191, 1209[45].

21. For the incident in Exeter, see Haigh, *English Reformations,* 143.

22. For the resistance of the canons at Hexham, see, chiefly, SP 1/106, fols. 222-24 (*LP* XI, 504); Haigh, *English Reformations,* 144; and the detailed narrative in

Madeleine Hope Dodds and Ruth Dodds, *The Pilgrimage of Grace, 1536-1537, and the Exeter Conspiracy, 1538,* 2 vols. (Cambridge, 1915), 1:192-97.

23. We briefly mentioned the Taunton rising in chapter 2. The relevant state papers documenting the events in Taunton are not to be found among the 1536 state papers; instead, they are gathered in the later papers of SP 1/239 and 1/240. For noting that these documents relate to the events of 1536, G. R. Elton must be credited. The documents are, then, SP 1/239, fols. 287-89, 292, and SP 1/240, fol. 5 (*LP Addendum* I.1, 1056, 1058, 1063, 1075). In his account of the riot Elton also cites an entry in the King's Bench, KB 27/1102/9 (*Policy and Police,* 108-09).

The state papers do include two letters from May 1536 that refer to the risings in Taunton; both are letters reporting rumors about who was responsible for the harshness of the judgment against those executed and about the king's supposed displeasure at what had transpired (see SP 1/20, fols. 73-77 [*LP* XII.2, 1194, 1195]).

24. There is some uncertainty about the number executed; accounts from Somerset number them at twelve, which is the figure Elton accepts; Wriothesley indicates that fourteen were actually executed. Wriothesley adds the specific statement that one of those executed was a woman.

25. SP 1/140, fols. 61-63 (*LP* XIII.2, 1010).

26. *LP* XII.2, 291.

27. SP 1/119, fols. 63-64 (*LP* XII.1, 1083).

28. For Bulmer's involvement in the risings of December 1536 and January 1537, see chapters 1 and 2.

29. 31 Henry VIII, c. 61.

30. On the "treason of buggery," see John Bellamy, *The Tudor Law of Treason: An Introduction* (Toronto, 1979), 42-43. In a brief discussion of Hungerford's "unnatural offences" Bellamy suggests that buggery had been held as treason at various times. But, even if buggery weren't treason, conjuring to know the length of the king's life definitely was. Elton indicates that Hungerford was a friend of Cromwell's and a victim of his fall (*Policy and Police,* 341 n. 1). Conjuring to find out how long the king would live figured among the charges against the duke of Buckingham, attainted for treason in 1521 (see chap. 4).

31. Charles de Marillac, quoted in George L. Kittredge, *Witchcraft in Old and New England* (1929; rpt. New York, 1956), 65.

32. Hall, *Triumphant Reign,* 2:308; Wriothesley, *Chronicle of England,* 1:120; *Chronicle of the Grey Friars,* 43-44. The "London Chronicle, 1523-1555 (ed. Charles L. Kingsford, in *Camden Miscellany XII* [London, 1910]) also notes the executions, with no additional information but with some misinformation, indicating that the executions took place on Tower Hill; this error also appears in Hopper, "London Chronicle," 15.

33. In the similar case of Edward Stafford, duke of Buckingham, who had been attainted for treason for having "imagined and compassed traitorously and unnaturally the destruction of the most royal person of our said Sovereign Lord" (14 and 15 Henry VIII c. 20), Stafford had been involved with a monk named Nicholas Hopkins, who had done the conjuring (see Barbara J. Harris, *Edward Stafford, Third Duke of Buckingham, 1478-1521* [Stanford, CA, 1986], 180-202). Although Hopkins was not punished for his part in Stafford's treason, Harris notes the contemporary belief that, because of his "deep attachment" to Buckingham, Hopkins died of a broken heart (189). On Stafford's involvement with prophecies, see chapter 4.

34. SP 1/160, fol. 192 (*LP* XV, 784); the *LP* identifies the hand in this vague letter as Wriothesley's. It's not clear who the recipient of the letter was.

35. The petition from John Knight, chaplain, is printed in full by C. Trice Martin, "Clerical Life in the Fifteenth Century, as Illustrated by Proceedings of the Court of Chancery," *Archaeologia: Or Miscellaneous Tracts Relating to Antiquity,* 60 (1907), 373-74.

36. Anthony Fletcher, *Tudor Rebellions* (1968; rpt., London, 1973), 47.

37. This incident is not mentioned in Mackie, Guy, or Elton (*England under the Tudors* [1955; rpt., London, 1991]), though Elton does refer to the conspiracy briefly in *Policy and Police,* 395. Fletcher indicates "about fifteen" were executed, while Elton says fourteen were executed.

38. See Eric Ives, *Faction in Tudor England* (London, 1979); and his biography *Anne Boleyn* (Oxford, 1986); as well as Retha Warnicke, *The Rise and Fall of Anne Boleyn: Family Politics at the Court of Henry VIII* (Cambridge, 1989).

39. For brief discussion, see Mackie, *Earlier Tudors,* 396, 418; and Scarisbrick, *Henry VIII,* 364-65; for a more detailed narrative, see Dodds and Dodds, *Pilgrimage of Grace,* 2:277-328 (two chaps., "The White Rose Party" and "The Exeter Conspiracy").

40. There are many surviving documents in the state papers: from 1538, *LP* XIII.2, 695, 696 (SP 1/138, fols. 12-27), 702 (SP 1/138, fols. 32-41), 732 (a list of "the names of all the nobility in England, their ages, and their activeness," now in the Archivo di Stato at Rome, which calls Exeter "lusty and strong of power, specially beloved, diseased often with the gout, and next unto the Crown of any man within England"), 743 (SP 1/138, fols. 92-93), 765 (SP 1/138, fols. 158-59, an examination of Gertrude Courtenay), 766 (SP 1/138, fols. 160-61, an examination of a woman named Elizabeth Darrell about Geoffrey Pole's conversations), 771 (SP 1/138, fols. 168-73), 772 (SP 1/138, fols. 174-75), 779 (SP 1/138, fols. 183-84), 796 (SP 1/138, fols. 189-90, an examination of Constance Pole), 797 (SP 1/138, fols. 191-205), 802 (SP 1/138, fol. 210, an examination of Constance Bontayne about the meeting of Gertrude Courtenay with Elizabeth Barton), 804

(SP 1/138, fols. 213-30, which include three examinations of Gertrude Courtenay), 805 (SP 1/138, fols. 231-36), 817 (examinations about the activities and conversations of the countess of Salisbury), 818 (SP 1/138, fols. 242-47, answers of the countess of Salisbury), 819[2-3] (SP 1/138, fols. 242-53, papers seized from the countess of Salisbury) and 819[3,4,5] (E 36/155, fols. 9-16), 822, 827 (SP 1/139, fols. 14-20), 828 (SP 1/139, fols. 21-24), 829 (SP 1/139, fols. 25-36), 830 (SP 1/139, fols. 37-75), 831 (SP 1/139, fols. 76-80), 835 (a letter from Southampton about repeated examinations of the countess of Salisbury and about her imprisonment at Cowdray), 838 (SP 1, 139, fols. 86-98, an inventory of the countess of Salisbury's goods), 855 (SP 1/139, fols. 131-34, a letter from Southampton on repeated attempts to get information from the countess of Salisbury), 875 (SP 1/139, fols. 152-55), 876, 884, 954 (SP 1/139, fol. 220, Cromwell's memoranda for indictments), 955 (SP 1/139, fols. 221-22, an abstract of evidence against Henry Pole, lord Montague), 956 (SP 1/139, fols. 223-24, Cromwell's notes about evidence against Exeter and Montague), 957 (SP 1/139, fols. 225-26, Cromwell's notes about evidence against Geoffrey Pole and Edward Neville), 958 (SP 1/139, fols. 227-28, counts to be inserted into indictment of Montague), 959 (SP 1/139, fols. 229-30, notes for the prosecution of Exeter and Montague), 960 (SP 1/140, fols. 1-2, charges against Montague), 61 (SP 1/140, fols. 3-8, charges against Exeter), 62 (SP 1/140, fols. 9-14, extracts of witnesses), 979 (KB 8/11/11, trials), 986 (KB 8/11/1, trials), 987 (E 36/120, fol. 38, declaration of Sir Edward Neville), 1056 (SP 1/140, fol. 97, proclamation "degrading" Exeter); from 1539, *LP* XIV.1, 37, 520 (Cotton Cleopatra E.iv, fols. 209-10, Wriothesley on the countess of Salisbury), 806 (letter from Cromwell to Henry VIII describing his examination of Gertrude Courtenay, printed in Roger Bigelow Merriman, *Life and Letters of Thomas Cromwell,* 2 vols. [1902; rpt., Oxford, 1968], vol. 2, letter 307), 867 (31 Henry VIII, c. 66, bill of attainder against all involved in the White Rose party, including Gertrude Courtenay and the countess of Salisbury), *LP* XIV.2, 212 (a letter of Cardinal Reginald Pole about Henry's actions against his family, in particular his mother: "not only has he condemned to death a woman of seventy, than whom he has no nearer relation except his daughter, and of whom he used to say there was no holier woman in his kingdom, but at the same time, her grandson, son of my brother [Henry Pole], a child, the remaining hope of our race. . . . At length it has come to women and innocent children, for not only my mother is condemned, but the wife of that marquis [Exeter] who was slain with my brother, whose goodness was famous and whose little son is to follow her"), 287 (SP 1/153, fols. 219-20), 401 (Richard Morison's official description of the "great and detestable vice, treason, wher[e]in the secret practices and traitorous workings of them that suffered of late are disclosed," printed in London, 1539), 554 (a list of prisoners held in the Tower, including the countess of Salisbury and Gertrude Courtenay); from 1540, *LP* XV, 487 (PRO 31/3, transcripts of a diplomatic letter of Marillac, dated 10 April 1540, indicating Gertrude Courtenay had been released from the Tower but that her son, the countess of Salisbury, and Montague's son remain in the Tower); from 1541, *LP* XVI, 868 (PRO 31/3, transcripts of a letter from Marillac to Francis I, dated 29 May 1541, informing the French king of the execution of the countess of Salisbury), 941 (PRO 31/3, letter from Marillac to Francis I with further mention of the countess's execution).

Chronicle accounts of the trials and executions include Hall, *Triumphant Reign,* 2:283-85; Wriothesley, *Chronicle of England,* 1:88, 91-92; and *Chronicle of King Henry VIII of England . . . Written in Spanish by an Unknown Hand,* ed. and trans. Martin A. Sharp Hume (London, 1889), 131-34.

Chapter 7

1. Mabel's case appears in SP 1/130, fols. 22-31 (in *Letters and Papers, Foreign and Domestic, of the Reign of Henry VIII,* ed. J. S. Brewer et al., 21 vols. and *Addenda* [London, 1862-1932], XIII.1, 487; hereafter referred to as *LP).* Her story is briefly mentioned by Madeleine Hope Dodds and Ruth Dodds, *The Pilgrimage of Grace, 1536-1537, and the Exeter Conspiracy, 1538,* 2 vols. (Cambridge, 1915), 2:301; G. R. Elton, *Policy and Police: The Enforcement of the Reformation in the Age of Thomas Cromwell* (Cambridge, 1972), 57-58; and Patricia Crawford, *Women and Religion in England, 1500-1720* (New York, 1993), 105 (who cites Elton as her source).
2. SP 1/130, fols. 24-25.
3. Dating the events in this case is difficult. For one thing, the sequence of events is itself confusing, and the witnesses, as we could expect, give conflicting testimony about what happened and when it occurred. Further complicating chronology is the witnesses' dating of events by their relation to saints' days or the days of religious feasts. Agnes, for example, dates Mabel's arrival at Reysome Grange as seven days before "Cross Days last"; the date of the Exaltation of the Holy Cross is 14 September, while the date of the Invention of the Holy Cross is 3 May. Since events seem to have taken place during the spring of the previous year, Agnes was likely referring to late April, about a week before 3 May.
4. SP 1/130, fol. 26.
5. SP 1/130, fols. 27-28. *St. Trinian* is an alternative spelling for Saint Ninian (ca. 360 - ca. 432), generally regarded as the first Christian missionary to Scotland. (See the reference to Saint Ninian and the fasting of John Scot, n. 18).

6. SP 1/130, fol. 26.

7. SP 1/130, fol. 27.

8. SP 1/130, fols. 27-28.

9. SP 1/130, fol. 28.

10. SP 1/130, fol. 30. Elizabeth Broune was not involved any further in the Council of the North's investigations.

11. SP 1/130, fol. 31.

12. SP 1/134, fol. 56 (*LP* XIII.1, 705).

13. Alice M. Cooke, *Act Book of the Ecclesiastical Court of Whalley* (London, 1901), 66-67. The case also appears in Paul Hair, ed., *Before the Bawdy Court: Selections from Church Court and Other Records Relating to the Correction of Moral Offences in England, Scotland, and New England, 1300-1800* (New York, 1972), 194.

14. These articles are printed by J. S. Purvis, *Tudor Parish Documents of the Diocese of York* (Cambridge, 1948), 13-15, in which they are printed between Durham injunctions dated 1559 and the Visitation articles of 1567, implying an earlier date. But the articles are for the "xixth yere of the Raigne of the Quenes Majestie that now is" (i.e., 1576).

    The articles were earlier printed by James Raine, ed., *The Injunctions and Other Ecclesiastical Proceedings of Richard Barnes, Bishop of Durham, from 1575 to 1587* (Durham, 1850), 17. In a note Raine describes the "St. Trinian" fast as a fast abstaining from meat, the "black fast" as a fast abstaining from "the *lacticinia*." According to Raine, a St. Trinian fast was observed during Lent, while a black fast "characterizes what is called a Black Lent." He gives no source for his information, however. One of Mabel Brigge's fasts had been described as a St. Trinian's fast, the other as a black fast. Her fasts were also described by those who observed them, the Lockers explaining what went on in Holmpton and William Fisher what happened later, in Welwick. But neither of Mabel Brigge's fasts correspond to Raine's descriptions: neither occurred during Lent, and the rituals involved with both involved far more than abstaining from meat or milk products.

15. C. L'Estrange Ewen, *Witchcraft and Demonianism: A Concise Account Derived from Sworn Depositions and Confessions Obtained in the Courts of England and Wales* (London, 1933), 292.

16. See, for example, Christopher Haigh, *English Reformations: Religion, Politics, and Society under the Tudors* (Oxford, 1993); and Susan Brigden, *London and the Reformation* (Oxford, 1989). Specific examples of such concerns can be found in the many presentments printed in Visitations records and decisions recorded in printed act-books (see bibliography.).

17. For additional examples, see presentments and act-books.

18. See Hyder E. Rollins, "Some Accounts of Miraculous Fasts," *Journal of American Folk-Lore,* 34 (1921), 357-76. About the books and pamphlets publishing the

stories of "miraculous fasting persons," Rollins writes, "The literature of the subject is enormous in quantity, and to it no brief article could begin to do justice." He "call[s] attention only to some of the more picturesque stories" (357).

One of the "miraculous fasting persons" whose name Rollins found in an eighteenth-century source but about whom he could find no detail was one John Scot. Rollins would certainly have included Scot among his "picturesque stories" if he had been able to, for Scot's story is nothing if not picturesque.

On 21 July 1532 Clement VII issued a bull for John Scot, of Glasgow, whose "competitors and enemies," hoping to obtain "certain estates and possessions belonging to him," had thrown Scot into prison. In prison Scot had been "sustained . . . during 33 days, without food and without drink or human consolation, remaining comforted solely by our Lord Jesus Christ, the blessed Virgin Mary, and by St. Ninian, bishop and confessor, whose miracles in Scotland become daily more and more resplendent." Released from prison but still persecuted by his enemies, Scot had taken refuge in the monastery of Holyrood, where he remained without food or drink for 106 days, vowing that if he were delivered from "such distresses and tribulations" he would undertake a pilgrimage not only to the relics of Saint Ninian (at the church of Whitehern, in Galloway) but also one to the Sepulchre of Christ. Clement's bull granted Scot and a companion license to visit Jerusalem and the Holy Land (*Calendar of State Papers and Manuscripts Relating to English Affairs Existing in the Archives and Collections of Venice and in Other Libraries in Northern Italy*, ed. J. Rawdon Brown et al. [London, 1864-1947], IV, 789; hereafter referred to as *Calendar of State Papers, Venetian*).

By 1 September the Bolognese Vianesio Albergati had met Scot and, in order to test him, asked him "whether he would abstain for some days from eating and drinking." After stripping Scot, "lest he should secrete anything whereby to recruit his strength and deceive" him, Albergati kept Scot for eleven days without food or drink—the "Glasgow Faster" passing Albergati's test successfully (*Calendar of State Papers, Venetian, IV, 801*). By 30 September Scot had passed yet another test, this one in Rome for Clement himself, and this time of thirteen days' duration (*Calendar of State Papers, Venetian, IV, 810*); this trial was reported to the Venetian senate by Marco Antonio Venier, ambassador at Rome on 5 October (*Calendar of State Papers, Venetian, IV, 812*). By 6 October Scot was in Venice, where a description of the Glasgow Faster was recorded: "He cannot speak [Italian]; is about 50 years old; long hair, red face, rather fat; is wrapped round the body in a very sorry cloth garment. . . . Many persons went to see him." Scot was to be locked up "in a chamber for 10 days without taking any food" in S. Giorgio Maggiore, after which fasting test a safe passage to Jerusalem was to be arranged for him (*Calendar of State Papers, Venetian, IV, 814*).

After this letter we lose sight of the amazing John Scot, the Glasgow Faster.

19. On fasting and its association with witchcraft, see Keith Thomas, *Religion and the Decline of Magic: Studies in Popular Beliefs in Sixteenth- and Seventeenth-Century England* (1971; rpt., London, 1980).

The ambivalence of fasting as a sign is discussed by Caroline Walker Bynum, *Holy Feast and Holy Fast: The Religious Significance of Food to Medieval Women* (Berkeley, CA, 1987); and Donald Weinstein and Rudolph Bell, *Saints and Society: The Two Worlds of Western Christendom, 1100-1700* (Chicago, 1982). See also William Monter, "Protestant Wives, Catholic Saints, and the Devil's Handmaid: Women in the Age of Reformations," *Becoming Visible: Women in European History* (New York, 1987), 203-19.

A brief but very good discussion of the connections between "candidates for sanctity and suspected witches" is found in Margaret L. King, *Women of the Renaissance* (Chicago, 1991), 152-55. A more recent treatment is in "Dangerous Beliefs: Magic, Prophecy and Mysticism," chapter 5 of Crawford, *Women and Religion in England.*

I will not attempt any discussion per se of witchcraft here, for the subject is complicated and the literature large (for an introduction to this literature, see the appropriate section in the biblio.).

I use the terms *witchcraft* and *sorcery* here to refer generally to the use of magic and conjuration typical of early sixteenth-century England rather to their (later) association with diabolism. Such usage is not uncommon; Richard Kieckhefer, for example, while defining carefully the three most common types of "witch belief"—"sorcery" (the practice of maleficent magic), "invocation" (the appeal to supernatural powers to have one's wishes executed), and "diabolism" (the deliberate worship of devils)—explicitly states that he uses the term *witchcraft* to refer generally to any or all of these practices, and the term witch to refer to any practitioners (*European Witch Trials: Their Foundations in Popular and Learned Culture, 1300-1500* [Berkeley, CA 1976], 5-8).

Keith Thomas, too, uses a similarly nontechnical working definition for *witchcraft*: "At a popular level every kind of magical activity . . . might be lumped together under the blanket title of 'witchcraft'" (517-18), including both maleficent and beneficent magic ("Witchcraft in England: The Crime and Its History," chap. 14 in *Religion and the Decline of Magic*). For a more technical discussion, see his appendix A, "The meaning of the term witchcraft" (551-54). Briefly, the witch exercised malevolent power by diabolic means (by "the devil's insinuation of himself," according to one writer in 1653), and witchcraft was "an occult power given by the Devil," while sorcery was the employment of maleficent magic (such as images or poisons) and could be practiced by anyone. In the cases discussed here we are not faced with Continental notions of demonology or with the prosecution of witches as devil worshipers.

For further discussion of terms, see also C. L'Estrange Ewen, *Witch Hunting and Witch Trials: The Indictments for Witchcraft from the Records of 1373 Assizes Held for the Home Circuit, A.D. 1559-1736* (London, 1929), 21-24.

20. For the case of Alianor Dulyne, see chapter 4, in which several women are noted for divining, also to be regarded as conjuring. For Johanna Benet, see William Hale, ed., *A Series of Precedents and Proceedings in Criminal Causes, 1475-1640, Extracted from Act-Books of Ecclesiastical Courts in the Diocese of London . . .* (London, 1847), 20. The charge reads: *Johanna vult acci[d]ere longitudinem hominis et facere in candelam ceri et offerri coram imagine, et sicut candelum consumit, sic debet homo consumere.*

21. The documents about Tanglost are printed by C. Trice Martin, "Clerical Life in the Fifteenth Century, as Illustrated by Proceedings of the Court of Chancery," *Archaeologia: Or Miscellaneous Tracts Relating to Antiquity,* 60 (1907), 374-75.

22. Tanglost's "answer" to the "bill of complaint of John, Bishop of St. David's," is printed by Martin, "Clerical Life," 375-76.

23. Thomas, *Religion and the Decline of Magic,* 317.

24. Hale, *Series of Precedents,* 10-11, 84.

25. Ibid., 139.

26. Purvis, *Tudor Parish Documents,* 199. Hair *(Before the Bawdy Court)* cites such a case from as late as the eighteenth century: in Elgin, Morayshire, Scotland, Agnes Urquhart was cited in 1724 for making a charm "for finding out things that were stolen," a practice she was said to have "done frequently. She was sentenced to public rebuke before the congregation (153).

27. For discussions of the kinds of women investigated—or persecuted—for witchcraft, see especially Christina Larner, *Witchcraft and Religion: The Politics of Popular Belief,* ed. Alan MacFarlane (Oxford, 1984); Marianne Hester, *Lewd Women and Wicked Witches: A Study of the Dynamics of Male Domination* (London, 1992); and Anne Llewellyn Barstow, *Witchcraze: A New History of the European Witch Hunts* (San Francisco, CA, 1994).

28. On the question of the "legal status of witchcraft in England," see Thomas, *Religion and the Decline of Magic,* appendix B, 554-58, in which he discusses the vexed question of jurisdiction: "The difficult problem is to ascertain whether the secular courts had independent jurisdiction over maleficent sorcery before the passing of the witchcraft statutes" (554). In brief, "Modern scholars have found very few cases of sorcery in the medieval records of lay courts. . . . Of the witch-trials which are known for certain to have occurred in the King's Bench or other temporal courts, several involved issues of fraud or treason and thus did not pose directly the problem of the legal status of maleficent sorcery" (555-56).

Still, "many contemporaries continued to find the precise legal situation obscure," and "legal practice had many vagaries" (556-57). Thomas concludes:

Even after the passing of the 1563 Act there were irregularities in its actual administration. A reasonable conclusion on the basis of this rather unsatisfactory evidence would be that, until the passing of the Witchcraft Acts, it was not a temporal offence to conjure spirits, or to engage in magical activity as such. But, if fraud was involved, a secular prosecution might well ensue, and if treason, murder or physical injury were alleged, the offence was in practice indictable. (557-58)

The first act of Parliament making witchcraft a felony—The Bill Against Conjurations and Witchcrafts and Sorcery and Enchantments—was passed in 1542, 33 Henry VIII c. 8 (see A. Luders et al, *Statutes of the Realm* [London, 1810-24], 3:837). The bill defined as a felony any "invocacions and conjuracions" to find treasure, the use of "wichecraftes, inchauntement, and sorceries to the distrucction of . . . personses and goodes," all kinds of image magic, and the use of magic "to declare and tell where thinges lost of stollen shulde be become." The penalty for all those found guilty was the "paynes of deathe" and the forfeiture of their property. This bill was repealed in 1547 (1 Edward VI c. 12). In 1563 Parliament again passed an act "agaynst conjuracions, inchantments, and witchecraftes" (5 Elizabeth c. 16).

Wunderli notes, "Witchcraft and sorcery were of much less concern as crimes than heresy to Yorkist and early Tudor Londoners. Only a few people were ever charged for sorcery" (*London Church Courts,* 126).

Chapter 8

1. SP 1/97, fols. 128-29 (in *Letters and Papers, Foreign and Domestic, of the Reign of Henry VIII,* ed. J. S. Brewer et al., 21 vols. and *Addenda* [London, 1862-1932], IX, 551; hereafter referred to as *LP*); printed in full by Henry Ellis, *Original Letters, Illustrative of English History* (London, 1846), 3rd ser., vol. 3, letter 268.

   This was not the first such case reported to Cromwell, but its political implication parallels more closely the situation of Mabel Brigge than, for example, a more general complaint in 1533 about a monk named Sheldon who had involved several people in conjuring in Huntingdonshire (SP 1/78, fol. 177 [*LP* VI, 1023]).

   A similar report with no clearly political connections is a report about an Oxford friar whose claims to know where lost or stolen property could be dug up were causing damage all around Oxford (cited by Elton, *Policy and Police: The Enforcement of the Reformation in the Age of Thomas Cromwell* [Cambridge, 1972], 48).

2. SP 1/126, fols. 177-78 (*LP* XII.2, 1102). We have looked at Cowpar's examination before, in chapter 4, for its details about the priest's alphabetic prophecies.

    Elton draws attention to the case of two men indicted in the King's Bench "for cheating three fools at Islington" by means of the kind of conjuring Cowpar seems to have been practicing. Although they were indicted, Elton concludes that there was probably no trial (*Policy and Police*, 48-49), nor were there any hints of any activities more serious than "cozening" their victims.

3. E 36/120, fol. 71 (*LP* XIII.1, 41).

4. SP 1/141, fol. 67 (*LP* XIII.2, 1200). There is no indication in the state papers who Guercey made his confession to nor who received it after it had been recorded.

5. SP 1/79, fol. 126 (*LP* VI, 1193).

6. See Madeleine Hope Dodds and Ruth Dodds, *The Pilgrimage of Grace, 1536-1537, and the Exeter Conspiracy, 1538*, 2 vols. (Cambridge, 1915), 1:87 n. E; Keith Thomas, *Religion and the Decline of Magic: Studies in Popular Beliefs in Sixteenth- and Seventeenth-Century England* (1971; rpt., London, 1980), 506; and David Loades, *Mary Tudor: A Life* (1989; rpt., Oxford, 1992), 76-77.

7. *LP* XII.1, 1156.

8. SP 1/120, fols. 108-11 (*LP* XII.1, 1214).

9. SP 1/124, fols. 151-54 (*LP* XII.1, 1246).

10. Curwen and Wharton report as well on a tenth case, that of Alexander Bank, who reportedly had been cut down by a man named John Dawson.

11. *LP* XII.1, 1257; printed in full in Roger Bigelow Merriman, *The Life and Letters of Thomas Cromwell*, 2 vols. (1902; rpt., Oxford, 1968), vol. 2, letter 188.

12. SP 1/135, fols. 53-55 (*LP* XIII.2, 62). The destination of Henry's pilgrimage is St. Michael's Mount, in Mount's Bay, just off the western coast of Cornwall. St. Michael's Mount was established in the eleventh century as a priory of Mont-Saint-Michel abbey.

13. An excellent discussion of the prohibitions of the Injunctions of 1536 and of 1538 is found in Eamon Duffy, *The Stripping of the Altars: Traditional Religion in England, 1400-1580* (New Haven, CT, 1992), 398-408. The texts of these injunctions are printed in Walter H. Frere and William McClure Kennedy, eds., *Visitation Articles and Injunctions of the Period of the Reformation* (London, 1910), vol. 2: "The First Royal Injunctions of Henry VIII, 1536," 1-11, and "The Second Royal Injunctions of Henry VIII, 1538," 34-43.

14. There are reports of similar incidents that might be included here, but they seem more exclusively to focus on official actions rather than popular reactions.

    For example, Charles Wriothesley describes the public "exposure" of the Rood of Grace, an "image of the crucifix of Christ which had been used of long continuance for a great pilgrimage at the Abbey of Boxley by Maidstone in Kent"

(*A Chronicle of England during the Reigns of the Tudors, from A.D. 1485 to 1559*, ed. William D. Hamilton, 2 vols. [London (Camden Society), 1875], 1:74). The image was set up at St. Paul's Cross on 24 February, 1538, and John Hilsey, bishop of Rochester, delivered a sermon on the Rood: "and so the people had been deluded and caused to do great idolatry by the said image, of long continuance, to the derogation of God's honor and great blasphemy of the name of God" (Wriothesley, *Chronicle of England,* 1:75). A letter to Cromwell described how this image had been "manipulated" by the abbot of Boxley:

> I found in the image of the rood called the Rood of Grace, the which heretofore hath been had in great veneration of people, certain engines and old wire, with old rotten sticks in the back of the same, that did cause the eyes of the same to move and stare in the head thereof, like unto a lively thing; and also the nether lip in like wise to move as though it should speak; which, so famed, was not a little strange to me and other that was present at the plucking down of the same, whereupon the abbot, hearing this bruit, did thither resort, whom to my little wit and cunning, with other of the old monks, I did examine of their knowledge of the premises, who do declare themselves to be ignorant of the same. (Ellis, *Original Letters,* 3rd ser., vol. 3, letter 322)

A similar "exposure" was involved later in the year, when Wriothesley described a sermon preached on 24 November, again by the bishop of Rochester, about the "blood of Hales," a relic that had been "proven" not to be blood at all but "honey clarified and colored with saffron" (*Chronicle of England,* 1:90). The blood of Hales had belonged to the abbey at Evesham. The "exposure" of the "miracle of the Blood of Hales" was made in a letter to Cromwell from Bishop Latimer:

> we have been boulting [sieving] and sifting the blood of Hales all this forenoon. It was wonderously closely and craftily enclosed and stopped up for taking of care. And it cleaves fast to the bottom of the little glass that it is in. And verily it seemeth to be an unctuous gum and a compound of many things. It hath a certain unctuous moistness, and though it seem somewhat like blood while it is in the glass, yet when any parcel of the same is taken out, it turneth to a yellowness and is cleaving like glue. (Ellis, *Original Letters,* vol. 3, letter 353)

In January 1540 Sir Roger Townsend wrote to Cromwell about yet another relic that had been denounced, the image of Our Lady of Walsingham. It was removed from Walsingham and taken to London, but Townsend was reporting that "a woman from Wells" had spread a story about a miracle that was effected by the image of Our Lady, even after it was taken to London. Townsend first put the woman in ward and then decided on her punishment:

> The next day after, being market day, there I caused her to be set in stocks in the morning, and about nine of the clock when the said market was fullest of people, with a paper set about her head, written with these words upon the same, "a reporter of false tales," was set in a cart and so carried about the marketstead and other streets in the town, staying in divers places where most people assembled, young people and boys of the town casting snowballs at her. This done and executed, [she] was brought to the stocks against, and there set till the market was ended. This was her penance; for I knew no law otherwise to punish her but by discretion, trusting it shall be a warning to other light persons in such wise to order themselves. (Ellis, *Original Letters*, 3rd ser., vol. 3, letter 318)

About the affair he concluded: "I cannot perceive but the said image is not yet out of some of their heads."

15. SP 1/134, fols. 133-34 (*LP* XIII.1, 1282[1]); and E 36/120, fols. 152-54 (*LP* XIII.1, 1350).

16. SP 1/133, fols. 241-42.

17. Caroline Walker Bynum, *Holy Feast and Holy Fast: The Religious Significance of Food to Medieval Women* (Berkeley, CA, 1987) notes a stereotypical view that "fasting as a religious activity is done primarily by women, although fasting as scientific experiment or as political protest is usually performed by men" (192). She argues instead that fasting was a way women "controlled their social and religious circumstances quite directly and effectively"; women could use fasting "to criticize powerful secular or religious authorities," and "to claim for themselves . . . reforming roles" (220).

18. Elton (*Policy and Police*, 57) suggests that Isabel Buck was probably pardoned.

Conclusion

1. In *Tudor England* (Oxford, 1986), John Guy writes: "The classic questions of the Middle Ages had centred on the relations between temporal and spiritual powers, but when Clement VII revoked Henry VIII's divorce suit to Rome, politics, humanism, evangelism, and legalism fused to ask the question, 'What is the state and how is it constructed?' It was Henry VIII and Parliament who gave the answer" (123).

2. A large number of the women whose names are in the state papers are recipients of grants and subsidies or involved in wardship suits (*Letters and Papers, Foreign and Domestic, of the Reign of Henry VIII,* ed. J. S. Brewer et al., 2 vols. and *Addenda* [London, 1862-1932]; hereafter referred to as *LP*). During the 1530s many of the women named in the state papers are included among the reports having to do with the dissolution of the monasteries: they are either reported as the "concubines" of priests or as nuns whose convents are being examined. Among the numerous examples: from 1534, *LP* VII, 527-29, 907; from 1536, *LP* IX, 406, 423, 457, 533, 607, 608, 668, 708, 954, 986, 1005, 1109, 1166; *LP* X, 136, 364, 562; *LP* XI, 174; from 1537, *LP* XII.1, 742; XII.2, 450; from 1538, *LP* XIII.2, 700, 716, 758, 767, 911, and *LP Addendum* I.2, 1343, 1369; from 1539, *LP,* XIV.2, 626.

    Women involved in the English reformation are also discussed, for example, in Christopher Haigh, *English Reformations: Religion, Politics, and Society under the Tudors* (Oxford, 1993); Susan Brigden, *London and the Reformation* (Oxford, 1989); and Patricia Crawford, *Women and Religion in England, 1500-1720* (New York, 1993).

3. For Margaret Bowgas, who was first reported for heresy in the Visitation of 1527, see James B. Oxley, *The Reformation in Essex to the Death of Mary* (Manchester, England, 1956), 7. She escaped punishment then, but she was arrested again in 1532, charged with the words quoted here, and carefully examined for what were believed to be Protestant sympathies (14-16). Eventually she abjured.

    Joan Baker's comments are cited by Brigden, *London and the Reformation,* 93. Alice Fonge's words were reported by two men who had come to her house asking for "charity" for the church; she was indicted for heresy (BL MS Cotton Cleopatra E.iv, fol. 124 [*LP* XII.2, 221]). Mrs. Cowper's conversation was with one Ellis, a servant of the marquis of Exeter (SP 1/139, fol. 1 [*LP* XIII.2, 820]).

    I will not attempt an exhaustive list of women accused of and executed for heresy. See, for example, the case of twenty-three Anabaptists, three of them women, arrested and tried for heresy in 1535—a man and a woman were burned at Smithfield on 4 June, while twelve others were taken to other towns and burned (*LP* VIII, 771, 826, 846; described by Charles Wriothesly, *A Chronicle of England during the Reigns of the Tudors, from A.D. 1485 to 1559,* ed. William D. Hamilton, 2 vols. [London, 1875], 1:28), or the extensive investigation of heretics in Kent by Cranmer in 1546, many of whom were women, including Joan French, Margaret Toftes senior and Margaret Toftes junior, Mrs. Starkey, Joan Boucher, and Joyce Benson (*LP* XVIII.2, 546 [291-378]; Johanna Merryweather, however, was examined for some kind of image magic involving a candle and "the dung" of the "young maid" she hoped to harm [300]).

The story of Anne Askew has been told often. For a succinct review, see the entry "Anne Askew Affair," in *Historical Dictionary of Tudor England.*

4. Brigden, *London and the Reformation*, 413-16.

5. See, for example, the cases before ecclesiastical courts noted in presentments and act-books cited in the bibliography. On the frequency of defamation charges between women, see Richard M. Wunderli, *London Church Courts and Society of the Eve of the Reformation* (Cambridge, MA, 1981); Laura Gowig, "Language, Power, and the Law: Women's Slander Litigation in Early Modern London," in *Women, Crime and the Courts,* ed. Jenny Kermode and Garthine Walker (Chapel Hill, NC, 1994); and Carol Z. Wiener, "Sex Roles and Crime in Late Elizabethan Hertfordshire," *Journal of Social History,* 8 (1975).

6. These are the conclusions originally posited by G.R. Elton, *Policy and Police: The Enforcement of the Reformation in the Age of Thomas Cromwell* (Cambridge, 1972), and my own experiences followed the path he outlines:

> The law, especially that of treason, was severe, reached far, and could punish even casual utterances with savagery. Its administration, though governed by comprehensive rules which imposed limits on the exercise of mere power, was intensive and precise. Police activity, in discovering and communicating suspects, was energetic and continuous. All this, one would suppose, should lend support to the notion that the 1530's produced a large tally of victims, of men and women almost innocently caught in the toils of the law and brought to the frightful end which execution for treason meant in the sixteenth century. That familiar assumption constituted the starting point of this enquiry. Yet . . . the story is a good deal more complex and less easily judged in terms of black and white. (383)

Elton concludes:

> The instruments of enforcement were used rigorously and stringently: no one would attempt to suggest that this government was of a gentle, merciful or tolerant disposition. But it worked to the facts which it made every effort to establish; it did not choose the easy solution of disposing of all, or even most, of the people it denounced. . . . [T]he evidence of investigations and of discrimination demonstrates that there was never any intention to do more than punish real guilt as defined by law. Treason was abhorred and to be rooted out, but treason also had to be properly proved in every case. There was a real revolution, but a revolution under the law, and while the first fact produced a severe law and energetic enforcement, the second ensured that there should be neither holocaust nor reign of terror. (399-400)

I do have some reservations about Elton's conclusions that those executed were always those about whom "real guilt as defined by law" had been "properly proved," but, given the number of those investigated for treason, relatively few were executed.

Elton constructs very useful tables for cases of treason between 1532 and 1540 (387, 394). The first charts those accused by kind of charge and by what is known to have resulted from the charges; the second graphs the charges by date. The results show the same pattern I have indicated here: a rise in charges from 1534 to a marked peak in 1536 and 1537, with a rapid fall in 1538. Briefly, delations rose from 4 in 1532 to 44 in 1534 to peaks of 110 and 128 in 1536 and 1537; in 1538 they fell to 89, by 1540 to 10. Further, between 1540 and Henry's death in 1547, Elton reports, only "a total of ninety-six persons are known to have come within the operation of the treason law" (395; this figure excludes those concerned in Catherine Howard's "treason").

7. See the very helpful discussion of "Gender and Power" in Merry E. Wiesner, *Women and Gender in Early Modern Europe* (Cambridge, 1993), 239-58, but especially the section "Gender and Political Power," 241-52.

8. Elton *(Policy and Police)* undertakes significant statistical analysis of all those who came "within the compass" of the treason laws, noting that further investigations would, of course, add to the numbers of those he included in his study. Further investigations will add to the number of women's stories that I have told here as well.

9. Women's roles in political and religious activities in the later sixteenth and seventeenth centuries have already been recognized; setting aside the debate about female rulers resulting from the reigns of Mary and Elizabeth Tudor, see, as only a few examples: Ellen A. McArthur, "Women Petitioners and the Long Parliament," *English Historical Review*, 24 (1909), 698-709; Keith Thomas, "Women and the Civil War Sects," *Past and Present*, 13 (1958), 42-62; Patrick Collinson, "The Role of Women in the English Reformation Illustrated by the Life and Friendships of Anne Locke," *Studies in Church History*, 2 (1965), 258-72; Claire Cross, "'He-Goats before the Flocks': A Note on the Part Played by Some Women in the Founding of Some Civil War Churches," *Studies in Church History*, 9 (1972), 195-202; Patricia Higgins, "The Reactions of Women," in *Politics, Religion and the English Civil War*, ed. Brian Manning (London, 1973), 179-22; Phyllis Mack, "Women as Prophets during the English Civil War," *Feminist Studies*, 8 (1982),19-45; Hilda L. Smith, *Reason's Disciples: Seventeenth-Century English Feminists* (Urbana, IL, 1982); Retha M. Warnicke, *Women of the English Renaissance and Reformation* (Westport, CT, 1983);Susan Dwyer Amussen, "Gender, Family and the Social Order, 1560-1725," in *Order and Disorder in Early Modern England*, ed. Anthony Fletcher and John Stevenson (Cambridge,

1985), 196-217; Susan Dwyer Amussen, *An Ordered Society: Gender and Class in Early Modern England* (London, 1988); Diane Willen, "Women and Religion in Early Modern England," in *Women in Reformation and Counter-Reformation Europe: Public and Private Worlds* (Bloomington, IN, 1989); Diane Willen, "Godly Women in Early Modern England: Puritanism and Gender," *Journal of Ecclesiastical History*, 43 (1992), 561-80; and Patricia Crawford, *Women and Religion in England, 1500-1720* (New York, 1993).

Some of the seditious words women are charged with having uttered at the time of the Restoration sound remarkably as if they had come from the mouth of Margaret Chanseler or Margery Cowpland; on 13 May 1660, for example, Margaret Dixon was charged with having said: "What! can they finde noe other man to bring in then a Scotsman? What! is there not some Englishman more fit to make a king then a Scott? There is none that loves him but drunk whores and whoremongers. I hope hee will never come into England, for that hee will sett on fire the three kingdomes as his father before him has done. God's curse light on him" (qtd. in James Raine, ed., *Depositions from the Castle of York, Relating to Offences Committed in the Northern Counties in the Seventeenth Centuries* [London, 1861], 83.

SELECTED BIBLIOGRAPHY

Full bibliographical references for all of the sources used in this book appear in the notes. This select bibliography lists principal manuscript and primary sources as well as the most frequently cited secondary works and the works most useful for those interested in further reading on the subjects of early modern England, Tudor reform and Reformation, political prophecy, European witchcraft, and women's activities during the early Tudor period.

Primary Sources, Manuscript

Public Record Office (London)

E 36	Exchequer, Treasury of Receipt, Miscellaneous Books
E 315	Exchequer, Augmentation Office, Miscellaneous Books
KB 8	King's Bench, Baga de Secretis
KB 29	King's Bench, Controlment Rolls
SP 1	State Papers, Henry VIII
SP 3	Lisle Letters
SP 60	State Papers, Ireland

British Library (London)

MS Cotton Caligula B.i
MS Cotton Cleopatra E.iv
MS Cotton Cleopatra E.vi
MS Cotton Otho C.x
MS Cotton Titus B.i
MS Cotton Faustina C.iii
MS Harley 282
MS Harley 6148

Primary Sources, Printed

Including contemporary writings, chronicles, printed collections of documents, and calendars.

Bowker, Margaret. *An Episcopal Court Book for the Diocese of Lincoln, 1514-1520.* Lincoln (Lincoln Record Society), 1967.

Brown, Rawdon. *Four Years at the Court of Henry VIII: Selection of Despatches Written by the Venetian Ambassador, Sebastian Giustinian, and Addressed to the Signiory of Venice, January 12th 1515, to July 26th 1519.* London, 1854.

Calendar of Letters, Documents and State Papers Relating to the Negotiations between England and Spain Preserved in the Archives at Simancas and elsewhere. Ed. G. A. Bergenroth et al. London, 1862-1965.

Calendar of State Papers and Manuscripts Relating to English Affairs Existing in the Archives and Collections of Venice and in other Libraries in Northern Italy. Ed. J. Rawdon Brown et al. London, 1864-1947.

Cavendish, George. *Thomas Wolsey, Late Cardinal, his Life and Death, Written by George Cavendish, his Gentleman-Usher.* Ed. Roger Lockyer. London, 1973.

Chronicle of the Grey Friars of London. Ed. John G. Nichols. London (Camden Society), 1852.

Chronicle of King Henry VIII of England, Being a Contemporary Record of Some of the Principal Events of the Reigns of Henry VIII and Edward VI, Written in Spanish by an Unknown Hand. Ed. and trans. Martin A. Sharp Hume. London, 1889.

Chronicle of the Years 1532-1537, Written by a Monk of St. Augustine's, Canterbury. Ed. John G. Nichols. In *Narratives of the Days of the Reformation.* London (Camden Society), 1859.

"A Chronicle, 1413-1536." In *Songs, Carols, and Other Miscellaneous Poems, from the Balliol MS 354, Richard Hill's Commonplace Book,* Ed. Roman Dyboski, 142-67. 1908. Reprint. London, 1937.

Clark, Andrew, ed. *Lincoln Diocese Documents, 1450-1544.* London (Early English Text Society), 1914.

Cooke, Alice M. *Act Book of the Ecclesiastical Court of Whalley, 1510-1538.* Chetham (Chetham Society), 1901.

Ellis, Henry. *Original Letters Illustrative of English History.* 3d Ser. London, 1846.

The Fabric Rolls of York Minster. Durham (Surtees Society), 1859.

Foster, Joseph, ed. *Pedigrees of the County Families of Yorkshire.* 2 vols. London, 1874.

――――. *The Visitation of Yorkshire, Made in the Years 1584/5.* . . . London, 1875.

Foxe, John. *The Acts and Monuments of John Foxe.* Ed. George Townsend. 8 vols. 1837-41. Reprint, New York, 1965.

Frere, Walter H., and William M. Kennedy, eds. *Visitation Articles and Injunctions of the Period of the Reformation.* 3 vols. London, 1910.

Gibbons, A. *Ely Episcopal Records: A Calendar and Concise View of the Episcopal Records Preserved in the Muniment Room of the Palace at Ely.* Lincoln, England 1891.

Hale, William, ed. *A Series of Precedents and Proceedings in Criminal Causes . . . from Act-Books of Ecclesiastical Courts in the Diocese of York.* London, 1847.

――――, ed. *A Series of Precedents and Proceedings in Criminal Causes, 1475-1640, Extracted from Act-Books of Ecclesiastical Courts in the Diocese of London.* . . . London, 1847.

Hall, Edward. *Chronicle Containing the History of England, during the Reign of Henry the Fourth.* . . . 1902. Reprint. New York, 1965.

――――. *The Triumphant Reign of Henry VIII.* . . . Ed. Charles Whibley. 2 vols. London, 1904.

Howell, T. B. *A Complete Collection of State Trials and Proceedings for High Treason.* . . . Vol. 1: 1163-1600. London, 1816.

Hughes, Paul L. and James F. Larkin, eds. *Tudor Royal Proclamations.* Vol. 1: The Early Tudors (1485-1553). New Haven, CT, 1964.

Jenkyns, Henry, ed. *The Remains of Thomas Cranmer, D.D., Archbishop of Canterbury.* 4 vols. Oxford, 1833.

Letters and Papers, Foreign and Domestic, of the Reign of Henry VIII. 21 vols. and *Addenda.* Ed. J. S. Brewer, et al. London, 1862-1910.

"A London Chronicle during the Reigns of Henry the Seventh and Henry the Eighth." Ed. Clarence Hopper. In *The Camden Miscellany IV.* London, 1859.

Longstaffe, W. Hylton Dyer, ed. *Heraldic Visitation of the Northern Counties in 1530, by Thomas Tonge, Norroy King of Arms.* Durham, 1863.

Merriman, Roger Bigelow, ed. *Life and Letters of Thomas Cromwell.* 2 vols. 1902. Reprint. Oxford, 1968.

Moore, A. Percival. "Proceedings of the Ecclesiastical Courts in the Archdeaconry of Leicester, 1516-1535." *Associated Architectural Societies, Reports and Papers,* 28 (1905-6), 593-661.

Ord, John W. *The History and Antiquities of Cleveland, Comprising the Wapentake of East and West Langbargh, North Riding, County York.* London, 1846.

Purvis, J. S., ed. *Tudor Paris Documents of the Diocese of York.* Cambridge, 1948.

Raine, Angelo, ed. *York Civic Records.* York Civic Records, vol. 4. York, 1945.

Raine, James, ed. *Depositions and Other Ecclesiastical Proceedings from the Courts of Durham, Extending from 1311 to the Reign of Elizabeth.* London, 1845.

———. *Depositions from the Castle of York, Relating to Offences Committed in the Northern Counties in the Seventeenth-Centuries.* London (Surtees Society), 1861.

———. *The Injunctions and Other Ecclesiastical Proceedings of Richard Barnes, Bishop of Durham, 1575 to 1587.* Durham, 1850.

Rogers, Elizabeth F., ed. *The Correspondence of Sir Thomas More.* Princeton, 1947.

Select Cases before the King's Council in the Star Chamber Commonly Called the Court of Star Chamber, Vol. 2: *1509-1544.* Ed. I. S. Leadam. London (Selden Society), 1911.

Statutes of the Realm. Ed. A. Luders, et al. London, 1810-24.

Stone, E. D., and B. Cozens-Hardy, eds. *Norwich Consistory Court Depositions, 1499-1512 and 1518-1530.* Norfolk (Norfolk Record Society), 1938.

Stowe, John. *A Summarie of the Chronicles of England, from the first comming of Brute into this land, vnto this present yeare of Christ, 1575.* London, 1575 (STC 23325; University Microfilms).

Strype, John. *Ecclesiastical Memorials, Relating Chiefly to Religion and the Reformation of It . . . Under Henry VIII.* Oxford, 1822.

Thompson, A. Hamilton, ed. *Visitations in the Diocese of Lincoln, 1517-31.* 3 vols. Lincoln (Lincoln Record Society), 1940-47.

"Two London Chronicles from the Collections of John Stow." Ed. Charles L. Kingsford. In *Camden Miscellany XII.* London, 1910.

Wright, Thomas, ed. *Three Chapters of Letters Relating to the Suppression of the Monasteries.* London, 1843.

Wriothesley, Charles. *A Chronicle of England During the Reigns of the Tudors, from A.D. 1485 to 1559.* Ed. William D. Hamilton. 2 vols. London (Camden Society), 1875.

Tudor England

Baker, J. H. "Criminal Courts and Procedure at Common Law, 1550-1800." In *Crime in England, 1550-1800,* ed. J. S. Cockburn, 15-48. Princeton, 1977.

Beer, Barrett. *Rebellion and Riot: Popular Disorder in England during the Reign of Edward VI.* Kent, OH, 1982.

Bellamy, John G. *Crime and Public Order in England in the Later Middle Ages.* London, 1973.

————. *The Law of Treason in England in the Later Middle Ages.* Cambridge, 1970.

————. *The Tudor Law of Treason: An Introduction.* Toronto, 1979.

Berkowitz, David S. *Humanist Scholarship and Public Order: Two Tracts against the Pilgrimage of Grace by Sir Richard Morison.* Washington, D.C., 1984.

Bernard, G. W. "The Fall of Ann Boleyn." *English Historical Review* (1991), 584-610.

Bowker, Margaret. *The Henrician Reformation: The Diocese of Lincoln under John Longland, 1521-1547.* Cambridge, 1981.

————. "Lincolnshire 1536: Heresy, Schism or Religious Discontent?" *Studies in Church History,* 9 (1973), 195-212.

Brigden, Susan. *London and the Reformation.* Oxford, 1989.

Chrimes, Stanley B. *Henry VII.* Berkeley, 1972.

————. *Lancastrians, Yorkists, and Henry VII.* London, 1964.

Cockburn, J. S. *A History of English Assizes, 1558-1714.* Cambridge, 1972.

Coleman, C., and D. R. Starkey, eds. *Revolution Reassessed: Revisions in the History of Tudor Government and Administration.* Oxford, 1986.

Davies, C. S. L. "The Pilgrimage of Grace Reconsidered." Past and Present, 41 (1968), 54-76. Reprinted in *Popular Protest and the Social Order in Early Modern England,* ed. Paul Slack, 16-38. Cambridge, 1984.

————. "Popular Religion and the Pilgrimage of Grace." In *Order and Disorder in Early Modern England,* ed. Anthony Fletcher and John Stevenson, 58-88. Cambridge, 1985.

Davis, J. F. *Heresy and Reformation in the South-East of England, 1520-1559.* London, 1983.

Davis, Natalie Zemon. *Fiction in the Archives: Pardon Tales and Their Tellers in Sixteenth-Century France.* Stanford, CA, 1987.

Dickens, A. G. *The English Reformation.* 1964. Reprint. London, 1989.

————. *Lollards and Protestants in the Diocese of York, 1509-1558.* Oxford, 1959.

————. "Secular and Religious Motivation in the Pilgrimage of Grace." *Studies in Church History,* 4 (1967), 39-64.

————. "Wilfred Holme of Huntingdon: Yorkshire's First Protestant Poet." *Yorkshire Archaeological Journal,* 39 (1956), 119-35.

Dodds, Madeleine Hope, and Ruth Dodds. *The Pilgrimage of Grace, 1536-1537, and the Exeter Conspiracy, 1538.* 2 vols. Cambridge, 1915.

Dubrow, Heather, and Richard Strier, eds. *The Historical Renaissance: New Essays on Tudor and Stuart Literature and Culture.* Chicago, 1988.

Duffy, Eamon. *The Stripping of the Altars: Traditional Religion in England, 1400-1580.* New Haven, CT, 1992.

Duggan, Christopher R. "The Advent of Political Thought-Control in England: Seditious and Treasonable Speech, 1485-1547." Ph.D. diss., Northwestern University, 1993.

Elton, G. R. *England Under the Tudors.* 1955. Reprint. London, 1991.

———. "The Law of Treason in the Early Reformation." *The Historical Journal,* 11 (1968), 211-36.

———. *Policy and Police: The Enforcement of the Reformation in the Age of Thomas Cromwell.* Cambridge, 1972.

———. "Politics and the Pilgrimage of Grace." In *Studies in Tudor and Stuart Politics and Government,* ed. G. R. Elton, 183-215. Cambridge, 1983.

———. *The New History of England.* Vol. 2: *Reform and Reformation: England, 1509-1558.* London, 1977.

———. *Reform and Renewal: Thomas Cromwell and the Common Weal.* Cambridge, 1973.

———. *Star Chamber Stories.* London, 1958.

———. *The Tudor Constitution: Documents and Commentary.* Cambridge, 1960.

———. *The Tudor Revolution in Government.* Cambridge, 1962.

Erickson, Carolly. *Great Harry: The Extravagant Life of Henry VIII.* New York, 1980.

Fines, J. "Heresy Trials in the Diocese of Coventry and Lichfield, 1511- 12." *Journal of Ecclesiastical History,* 14 (1963), 160-74.

Fletcher, Anthony. *Tudor Rebellions.* 1968. Reprint. London, 1980.

Fletcher, Anthony, and John Stevenson, eds. *Order and Disorder in Early Modern England.* Cambridge, 1985.

Fox, Alistair. *Politics and Literature in the Reigns of Henry VII and Henry VIII.* Oxford, 1985.

Fox, Alistair, and John Guy, eds. *Reassessing the Henrician Age: Humanism, Politics, and Reform, 1500-1550.* Oxford, 1986.

Fraser, Antonia. *The Wives of Henry VIII.* New York, 1993.

Froude, James A. *History of England from the Fall of Wolsey to the Defeat of the Spanish Armada.* 12 vols. London, 1893.

Guy, John. *Tudor England.* Oxford, 1986.

Gwyn, Peter. *The King's Cardinal: The Rise and Fall of Thomas Wolsey.* London, 1990.

Haigh, Christopher. "Anticlericalism and the English Reformation." *History,* 68 (1983), 391-407.

———. *The English Reformation Revised.* Cambridge, 1987.

———. *English Reformations: Religion, Politics, and Society under the Tudors.* Oxford, 1993.

———. *Reformation and Resistance in Tudor Lancashire.* Cambridge, 1975.

———. "Revisionism, the Reformation and the History of English Catholicism." *Journal of Ecclesiastical History,* 36 (1985), 394-405.

Harris, Barbara J. *Edward Stafford, Third Duke of Buckingham, 1478-1521.* Stanford, CA, 1986.

Harrison, Scott M. *The Pilgrimage of Grace in the Lake Counties, 1536-37.* London, 1981.

Helm, P. J. *England under the Yorkists and Tudors, 1471-1603.* New York, 1968.

Hodgett, G. A. J. *Tudor Lincolnshire.* Lincoln, 1975.

Holdsworth, W. *A History of English Law,* vol. 4. 1924. Reprint. London, 1937.

Hughes, Paul L., and James F. Larkin. *Tudor Royal Proclamations.* Vol. 1: *The Early Tudors (1485-1553).* New Haven, CT, 1964.

Ives, Eric W. Anne Boleyn. Oxford, 1986.

———. *Faction in Tudor England.* London, 1979.

James, Mervyn E. "Obedience and Dissent in Henrician England: the Lincolnshire Rebellion of 1536." *Past and Present,* 48 (1970), 3-78. Reprinted in *Society, Politics and Culture: Studies in Early Modern England* by M. E. James, 188-269. Cambridge, 1986.

———. *Society, Politics and Culture, 1485-1640: Essays and Studies.* Cambridge, 1986.

Jones, W. Garmon. "Welsh Nationalism and Henry Tudor." *Transactions of the Honourable Society of Cymmrodorion* (Sess. 1917-18), 1-59.

Lehmberg, S. E. *The Later Parliaments of Henry VIII, 1536-47.* Cambridge, 1977.

———. *The Reformation Parliament, 1529-1536.* Cambridge, 1970.

Levine, Mortimer. *Tudor Dynastic Problems, 1460-1571.* New York, 1973.

Levy, F. J. "The Fall of Edward, Duke of Buckingham." In *Tudor Men and Institutions,* ed. A. J. Slavine, 32-48. Baton Rouge, LA 1972.

———. *Tudor Historical Thought.* San Marino, CA 1967.

Lindsey, Karen. *Divorced, Beheaded, Survived: A Feminist Reinterpretation of the Wives of Henry VIII.* Reading, MA 1995.

Loades, David M. *Politics and the Nation, 1450-1660: Obedience, Resistance, and Public Order.* London, 1974.

————. *Politics, Censorship, and the English Reformation.* New York, 1991.

Lockyer, Roger. *Tudor and Stuart Britain, 1471-1714.* New York, 1974.

MacCulloch, Diarmaid. "The Myth of the English Reformation." *Journal of British Studies,* 30 (1991), 1-19.

————. *Suffolk and the Tudors: Politics and Religion in an English County, 1500-1600.* Oxford, 1986.

Mackie, J. D. *The Oxford History of England.* Vol. 7: *The Earlier Tudors, 1485-1558.* Oxford, 1952.

Manning, Roger B. "Violence and Social Conflict in Mid-Tudor Rebellions." *Journal of British Studies,* 16 (1977), 18-40.

Miller, Helen. *Henry VIII and the English Nobility.* Oxford, 1986.

Nuttall, Geoffrey. "The English Martyrs, 1535-1680: A Statistical Review." *Journal of Ecclesiastical History,* 22 (1971), 191-97.

Oxley, James B. *The Reformation in Essex to the Death of Mary.* Manchester, 1965.

Palliser, D. M. *The Reformation in York, 1534-53.* York, 1971.

Pollard, A. F. *Henry VIII.* 1905. Reprint. London, 1951.

Ridley, Jasper. *Henry VIII.* London, 1984.

Scarisbrick, J. J. *Henry VIII.* Berkeley, CA, 1968.

————. *The Reformation and the English People.* Oxford, 1984.

Simons, Eric N. *Henry VII: The First Tudor King.* London, 1968.

Slack, Paul, ed. *Rebellion, Popular Protest and the Social Order in Early Modern Europe.* Cambridge, 1984.

Smith, Lacey Baldwin. "English Treason Trials and Confessions in the Sixteenth Century." *Journal of the History of Ideas,* 15 (1954), 471-98.

————. *Henry VIII: The Mask of Royalty.* 1971. Reprint. Chicago, 1982.

————. *Treason in Tudor England: Politics and Paranoia.* Princeton, 1986.

Smith, R. B. *Land and Politics in the England of Henry VIII: The West Riding of Yorkshire, 1530-46.* Oxford, 1970.

Thomas, Keith. *Religion and the Decline of Magic: Studies in Popular Beliefs in Sixteenth- and Seventeenth-Century England.* 1971. Reprint. London, 1980.

Walker, Greg. *John Skelton and the Politics of the 1520s.* Cambridge, 1988.

Warnicke, Retha M. *The Rise and Fall of Anne Boleyn: Family Politics at the Court of Henry VIII.* Cambridge, 1989.

Weir, Alison. *The Six Wives of Henry VIII.* New York, 1991.

Weisser, Michael R. *Crime and Punishment in Early Modern Europe.* Atlantic Highlands, NJ, 1976.

Williams, Glanmor. *Recovery, Reorientation, and Reformation: Wales c. 1415-1642.* Oxford, 1987.

————. *The Welsh Church from Conquest to Reformation.* Cardiff, 1962.

Williams, Neville. *Henry VIII and His Court.* New York, 1971.

Williams, W. L. "A Welsh Insurrection." *Y Cymmrodor,* 16 (1903), 33-41.

Woodcock, Brian L. *Medieval Ecclesiastical Courts in the Diocese of Canterbury.* Oxford, 1952.

Wunderli, Richard M. *London Church Courts and Society on the Eve of the Reformation.* Cambridge, MA, 1981.

Zagorin, Perez. *Rebels and Rulers, 1500-1660.* 2 vols. Cambridge, 1982.

Zeeveld, W. Gordon. *Foundations of Tudor Policy.* Cambridge, MA 1948.

General Works on Political Prophecies

Berdan, John M. *Early Tudor Poetry, 1485-1547.* New York, 1920.

Dodds, Madeleine Hope. "Political Prophecies in the Reign of Henry VIII." *Modern Language Review,* 11 (1916), 276-84.

Fox, Alistair. "Prophecies and Politics in the Reign of Henry VIII." In *Reassessing the Henrician Age; Humanism, Politics and Reform, 1500-1550,* ed. Alistair Fox and John Guy, 77-94. Oxford, 1986.

Frazer, N. L. *English History in Contemporary Poetry: The Tudor Monarchy (1485-1588).* London, 1930.

Herrmann, Erwin. "Spätmittelalterliche englische Pseudoprophetien." *Archiv für Kulturgeschichte,* 57 (1975), 87-116.

Jansen, Sharon L. [Jaech]. "English Political Prophecy and the Dating of MS Rawlinson C.813." *Manuscripta,* 25 (1981), 141-50.

————. *Political Protest and Prophecy under Henry VIII.* Suffolk, England, 1992.

Kinghorn, A. M. *The Chorus of History: Literary-Historical Relations in Renaissance Britain, 1485-1559.* New York, 1971.

Robbins, Rossell H. "Political Prophecies." In *A Manual of the Writings in Middle English, 1050-1500,* vol. 5., ed. J. Burke Severs, 1516-36, 1714-25. New Haven, CT, 1975.

Scattergood, V. J. *Politics and Poetry in the Fifteenth Century.* New York, 1972.

Southern, R. W. "Aspects of the European Tradition of Historical Writing: 3. History as Prophecy." *Transactions of the Royal Historical Society,* 5th ser., 22 (1972), 159-80.

Taylor, Rupert. *The Political Prophecy in England.* New York, 1911.

Williams, Glanmor. "Prophecy, Poetry, and Politics in Medieval and Tudor Wales." *In British Government and Administration: Studies Presented to S. B. Chrimes, ed. H. Hearder and H. R. Loyn,* 104-16. Cardiff, 1974.

Witchcraft and Magic

The literature on witchcraft is vast. These are representative studies; their bibliographies indicate further sources for the interested reader.

Barstow, Anne Llewellyn. *Witchcraze: A New History of the European Witch Hunts.* San Francisco, CA, 1994.

Brain, James L. "An Anthropological Perspective on the Witchcraze." In *The Politics of Gender in Early Modern Europe,* ed. Jean R. Brink, Allison P. Coudert, and Maryanne C. Horowitz, 15-27. Kirksville, MO, 1989.

Coudert, Allison P. "The Myth of the Improved Status of Protestant Women: The Case of the Witchcraze." In *The Politics of Gender in Early Modern Europe,* ed. Jean R. Brink, Allison P. Coudert, and Maryanne C. Horowitz, 61-89. Kirksville, MO, 1989.

Currie, Elliott P. "The Control of Witchcraft in Renaissance Europe." In *The Social Organization of Law,* ed. Donald Black and Maureen Mileski, 344-67. New York, 1973.

Ewen, C. L'Estrange. *Witch Hunting and Witch Trials: The Indictments for Witchcrafrt from the Records of 1,373 Assizes Held for the Home Circuit, A.D. 1559-1736.* London, 1929.

———. *Witchcraft and Demonianism: A Concise Account Derived from Sworn Depositions and Confessions Obtained in the Courts of England and Wales.* London, 1933.

———. *Witchcraft in the Star Chamber.* N.p., 1938.

Gibson, Joyce. *Hanged for Witchcraft: Elizabeth Lowys and Her Successors.* Canberra, Australia 1988.

Ginzburg, Carlo. *The Night Battles: Witchcraft and Agrarian Cults in the Sixteenth and Seventeenth Centuries.* Trans. John and Anne Tedeschi. New York, 1985. (*I Benandanti: Stregonerie e culti agrari tra Cinque-cento e Seicento* [Rome, 1966].)

Hester, Marianne. "The Dynamics of Male Domination Using the Witch Craze in Sixteenth- and Seventeenth-Century England as a Case Study." *Women's Studies International Forum,* 13 (1990), 9-19.

———. *Lewd Women and Wicked Witches: A Study of the Dynamics of Male Domination.* London, 1992.

Keickhefer, Richard. *European Witchtrials: Their Foundations in Popular and Learned Culture, 1300-1500.* London, 1976.

———. *Magic in the Middle Ages.* Cambridge, 1990.

Kittredge, George L. *Witchcraft in Old and New England.* 1929. Reprint. New York, 1956.

Larner, Christina. *The Enemies of God: The Witch-hunt in Scotland.* Oxford, 1983.

———. *Witchcraft and Religion: The Politics of Popular Belief.* Ed. Alan MacFarlane. Oxford, 1984.

Levack, Brian P. *The Witch-Hunt in Early Modern Europe.* New York, 1987.

MacFarlane, Alan D. J. *Witchcraft in Tudor and Stuart England: A Regional and Comparative Study.* New York, 1970.

———. "Witchcraft in Tudor and Stuart Essex." In *Witchcraft Confessions and Accusations,* ed. Mary Douglas, 81-99. New York, 1970.

Notestein, Wallace. *A History of Witchcraft in England From 1558 to 1713.* 1911. Reprint. New York, 1968.

Richards, Jeffrey. *Sex, Dissidence, and Damnation: Minority Groups in the Middle Ages.* Chap. 4: "Witches," 74-83. New York, 1991.

Robbins, Rossell H. *Encyclopedia of Witchcraft and Demonology.* New York, 1959.

Ruggiero, Guido. *Binding Passion: Tales of Magic, Marriage, and Power at the End of the Renaissance.* New York, 1993.

Russell, Jeffrey Burton. *Witchcraft in the Middle Ages: Witchcraft and the Medieval Mind.* Ithaca, NY 1972.

Sharpe, Jim. "Women, Witchcraft and the Legal Process." In *Women, Crime and the Courts in Early Modern England,* ed. Jenny Kermode and Garthine Walker, 106-24. Chapel Hill, NC 1994.

Women in the Early Modern Period

Amussen, Susan D. "Gender, Family and the Social Order, 1560-1725." *In Order and Disorder in Early Modern England,* ed. Anthony Fletcher and John Stevenson, 196-217. Cambridge, 1985.

———. *An Ordered Society: Gender and Class in Early Modern England.* Oxford, 1988.

Anderson, Bonnie S., and Judith P. Zinsser. *A History of Their Own: Women in Europe from Prehistory to the Present*. Vol. 1. London, 1988.

Atkinson, Clarissa W. "The Modesty of the Elephant: Marriage, Families, and Holiness in the Sixteenth Century." *Reflections* (1991), 1-10.

Bainton, Roland. *Women of the Reformation in France and England*. Minneapolis, 1973.

Beard, Mary R. *Woman as Force in History: A Study in Traditions and Realities*. 1946. Reprint. New York, 1981.

Bridenthal, Renate, and Claudia Koonz, eds. *Becoming Visible: Women in European History*. 1977. Reprint. Boston, 1987.

Brink, Jean R., Allison P. Condert, and Maryanne C. Horowitz, eds. *The Politics of Gender in Early Modern Europe*. Kirksville, MO 1989.

Carlton, C. "The Widow's Tale: Male Myths and Female Reality in Sixteenth and Seventeenth Century England." *Albion,* 10 (1978), 118-29.

Clark, Alice. *Working Life of Women in the Seventeenth Century*. London, 1919.

Crawford, Patricia. *Women and Religion in England, 1500-1720*. New York, 1993.

Cross, Claire. "'Great Reasoners in Scripture': The Activities of Women Lollards, 1380-1530." In *Medieval Women,* ed. Derek Brewer, 359-80. Oxford, 1978.

Davis, Natalie Zemon. "Women on Top." *Society and Culture in Early Modern France: Eight Essays,* 124-51. Stanford, CA 1975.

Dolan, Frances E. *Dangerous Familiars: Representations of Domestic Crime in England, 1550-1700*. Ithaca, NY 1994.

Dowling, Maria, and Joy Shakespeare. "Religion and Politics in Mid Tudor England through the Eyes of an English Protestant Woman: the Recollections of Rose Hickman." *Bulletin of Historical Research,* (1982), 94-102.

Duby, Georges. "Affadavits and Confessions." In *A History of Women in the West.* Vol. 2: *Silences of the Middle Ages,* ed. Christiane Klapisch-Zuber, 483-91. Cambridge, MA, 1992.

Farge, Arlette. "Protesters Plain to See." In *A History of Women in the West.* Vol. 3: *Renaissance and Enlightenment Paradoxes,* ed. Natalie Zeamon Davis and Arlette Farge, 489-505. Cambridge, MA 1993.

Farrell, Kirby, Elizabeth H. Hageman, and Arthur F. Kinney, eds. *Women in the Renaissance: Selections from English Literary Renaissance*. Amherst, MA 1988.

Ferguson, Margaret W., et al., eds. *Rewriting the Renaissance: The Discourses of Sexual Difference in Early Modern Europe*. Chicago, 1986.

Hanawalt, Barbara. "The Female Felon in Fourteenth-Century England." In *Women in Medieval Society,* ed. Susan Mosher Stuard, 125-40. Philadelphia, 1976.

———. "Lady Honor Lisle's Networks of Influence." In *Women and Power in the Middle Ages,* ed. Mary Erler and Maryanne Kowaleski, 188-212. Athens, GA, 1988.

———. *The Ties That Bound: Peasant Families in Medieval England.* New York, 1986.

———, ed. *Women and Work in Pre-Industrial Europe.* Bloomington, IN, 1986.

Hanmer, Jalna. "Violence and the Social Control of Women." In *Power and the State,* ed. Gary Littlejohn et al., 217-38. London, 1978.

Hanmer, Jalna, and Mary Maynard. *Women, Violence, and Social Control.* New York, 1987.

Hannay, Margaret. *Silent But for the Word: Tudor Women as Patrons, Translators, and Writers of Religious Works.* Kent, OH, 1985.

Harris, Barbara. "Women and Politics in Early Tudor England." *The Historical Journal,* 33 (1990), 259-81.

Harris, Barbara, and JoAnn McNamara, eds. *Women and the Structure of Society.* Durham, NC, 1984.

Henderson, Katherine, and Barbara F. McManees. *Half Humankind: Contexts and Texts of the Controversy about Women in England, 1540-1640.* Urbana, IL, 1985.

Herlihy, David. "Did Women Have a Renaissance? A Reconsideration." *Medievalia et Humanistica,* n.s. 13 (1985), 1-22.

———. *Women, Family and Society in Medieval Europe: Historical Essays, 1978-1991.* Oxford, 1995.

Hogrefe, Pearl. "Legal Rights of Tudor Women and the Circumvention by Men and Women." *Sixteenth Century Journal,* 3 (1972), 97-105.

———. *Tudor Women: Commoners and Queens.* Ames, IA 1975.

———. *Women of Action in Tudor England.* Ames, IA 1977.

Hufton, Olwen. *The Prospect Before Her: A History of Women in Western Europe.* Vol. 1: 1500-1800. London, 1995.

Hull, Suzanne W. *Chaste, Silent, and Obedient: English Books for Women, 1475-1640.* San Marino, CA 1982.

Jankowski, Theodora A. "Women in Early Modern England: Privileges and Restraints." *Women and Power in the Early Modern Drama,* 22-53. Urbana, IL 1992.

Jordan, Constance. *Renaissance Feminism: Literary Texts and Political Models.* Ithaca, NY, 1990.

Kelly-[Gadol], Joan. "Did Women Have a Renaissance?" In *Becoming Visible: Women in European History,* ed. Renate Bridenthal and Claudia Koonz, 175-201. 1977. Reprint. Boston, 1987. Reprinted by Joan Kelly, *Women, History, and Theory,* 19-50. Chicago, 1984.

Kermode, Jenny, and Garthine Walker, eds. *Women, Crime and the Courts.* Chapel Hill, NC, 1994.

Kinnear, Mary. *Daughters of Time: Women in the Western Tradition.* Ann Arbor, MI, 1982.

Klein, Joan Larsen, ed. *Daughters, Wives, and Widows: Writings by Men about Women and Marriage in England, 1500-1640.* Urbana, IL, 1992.

LaBalme, Patricia H. *Beyond Their Sex: Learned Women of the European Past.* New York, 1980.

Laslett, Peter, and Richard Wall. *Household and Family in Past Time.* Cambridge, 1972.

Lerner, Gerda. *The Majority Finds Its Past: Placing Women in History.* Oxford, 1979.

Levin, Carole. "Queens and Claimants: Political Insecurity in Sixteenth-Century England." In *Gender, Ideology, and Action: Historical Perspectives on Women's Public Lives,* ed. Janet Sharistanian, 41-66. Bloomington, IN, 1989.

———. "Women in The Book of Martyrs as Models of Behavior in Tudor England." *International Journal of Women's Studies,* 4 (1981), 196-207.

Levin, Carole, and Jeanie Watson. *Ambiguous Realities: Women in the Middle Ages and the Renaissance.* Detroit, 1987.

Levine, Mortimer. "The Place of Women in Tudor Government." In *Tudor Rule and Tudor Revolution: Essays for G. R. Elton from His American Friends,* ed. Delloyd J. Guth and John McKenna, 109-23. Cambridge, 1982.

Lewalski, Barbara Kiefer. "Women, Writing, and Resistance in Jacobean England." *Writing Women in Jacobean England,* 1-11. Cambridge, MA, 1993.

Lucas, Angela M. *Women in the Middle Ages: Religion, Marriage, and Letters.* New York, 1983.

Mack, Phyllis. "Women as Prophets during the English Civil Wars." *Feminist Studies,* 8 (1982), 19-45.

Maclean, Ian. *The Renaissance Notion of Woman: A Study in the Fortunes of Scholasticism and Medical Science in European Intellectual Life.* 1980. Reprint. Cambridge, 1988.

Marshall, Sherrin, ed. *Women in Reformation and Counter-Reformation Europe: Public and Private Worlds.* Bloomington, IN, 1989.

Mendelson, Sara Heller. *The Mental World of Stuart Women: Three Studies.* Amherst, MA, 1987.

Monter, William. "Protestant Wives, Catholic Saints, and the Devil's Handmaid." In *Becoming Visible: Women in European History,* ed. Renate Bridenthal and Claudia Koonz, 203-19. 1977. Reprint. Boston, 1987.

Orlin, Lena Cowen. *Private Matters and Public Culture in Post-Reformation England.* Ithaca, NY, 1994.

Ozment, Steven. *When Fathers Ruled: Family Life in Reformation Europe.* Cambridge, MA, 1983.

Perrot, Michelle, ed. *Writing Women's History.* Trans. Felicia Pheasant. Oxford, 1984.

Pitkin, Hanna Fenichel. *Fortune Is a Woman: Gender and Politics in the Thought of Niccol Machiavelli.* Berkeley, CA, 1984.

Plowden, Alison. *Tudor Women: Queens and Commoners.* New York, 1979.

Prior, M., *Women in English Society, 1500-1800.* London, 1985.

Rose, Mary Beth, ed. *Women in the Middle Ages and the Renaissance: Literary and Historical Perspectives.* Syracuse, NY, 1985.

Rosenthal, Joel T. "Aristocratic Widows in Fifteenth-Century England." In *Women and the Structure of Society,* ed. Barbara J. Harris and JoAnn K. McNamara, 36-47. Durham, NC 1984.

Saxonhouse, Arlene W. *Women in the History of Political Thought: Ancient Greece to Machiavelli.* New York, 1985.

Shepherd, Simon, ed. *The Women's Sharp Revenge: Five Women's Pamphlets from the Renaissance.* New York, 1975.

Stone, Lawrence. *The Family, Sex and Marriage in England, 1500-1800.* 1977. Reprint. London, 1990.

Thomas, Keith. "Women and the Civil War Sects." *Past and Present,* 13 (1958), 42-62.

Travitsky, Betty S. "Placing Women in the English Renaissance." In *The Renaissance Englishwoman in Print: Counterbalancing the Canon,* ed. Anne M. Haselkorn and Betty S. Travitsky, 3-41. Amherst, MA, 1990.

―――, ed. *The Paradise of Women: Writings by Englishwomen of the Renaissance.* London, 1981.

Travitsky, Betty S., and Adele F. Seeff, eds. *Attending to Women in Early Modern England.* Newark, NJ, 1994.

Warnicke, Retha M. "Private and Public: The Boundaries of Women's Lives in Early Stuart England." In *Privileging Gender in Early Modern England,* ed. Jean R. Brink, 123-40. Kirksville, MO, 1993.

————. *Women of the English Renaissance and Reformation.* Westport, CT 1983.

Weigall, David. "Women Militants in the English Civil War." *History Today,* 22 (1972), 434-38.

Weinstein, Donald, and Rudolph Bell. *Saints and Society: The Two Worlds of Western Christendom, 1000-1700.* Chicago, 1982.

Weinstein, Minna F. "Reconstructing Our Past: Reflections on Tudor Women." *International Journal of Women's Studies,* 1 (1978), 133-40.

Wiener, Carol Z. "Sex Roles and Crime in Late Elizabethan Hertfordshire." *Journal of Social History,* 8 (1975), 38-60.

Wiesner, Merry E. *Women and Gender in Early Modern Europe.* Cambridge, 1993.

————. *Working Women in Renaissance Germany.* New Brunswick, NJ, 1986.

Yost, John. "The Value of Married Life for the Social Order in the Early English Renaissance." *Societas,* 6 (1976), 25-39.

INDEX